Distributing Applications Across
DCE *and*
WINDOWS NT

Distributing Applications Across

DCE *and*
WINDOWS NT

WARD ROSENBERRY
JIM TEAGUE
Digital Equipment Corporation

O'Reilly & Associates, Inc.
103 Morris Street, Suite A
Sebastopol, CA 95472

Distributing Applications Across DCE and Windows NT
by Ward Rosenberry and Jim Teague

Cover Design by Edie Freedman
Cover Illustration by Chris Reilley

Editor: Andy Oram

Production Editor: Stephen Spainhour

Printing History:

      November 1993: First Edition.

Many of the designations used by manufacturers and sellers to distinguish their products are claimed as trademarks. Where those designations appear in this book, and O'Reilly & Associates, Inc. was aware of a trademark claim, the designations have been printed in caps or initial caps.

While every precaution has been taken in the preparation of this book, the publisher assumes no responsibility for errors or omissions, or for damages resulting from the use of the information contained herein.

This book is printed on acid-free paper with 50% recycled content, 10-15% post-consumer waste. O'Reilly & Associates is committed to using paper with the highest recycled content available consistent with high quality.

ISBN: 1-56592-047-3

Table of Contents

Chapter 5: Writing Clients   *75*

Chapter 6: Writing a Server   *105*

Figures

Examples

Tables

Preface

If you are a programmer using either the Distributed Computing Environment (DCE) or Microsoft's Windows NT, then you have probably heard that the two environments are "compatible" or "interoperable" by virtue of remote procedure calls (RPC). But it's hard to find out exactly what this means. What can be passed between the environments, and what does it allow you to do?

This book describes the nitty-gritty technical realities behind some popular marketing buzzwords. Yes, DCE and Microsoft environments—Windows NT, Windows 3.x, and MS-DOS—can share applications. You can run a client on one system and a server on another, calling functions on the remote system and passing data back and forth without regard for architectural differences. This is a very powerful facility, made possible largely by a compatible RPC in the two environments. And this book tells programmers how to make it work (along with some advice for administrators).

Writing cross-environment applications is not hard, but you have to know what each environment contains. For instance, the compatibility between Microsoft and DCE lies only on the protocol level (where the client and server exchange data over the network). The two types of RPC differ at the source code level. Luckily, there is a simple way to work around the difference using the C preprocessor, and the technique is one of many where you'll find this book invaluable.

If you are unfamiliar with RPC in either environment, you should read this book twice. First read it to gain a quick overview of what RPC programming is. Then go to the vendor literature—the DCE or Microsoft programming manuals—and learn to write an application on one environment. After that, come back and read this book again to learn the differences and special techniques you need to write cross-environment applications.

O'Reilly & Associates has some books that can help you understand DCE and RPC better:

- *Understanding DCE*, by Ward Rosenberry, David Kenney and Gerry Fisher, 266 pages, ISBN: 1-56592-005-8

- *Guide to Writing DCE Applications*, by John Shirley, 282 pages, ISBN: 1-56592-004-X

Many people find *Guide to Writing DCE Applications* useful for understanding Microsoft RPC, even though it was written for the DCE environment, because the two types of RPC are almost identical.

In the DCE document set, the books that discuss RPC programming are:

- *Application Development Guide*

- *Application Development Reference*

In the Microsoft Win32 Software Development Kit for Windows NT, consult the *RPC Programmer's Guide and Reference*.

If you already program either DCE RPC or Microsoft RPC, the book you're now holding can make you an expert at cross-environment applications very quickly. The differences and traps are clearly explained. Chapter 4, *Administration*, details the administrative tasks that will make the environments work together more smoothly. The book lists and explains lots of sample code, which you can also download from CompuServe or an Internet anonymous ftp site, as described later in this preface.

Book Organization

This book starts with an overview of the broad ocean of RPC, so you won't drown in details later. Thus, the first two chapters present general concepts, such as the reason for using RPC and a simple application. Starting with Chapter 3, we get more focused and go into detail about the differences between DCE RPC and Microsoft RPC. Complete examples and other useful source code appear in the appendices.

In Chapter 1, *Building Bridges*, we provide some reasons why programmers will want to develop distributed applications that span the Microsoft RPC and the DCE environments. Then we highlight the terrain programmers will be working in by describing both the Microsoft RPC and the DCE environments.

In Chapter 2, *Developing a Cross-Environment Application*, we describe a sample cross-environment application that demonstrates several aspects of cross-environment applications.

Chapter 3, *Writing Interface Definitions*, shows how to write interface definitions.

Chapter 4, *Administration*, describes the administration tasks you'll need to follow so that Microsoft clients and servers can interact with several DCE services.

Chapter 5, *Writing Clients*, describes how to write client applications that execute on DCE systems as well as Microsoft Windows NT, Microsoft Windows, and Microsoft DOS systems.

Chapter 6, *Writing a Server*, shows the ins and outs of developing server applications that run on DCE or Windows NT.

Chapter 7, *A Remodeling Handbook for Existing Local Applications*, shows a simple way to convert existing stand-alone applications to work in a distributed environment.

Appendix A, *API Differences*, lists differences between Microsoft RPC and OSF DCE.

Appendix B, *The Simple Phonebook Application*, shows some basic distributed operations using Microsoft RPC and OSF DCE.

Appendix C, *The Complete Phonebook Application*, builds on the simple application used in Appendix B to show some advanced distributed operations using Microsoft RPC and OSF DCE.

Appendix D, *The Remote Search Application*, illustrates the use of customized binding handles.

Appendix E, *DCEPORT.H API Mapping File*, includes the C preprocessor directives that translate the Microsoft RPC API to the DCE API.

Conventions

Information in this document conforms to the following conventions:

`Constant width`	Indicates a keyword in the C or IDL language, and is used in examples for all source code and system output.
`Constant bold`	In examples, shows user input.
Italic	Used for filenames, functions, commands, variables, emphasis, and new terms.
`Constant italic`	Used for variables in code or input which the user specifies (i.e., `filename`).

Obtaining the Example Programs

The example programs in this book are available electronically in a number of ways: by FTP, FTPMAIL, BITFTP, UUCP, and CompuServe. The cheapest, fastest, and easiest ways are listed first. If you read from the top down, the first one that works for you is probably the best.

Use *FTP* if you are directly on the Internet. Use FTPMAIL if you are not on the Internet but can send and receive electronic mail to internet sites (this includes CompuServe users). Use BITFTP if you send electronic mail via BITNET. Use UUCP if you are on a UNIX system and none of the above works. Use CompuServe if you are accustomed to getting Microsoft-related software that way.

FTP

To use FTP, you need a machine with direct access to the Internet. A sample session is shown, with what you should type in boldface.

```
% ftp ftp.uu.net
Connected to ftp.uu.net.
220 ftp.UU.NET FTP server (Version 6.34 Thu Oct 22 14:32:01 EDT 1992) ready.
Name (ftp.uu.net:andyo): anonymous
331 Guest login ok, send e-mail address as password.
Password: andyo@ora.com     (use your user name and host here)
230 Guest login ok, access restrictions apply.
ftp> cd /published/oreilly/dce/dce_nt
250 CWD command successful.
ftp> binary      (Very important! You must specify binary transfer for compressed files.)
200 Type set to I.
ftp> prompt      (Convenient, so you are not queried for every file transferred)
Interactive mode off.
ftp> mget *
200 PORT command successful.
      .
      .
      .
ftp> quit
221 Goodbye.
%
```

Each .Z archive contains all the source code and configuration information required for building one example. Extract each example through a command like:

```
% zcat phnbk.oct93.tar.Z | tar xf -
```

System V systems require the following tar command instead:

```
% zcat phnbk.oct93.tar.Z | tar xof -
```

If *zcat* is not available on your system, use separate *uncompress* and *tar* commands.

The *tar* command creates a subdirectory that holds all the files from its archive. The README file in this subdirectory describes the goals of the example and how to build and run it; the text is an ASCII version of the introductory material from the corresponding appendix in this book.

FTPMAIL

FTPMAIL is a mail server available to anyone who can send and receive electronic mail to and from Internet sites. This includes most workstations that have an email connection to the outside world, and CompuServe users. You do not need to be directly on the Internet. Here's how to do it.

You send mail to *ftpmail@online.ora.com.* (Another popular server is *ftpmail@decwrl.dec.com,* but the *online.ora.com* server is much faster for retrieving O'Reilly examples). In the message body, give the name of the anonymous FTP host and the FTP commands you want to run. The server will run anonymous FTP for you and mail the files back to you. To get a complete help file, send a message with no subject and the single word "help" in the body. The following is an example mail session that should get you the examples. This command sends you a listing of the files in the selected directory and the requested example files. The listing is useful in case there's a later version of the examples you're interested in.

```
% mail ftpmail@online.ora.com
Subject:
reply andyo@ora.com            (where you want files mailed)
connect ftp.ora.com
chdir /published/oreilly/dce/dce_nt
dir
get README.oct93
get dceport.h.oct93
binary
uuencode            (or btoa if you have it)
get phnbk.oct93.tar.Z
get phnbk2.oct93.tar.Z
get search.oct93.tar.Z
quit
%
```

A signature at the end of the message is acceptable as long as it appears after "quit."

All retrieved files will be split into 60KB chunks and mailed to you. You then remove the mail headers and concatenate them into one file, and then *uudecode* or *atob* it. Once you've got the desired .Z files, follow the directions under FTP to extract the files from the archive.

VMS, MS-DOS, and Macintosh versions of *uudecode, atob, uncompress,* and *tar* are available. The VMS versions are found on *gatekeeper.dec.com* in */archive/pub/VMS.*

BITFTP

BITFTP is a mail server for BITNET users. You send it electronic mail messages requesting files, and it sends you back the files by electronic mail. BITFTP currently serves only users who send it mail from nodes that are directly on BITNET, EARN, or NetNorth. BITFTP is a public service of Princeton University. Here's how it works.

To use BITFTP, send mail containing your FTP commands to *BITFTP@PUCC.* For a complete help file, send HELP as the message body.

The following is the message body you should send to BITFTP:

```
FTP  ftp.uu.net  NETDATA
USER  anonymous
PASS your Internet email address (not your bitnet address)
CD  /published/oreilly/dce/dce_nt
DIR
GET README.oct93
GET dceport.h.oct93
BINARY
GET phnbk.oct93.tar.Z
GET phnbk2.oct93.tar.Z
GET search.oct93.tar.Z
QUIT
```

Once you've got the desired .Z files, follow the directions under FTP to extract the files from the archive. Since you are probably not on a UNIX system, you may need to get versions of *uudecode, uncompress, atob,* and *tar* for your system. VMS, DOS, and Mac versions are available. The VMS versions are on *gatekeeper.dec.com* in */archive/pub/VMS.*

Questions about BITFTP can be directed to Melinda Varian, *MAINT@PUCC* on BITNET.

UUCP

UUCP is standard on virtually all UNIX systems, and is available for IBM-compatible PCs and Apple Macintoshes. The examples are available by UUCP via modem from UUNET; UUNET's connect-time charges apply.

You can get the examples from UUNET whether you have an account or not. If you or your company has an account with UUNET, you have a system with a direct UUCP connection to UUNET. Find that system and type:

```
uucp uunet\!~/published/oreilly/dce/dce_nt/ yourhost\!~/yourname/
```

The backslashes can be omitted if you use the Bourne shell (*sh*) instead of *csh*. The files should appear some time later (up to a day or more) in the directory */usr/spool/uucppublic/yourname*. If you don't have an account but would like one so that you can get electronic mail, then contact UUNET at 703-204-8000.

If you don't have a UUNET account, you can set up a UUCP connection to UUNET using the phone number 1-900-468-7727. As of this writing, the cost is 50 cents per minute. The charges will appear on your next telephone bill. The login name is "uucp" with no password. For example, an *L.sys/Systems* entry might look like:

```
uunet Any ACU 19200 1-900-468-7727 ogin:--ogin: uucp
```

Your entry may vary depending on your UUCP configuration. If you have a PEP-capable modem, make sure s50=255s111=30 is set before calling.

Once you've got the desired .Z files, follow the directions under FTP to extract the files from the archives.

CompuServe

Sample programs from this book are available in the same CompuServe forum as other documents and code related to Microsoft RPC. Go to mswin32, ask for the Libraries Menu, and choose the API-WinNet/RPC item from the menu.

The sample code consists of three examples in zip format—*phnbk.zip*, *phnbk2.zip*, and *search.zip*—and one header file, *dcepor.h*. The four files are also available together in *oradce.zip*.

Here is a captured CompuServe session showing how to obtain one of the files:

```
CompuServe Information Service
 15:35 PDT Monday 25-Oct-93 P
     (Executive Option)
Last access: 15:00 25-Oct-93

     Copyright (c)puServe Incorporated
     All Rights Reserved


OK
go mswin32
```

```
One moment please...
MicrosoftMSWIN32


One moment please...
Welcome to Microsoft Win32 SDK Forum, V. 3A(131)

Hello,
Last visit:  25-Oct-93  15:00:23

Forum messages:  58594 to  59686
Last message you've read:  38985

Section(s) Selected: [ 1 3 4 5 6 7 8 9 10 11 12 13 14 15 16 17 ]

No members are in conference.

Forum !lib
Libraries Menu
 0  1  2  3  4  5  6  7  8  9 10 11 12 13 14 15 16 17
Enter choice !?
Libraries Menu

 0 Sysop Library
 1 MS Info and Index
 2 open
 3 Far East Win32-beta
 4 API-User/GUI
 5 API-Graphics/GDI
 6 API-Base/Console
 7 API-Security
 8 Tools-Win32 SDK
 9 Tools-SCT
10 Tools-MS Test/Setup
11 Porting-OS/2 & UNIX
12 API-WinNet/RPC
13 Windows NT DDK
14 API-Win32s
15 API-Unicode/NLS
16 Tools-Third Party
17 FAQ Library

Enter choice !12

LIB 12 !?

BRO, DIR, LIS, DOW, UPL, REA,
ERA, KEY

LIB 12 !lis

ORADCE.ZIP 12 18K 25-Oct-93 All Examples "Windows NT DCE Programming"
RPC.ZIP    12    4K 20-Oct-93 RPC.zip
NETBRS.    12   11K 18-Oct-93 Network Browser
SOCK_T.C   12    8K 10-Sep-93 WinSockets & select
WSAT.ZIP   12   41K 01-Sep-93 wsat.zip
COMER.ZIP  12   12K 24-May-93 Port of Comer's sample TCP/IP code to NT
WLTC3D.ZIP 12    4K 05-May-93 Replacement for rpcwltc3.dl_
```

```
RPCNDR.ZIP 12      5K 04-May-93 Replacement rpcndr.h_ March 93 CD
RCMDD.ZIP  12      7K 03-May-93 Executable for the Dos client of RSHELL
LMAPI.ZIP  12    493K 07-Apr-93 Lan Manager APIs, March Win32 SDK/Windows NT
WSOCK0.ZIP 12     33K 19-Jan-93 Sample WinSock application - listens and connects
WHLO16.ZIP 12     25K 19-Nov-92 Whelloc.exe 16-bit client
TTY32.ZIP  12     25K 26-Oct-92 TTY sample allowing TELNET connections
WNSOCK.ZIP 12    196K 17-Sep-92 Windows Sockets API
WSOCTX.ZIP 12     78K 19-Aug-92 Windows Sockets API Specs - ASCII Text Format
WSOCRT.ZIP 12     90K 19-Aug-92 Windows Sockets API Specs - RTF Format
WSOCPS.ZIP 12    167K 19-Aug-92 Windows Sockets API Specs - Postscript Format
WSOCHP.ZIP 12    118K 19-Aug-92 Windows Sockets API Specs - WinHelp 3.1 Format
WSOCDC.ZIP 12     98K 19-Aug-92 Windows Sockets API Specs - WinWord 2.0 Format

LIB 12 !dow proto:x1k oradce.zip

File TTY32.ZIP, 25387 Bytes, Lib 12

Starting 1K XMODEM send.
Please initiate 1K XMODEM receive
and press <CR> when the transfer
is complete.


LIB 12 !off

Thank you for using CompuServe!

Off at 15:37 PDT 25-Oct-93
Connect time = 0:02

NO CARRIER
```

After you obtain the examples, unzip them and look at the READ.ME file for explanations of their contents.

Acknowledgments

Any major undertaking is usually the result of lots of people working together. That's certainly true for this book. Although Jim and I get the credit on the cover, this work couldn't have been completed without the efforts of many.

First, we want to thank our editor at O'Reilly & Associates, Andy Oram, whose ideas, suggestions, and reviews contributed greatly to the book's shape and purpose.

A project like this always has a few folks who have held central roles in its development. We owe a special thanks to Michael Blackstock, for lots of work on the examples, to Jerry Harrow, for his thorough reviews, and to Ram Sudama, for his high level of technical expertise and helpfulness. Benn Schreiber and Jeff Schriesheim at Digital Equipment Corporation also deserve our heartfelt appreciation for their willingness to let Jim spend time on this project.

We also thank Digital Equipment Corporation and Microsoft Corporation for the spirit of enthusiastic cooperation and synergy they demonstrated during Microsoft's development of their RPC. We owe sincere thanks to people at these two companies both for their technical consulting and for supporting the cooperative work between companies. Those at Digital include Ken Ouellette, David Magid, Steve Miller, Al Simons, Wei Hu, Laura McCauley, Brian Schimpf, Howard Mayberry, Peter Hurley, Sumner Blount, and Mary Ellen Lewandowski. At Microsoft, we thank Dov Harel, Paul Leach, and Debbie Black for making Jim's productive stay at Microsoft possible. We also thank Mike Montague, Vibhas Chandorkar, and Donna Liu for their close work with Jim in some of the earliest days of the Microsoft RPC development project. Brian Moran at Microsoft enthusiastically championed our book there.

Many other people helped shape this book, supplying on-the-spot reviews and various contributions of software, testing examples, and participating in countless hallway conversations. At Digital, these people include Steve Jenness, Charlie Wickham, Will Lees, Stan Gazaway, Emilie Schmidt, Peter Keegan, Andy Ferris, Judy Egan, Janet McCann, Laura Holly, Darrell Icenogle, Mary Ellen Zurko, Clayton Martin, Mark Fox, Joe Comuzzi, John Wray, and Davie Robinson. Their counterparts at Microsoft include Bharat Shah, Mario Goertzel, Steve Zeck, Bruce McQuistan, Jeff Roberts, Ryszard Kott, and John Murray.

We are especially indebted to the folks at O'Reilly & Associates for their craft in turning our drafts into a real book. These creative people include Chris Reilley for his fine artwork, Edie Freedman for the wonderful cover design, Steve Spainhour for his precise copy editing, Ellie Cutler for producing the index, and Linda Walsh for managing the business end of things. We also owe a special thanks to Tim O'Reilly whose insights were invaluable in developing the final manuscript.

Finally, we owe our deepest gratitude to Frank Willison, who dreamed up the idea of this book and who imagined Jim and me as its authors.

1

Building Bridges

Despite many attempts over the years to get different types of computers to work together, lots of networked systems remain segregated. UNIX talks to UNIX, and PCs keep to themselves.

But recently, a lot of progress has been made on getting heterogeneous systems to work together in standard ways. The Open Software Foundation's Distributed Computing Environment represents one attempt to provide a common set of libraries that supports the development, use, and maintenance of distributed client-server applications on heterogeneous networked computers. Meanwhile, Microsoft is developing Windows NT, another environment designed to provide seamless connections among multiple systems.

To use a geographical metaphor, let's think of OSF DCE and the Microsoft environment as two continents separated by a body of water. Moving between these distinct continents has been difficult, so the cultures of each have remained relatively isolated from one another. Each continent has its own infrastructure built from and serving the cultural needs of its user-citizens. Operating in splendid isolation has its advantages; the population can conduct business quite efficiently in its native language while being protected from dealing with the problems of foreign cultures. But they're also denied the benefits of diversity. While each culture has its strengths, it also has weaknesses that could be offset by inherent strengths of the foreign culture.

Now it's possible to build bridges between these two continents. The governments of each continent share common architectural specifications and have manufactured special tools needed to build the bridges. All that's needed now are talented engineers who know how to use the tools. This is where you come in. Equipped with the information we provide here, you'll be well-prepared to develop cross-environment applications that bridge these similar-yet-different environments.

Let's look briefly at the two environments—DCE and Windows NT—and see what makes it possible to tie them together.

DCE   A diverse collection of libraries, tools, and runtime services that, together, make a network appear like a single system.

Mostly associated with the UNIX operating system, DCE is actually system-independent. Gradient Technologies has a version called PC-DCE that runs on Windows 3.1 making it possible for a PC to be a DCE client.

The glue that holds DCE together is its Remote Procedure Call (RPC) mechanism. RPC allows programs on one system to call functions that run on another system. All communication between different runtime parts of DCE use RPC, and it is the foundation for user applications as well. Differences in architectures, network transport protocols, and physical location are all hidden by RPC.

Windows NT

A modern operating system that can run both on high-end PCs and on workstation architectures. Windows NT covers all parts of the computing platform: the OS, the windowing system, and network communications.

Into Windows NT, Microsoft has incorporated an RPC mechanism that is compatible with DCE. This may be a small point of connection, but it's a critical one, given RPC's ability to mask architectural differences. To magnify the role of RPC even more, Microsoft is making it available for versions of MS-DOS and Windows 3.x.

What does this all mean in terms of distributed applications? If you can write a program using DCE RPC and Microsoft RPC, you can run it on multiple systems of many different types:

- DCE servers communicating with Windows NT clients

- Windows NT servers communicating with DCE clients

- DCE servers communicating with clients on MS-DOS, with or without Windows

And all this is possible using a single set of highly portable source files, with minimal attention to architectural differences!

While most of this book concentrates on the mechanics of developing cross-environment applications, we'll take a couple of minutes now to compare alternatives in distributed computing (that is, we will talk about current offerings in the industry and show what is special about using DCE and Windows NT together). Then we'll describe what is offered in each environment (DCE and Microsoft) by itself. Finally, we'll describe the basic components that can tie the two environments together.

Comparing Alternatives

Distributed computing has become a major buzzword for computing in the 1990s. The term has become closely associated with *downsizing*—another trendy buzzword denoting corporate migration from centralized mainframe environments towards networks of workstations, minicomputers, and personal computers.

In this section, we'll try to provide a framework for judging what the industry is doing, and what each alternative offers. Of course there's little doubt about where we'll end up—this whole book is based on the assumption that you're programming for both DCE and the Microsoft environment. But we'll do our best to be objective.

Partial Solutions

Early distributed applications included network fileservers that enabled network users to access each other's files as if the files were on local disks. Network database applications soon arrived with powerful data management and delivery mechanisms built on the client-server model. LAN products like Novell NetWare and Microsoft LAN Manager deliver integrated file, printing, and mail services. But while these vertical solutions are extremely efficient at their prescribed tasks, they are narrowly focused and don't easily adapt to alternative uses.

Frameworks for More Complete Solutions

If you've bought this book, you've probably decided that off-the-shelf partial solutions don't meet your organization's needs. You are willing to put resources into writing your own applications that provide specialized services. You need a general programming interface in two senses: general in its scope so you can make it do anything you want, and general in its architectural support, so you can get different types of systems working together. And one more thing, you'd probably like to spend your time writing the application itself rather than deal with managing network communications between distributed parts of your program.

There are tools that can deliver these capabilities into your hands. Distinct from narrowly-focused distributed applications like the partial solutions we mentioned earlier, these tools support more general frameworks that enable the implementation and deployment of broad classes of solutions.

RPC is one such framework. It enables processes on one system to share data with and invoke processes on remote systems—even dissimilar ones. Message queueing services represent another kind of general purpose framework, but message queueing is better suited to operations that take a long time to complete—like compiling a program or printing a file. RPC is better suited to shorter, atomic operations—like crunching some numbers, or returning some stored data in response to a client request. Its programming semantics offer more control over operations than you'll find with message queueing services. Now let's take a look at some of the RPC options you have to choose from.

RPC choices

Sun Microsystems was among the first to offer a distributed application utilizing an RPC technology. Their popular Network File System (NFS), which still rules the roost in many networks, runs over RPC and uses the Network Information Service (NIS) to locate file servers. Sun is also making NFS, and its underlying RPC mechanism, available on Windows NT. Thus, people who want to use Sun RPC will be able to make it work on nearly any system, UNIX, MS-DOS, or Windows NT.

OSF DCE relies on another type of RPC as the basis for distributing applications across heterogeneous systems. DCE RPC is based on the Network Computing System, a joint development effort by Apollo Computer (now part of Hewlett-Packard, Inc.) and Digital Equipment Corporation. OSF DCE provides a comprehensive set of services that enable secure (authenticated) operation between distributed processes in a network. DCE is gaining increasingly wide acceptance as more vendors port it to their critical platforms.

Of these two types of RPC, the one you choose will likely depend on what else you want in your environment—for instance, do you want NFS and NIS, or the DCE file system and other DCE services? At any rate, if you choose DCE, you'll still have access to the Microsoft environment.

DCE and the Microsoft environment

Microsoft has recently jumped onto the RPC bandwagon with Microsoft RPC. Largely compatible with the Open Software Foundation's DCE RPC, Microsoft RPC is available for PCs running Microsoft Windows NT, Microsoft Windows, or Microsoft DOS. It's bundled with Microsoft Windows NT, and it'll be widely available for Microsoft Windows and Microsoft DOS, so you can expect it to be just about everywhere. Because Microsoft RPC is compatible with OSF's DCE RPC, most PCs and systems running OSF DCE can share resources in a standard and consistent manner.

From DCE systems, you can get access to Microsoft systems in two ways. One is the method used in this book, where you depend on native support for Microsoft RPC in Windows NT, MS-DOS, and 16-bit Windows. The other is to run Gradient Technologies Inc.'s PC-DCE on each PC running Windows 3.1. Gradient's product is pretty impressive: it includes support for the client side of every service, including the DCE Security Service, the largest hole in this book's solution. It also supports application servers on PCs.

It's not our job to figure costs and benefits, or to propose what you should do. Our book is for people who want to write an application that works equally well in a pure Microsoft environment, a DCE environment, or on a mixture of systems that crosses the two environments. But before we get into the mechanics of writing cross-environment applications, we'll just take another moment here to offer two compelling reasons why you might consider writing them. The reasons can be summed up with two (possibly overused but quite appropriate here) aphorisms: "strength in numbers" and "getting the benefits of diversity."

We believe the most viable cross-environment applications will give users the consistency, pervasiveness, and attractiveness of a low-cost Microsoft Windows client front end that is backed up by the power and information resources of DCE server machines. The vast numbers of Microsoft Windows systems sitting on desktops suggests these as the natural client platform. And though Microsoft Windows NT makes a powerful RPC server, relying on NT alone denies your clients the often-complementary strengths found in foreign operating systems. Thus Microsoft RPC client-to-DCE server is a very natural and cost-effective configuration.

A Map of the Territory: Technical Summaries

So far, we've suggested some reasons why you might want to develop applications that span the Microsoft RPC and DCE environments, but we really haven't focused on how these environments work together. Now, to give you an idea of the terrain we'll be working in, we'll review the RPC model. Then we'll give you a bird's eye view of the DCE and Microsoft RPC environments. Seeing these two environments side by side will give you a sense of the ground this book will cover.

Remote Procedure Call

RPC is a distributed programming method wherein an application executing on one system (a client) calls a procedure that resides on another remote system (a server) in the network.

RPC keeps development cycles fairly simple; it masks differences among heterogeneous computers by managing data conversion needs. Its development tools also generate the code (called client and server stub code) that can manage most aspects of network communications, thus freeing programmers to concentrate on developing the application itself.

Figure 1-1 shows the major steps of a remote procedure call.

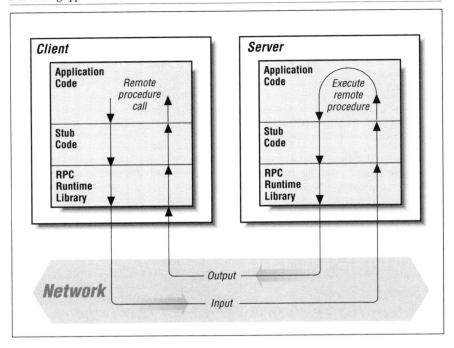

Figure 1-1: Remote procedure call model

The process contains many steps, but they fall into three stages:

1. The client application calls a procedure in the normal way but the RPC development process has substituted a stub procedure in place of the actual procedure, which resides on a remote system in the network. The client stub and RPC runtime library organize the parameters and transmit them to the server system on the network.

2. The server stub and RPC runtime library receive the parameters and invoke the remote procedure on the server, reorganizing and transmitting the results back to the client system.

3. The client stub and RPC runtime library receive the results from the server and pass them back to the calling code in the client application.

To get clients and servers working together, you have to make sure that they recognize the same calls and that the client can find the right host system and port for the server. DCE and Microsoft have similar solutions to these problems, but there are differences which we describe later in this chapter.

The Interface Definition Language

For a client's call to succeed, programmers need to make sure that the server is actually offering that remote procedure. That is, the server must be coded to a specification. It promises, "If a client issues such-and-such a call with such-and-such arguments, the server can handle it."

Such a specification is called an *interface definition.* In DCE, the language you use to write the specification is called the Interface Definition Language (IDL). Microsoft calls their language MIDL (for Microsoft IDL). The two are very similar, but they have a few differences which we'll explore in Chapter 3, *Writing Interface Definitions.* The interface definition basically looks like a set of ANSI C prototypes but contains extra keywords that make data transfers over the network more efficient.

Binding information

When you issue a remote procedure call in your client, how does it find a remote host and determine which server to connect to on that host? Most of the work is hidden in the stub code that is generated by the RPC development tools. But your client must somehow get some information about the server; this is called a *binding.* The information includes the transport mechanism used (such as TCP/IP), the name of the host, and the endpoint at which the server is listening (such as a TCP port).

In its simplest form, binding information could be hardcoded in an application, entered by the user, or retrieved from a file. You might even use one of those crude methods for the debugging phase of your application. But for industrial-strength use, you want the flexibility of updating information and choosing a server at any time. This requires a database maintained by an independent service.

Both DCE and Microsoft offer a runtime service called a name service, where the client submits a server name and is furnished the corresponding binding information. The two environments use different name services, but we shall show later in this chapter how to resolve this discrepancy. Figure 1-2 shows how the server and client find each other using a name service. These are the steps noted in the figure:

❶ Servers *export* binding information to the name service.

❷ Clients *import* binding information from the name service.

❸ Clients use the binding information to make a remote procedure call to the server. Clients also have to know which process to communicate with once they reach the server system; this is accomplished by referring to an endpoint map, not shown here.

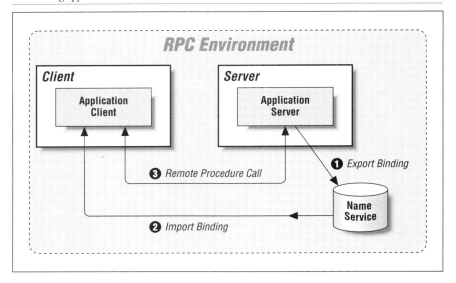

Figure 1-2: How clients find servers

To export and import binding information, programs call special routines that handle the internal details of the name service. These routines are called Name-Service Independent (NSI) and they make cross-environment applications much easier to develop. As we'll see, DCE and Microsoft provide different name services, but the NSI routines keep programmers from having to deal with the differences.

RPC is just one small part of distributed computing. It's important now to see what else you get with DCE and Microsoft Windows NT and where they overlap. Generally, the features that are common to both environments are the only features you can use in a cross-environment application. In some cases, you are lucky and are allowed to use the best of both worlds.

The DCE Environment

The OSF DCE is a comprehensive distributed environment; it uses RPC technology to distribute applications across multiple networked computers, and it also supplies a set of services that fulfill many additional distribution needs.

DCE Security Service
> This lets a process on one system verify the identity of a process on another system and selectively give access to resources. DCE offers this service because the underlying operating system is not expected to do all the things that are necessary to make distributed security work. Distributed security requires an independent service

that exchanges secret passwords with both the client's user and the server and checks their identities against a central database.

Microsoft systems provide their own form of distributed security, but as shown in the next section, it does not work with DCE.

DCE Directory Service

The name service in DCE is called the Cell Directory Service. DCE uses the term *cell* for the set of systems that are administered together. The concept is like that of a "domain" in Windows NT or Sun's NIS.

As we have described, CDS provides information to clients on how to reach servers. It actually has a much broader potential than that—it could be a global addressing system for any kind of object—but for the purposes of this book we'll stick to its most common use as a storage place for server information.

Microsoft systems can use CDS through a set-up we'll describe later.

Distributed File Service (DFS)

This imposes a single directory structure across all systems in a cell. DFS is a critical service for users, who can specify the same file name no matter what system they log into. It is not so important for programs, because in client-server computing it is natural to locate a server on the same system as the file containing the desired data.

Microsoft provides a uniform file system in Windows NT that covers MS-DOS as well. The file system is not compatible with DFS.

Distributed Time Service (DTS)

This keeps all systems synchronized. Processes on different systems can request the time from DTS and be assured of receiving the same answer. This service is used by specialized applications that have real-time constraints. Microsoft does not provide a time service.

Figure 1-3 shows how clients and servers interact with the two main DCE services, Security and CDS, with the following steps:

❶ A user logs into DCE, supplying a password to verify his or her identity to the Security service. The user can then invoke a client that takes on that user's identity.

❷ When the server starts, it also logs into DCE through a programming call to verify its identity.

❸ The DCE directory service (CDS) verifies its identity, too. This lets servers verify that they're putting their binding information into the authentic name service.

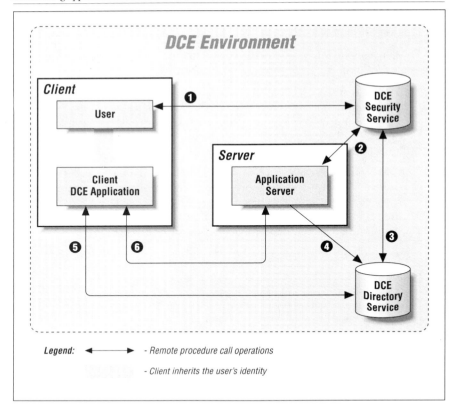

Figure 1-3: How DCE works

❹ The server places its binding information into CDS.

❺ The client obtains the server's binding information from CDS.

❻ The client makes a remote procedure call—what this book is all about.

The Microsoft RPC Environment

Since Microsoft RPC is integrated into its surrounding operating system, it depends on this operating system for most of the services that exist independently in DCE. Thus, security is available to RPC applications, but only over named pipes. This is because a named pipe is part of the file system, and Microsoft has built distributed security into its file system.

Unfortunately, DCE systems cannot use named pipes—the only transport that Microsoft and DCE consistently share is TCP/IP. Because Microsoft and DCE must use TCP/IP for their transport, and because Microsoft does not currently support DCE's security, the two forms of security offer almost no protection for cross-environment applications. In Chapter 6, *Writing a*

Server, we'll see how DCE security does offer a small way to control Microsoft RPC access to the DCE directory service.

Microsoft RPC also provides its own name service called the locator. Unlike the DCE directory service, the locator's namespace organization is flat rather than hierarchical in nature, limiting its ability to accommodate large naming environments. The locator implements the Microsoft Windows NT concept of the network domain, which is a group of Windows NT servers that share a common user security database. Figure 1-4 shows how servers and clients use the locator to pass binding information.

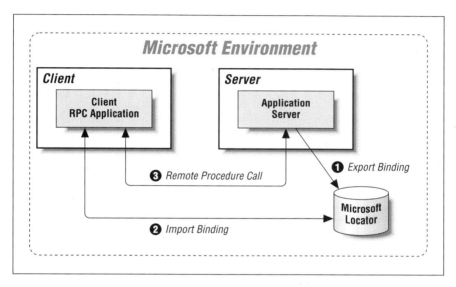

Figure 1-4: How the Microsoft RPC environment works

❶ Servers export binding information to the name service.

❷ Clients import binding information from the name service.

❸ Clients use the binding information to make a remote procedure call to the server.

A Note About Threads

The use of threads is an increasingly popular way to improve program performance. Programmers use a library of threads routines to interleave suspended operations with active ones, keeping the processor in constant use.

In DCE, threads are primarily used by servers so they can handle multiple, simultaneous requests from multiple clients. The threads implementation is based on the POSIX 1003.4a (Draft 4) standard.

Threads are also available as part of the Microsoft NT operating system. The NT implementation is not POSIX 1003.4 compliant, so modifications will likely be needed for server portability to other operating systems. Microsoft RPC does not provide threads for Microsoft Windows or DOS machines. Because Microsoft RPC treats Microsoft Windows and DOS as client-only operating systems, the lack of threads does not pose problems. Microsoft plans to bring threads to Microsoft Windows platforms with their WIN32S software developer's kit due out sometime this year. But it's too soon to tell how this will affect Microsoft RPC operation on Microsoft Windows platforms.

This book discusses threads as they are used by servers for handling multiple client requests. Although we provide some basic guidelines, threads is a complicated subject, and we leave more sophisticated use of threads to other relevant books.

Cross-Environment Applications Use the CDS Name Services

Microsoft RPC and DCE RPC need a consistent way for servers to pass binding information to clients, so both environments rely on the DCE directory service. However, while DCE systems use the DCE directory service by default, Microsoft RPC systems must be redirected from using the Microsoft locator to using the DCE directory service. In Chapter 4, we'll see how to redirect Microsoft RPC systems.

In your code, you don't have to do anything special to use CDS. This is because it's all built in to the NSI routines that you call from your client and server. That is, your code can run without change whether you use the Microsoft locator or CDS. The choice is made at the administrative level.

DCE client and server applications interact with the DCE directory service using an intermediary called the CDS clerk. The clerk relieves applications from the complicated task of using the name service directly. But because the locator is simpler than the DCE directory service, Microsoft RPC clients and servers do not provide an intermediary process like the CDS clerk. So DCE provides this function for Microsoft RPC systems in a special proxy agent called the name service interface daemon (*nsid*). The *nsid*, running on a DCE system, accepts NSI calls from Microsoft RPC systems. It performs the requested DCE directory service operation and returns any results to the Microsoft RPC system.

To the Microsoft RPC system, the *nsid* looks like a server process. To the DCE directory service's CDS server, the *nsid* looks just like any other CDS clerk on a DCE machine.

Figure 1-5 shows how a cross-environment application's PC client uses the *nsid* to interact with the DCE directory service.

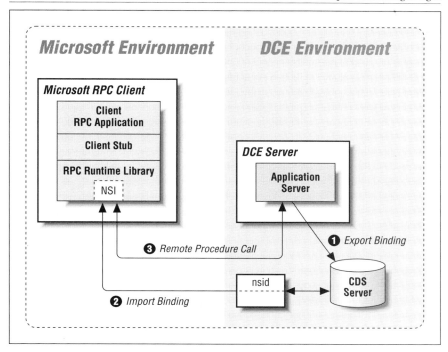

Figure 1-5: How a cross-environment application works

❶ The DCE server exports binding information to the Cell Directory Service.

❷ The Microsoft client issues Name-Service Independent calls to find binding information. These calls query the *nsid*, which formulates the queries so that CDS can handle them.

❸ The client uses the binding information to make a remote procedure call to the server.

What's Next?

OSF DCE and Microsoft RPC use the same protocols internally, but their programming interfaces look different. You can resolve most of these differences by using the C preprocessor so the same code can be compiled on either platform. The next chapter offers a concrete example application to get you up and running quickly.

2

Developing a Cross-Environment Application

Writing a distributed cross-environment application is, in most ways, very similar to developing a pure DCE or a pure Microsoft RPC application. The client and server share an interface file that defines the things both sides have to agree on, such as argument data types. An optional attribute configuration file (ACF) on each side can tune some compilation and networking issues without affecting the other side. In regular C code, you write routines for each side that look just like a traditional, local application. Finally, because some aspects of distributed computing cannot be fully automated, you have to provide some special code covering initialization (for servers only), error recovery, and other scattered programming tasks.

But there are also differences. While this book focuses on writing applications that rely on the strengths of the two environments, we need to know how to deal with environment differences so that your program will build and execute successfully.

We will use this chapter to walk through the development of a basic client-server application to get you up and running. Along the way, we'll encounter some of the differences you'll need to manage.

The pace is rather fast—we won't try to justify everything we're doing—so if this is your first encounter with RPC, you'll have to take a few things on faith. You are expected to augment your background with readings on other books about Microsoft RPC and OSF/DCE (see the preface for suggestions).

Managing Differences Between DCE RPC and Microsoft RPC

Although DCE and Microsoft RPC are very similar, there are some differences. Here are some obvious ones:

- The APIs use different notation conventions. While the DCE APIs divide function names, separating segments with underscores like *rpc_ns_binding_import_next*, Microsoft RPC omits the underscores, capitalizing the first letter in each segment as in *RpcNsBindingImportNext*.

- The interface definition languages are not identical. Each has a few features that the other does not support.

- DCE provides distributed services that include a directory service, a security service, and a time service to aid in operating distributed applications over a variety of transports. The Microsoft environment provides a simple directory service called the locator, and security is implemented directly in the named pipes transport layer.

You can deal with these and other differences by masking them where possible, and by relying only on capabilities and services that are equally available in both environments.

The sample application we build in this chapter is quite simple so it bumps into only a few of the differences. But we are pointing out the obvious ones here so you'll be aware of the larger issues we'll face in later chapters.

Cross-Environment Application Development Overview

A simplified development process for a cross-environment distributed application is shown in Figure 2-1. The darker shaded region of the diagram highlights the code you write. The lighter shaded regions define the platforms where code is written or compiled.

An interface definition contains just the things that both sides need to know so they can exchange information. C code contains the local parts of the application executed by each side, along with RPC initialization and other tasks that have to be performed on a particular side. In between these two types of code lies the ACF, which controls aspects of application building that matter only on one side. Finally, you should have a makefile on each side to coordinate the various stages of building.

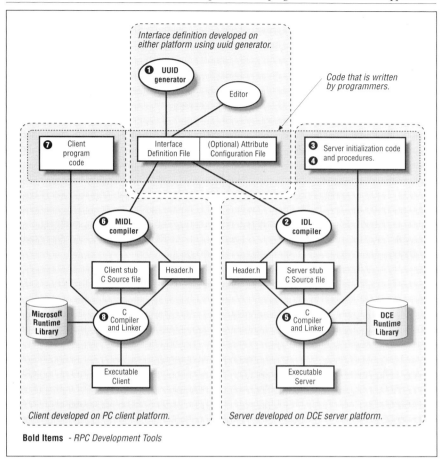

Figure 2-1: Developing a PC client, DCE server distributed application

Here are some general steps you can follow to write a distributed cross-environment application. These steps are shown by callouts in the figure.

❶ Use *uuidgen* to create a template for an interface definition file. *uuidgen* creates a unique identifier called a UUID to mark your application. Then use your favorite editor to complete the interface definition by including procedure declarations for each remote procedure offered by the server. You can also create an optional attribute configuration file (ACF) to control things like the method a client uses to find and communicate with a server.

❷ Use the IDL compiler on the DCE server to compile the interface definitions, producing the server stub file and header file.

❸ Write the server initialization code that prepares the server to receive incoming remote procedure calls.

❹ Write the server procedures (manager procedures). This is the code that implements the remote procedures.

❺ Use the C compiler on the DCE server to compile and link the server code, stub file, and header file with the DCE runtime library, producing an executable server.

❻ Use the MIDL compiler on the PC to compile the interface definitions, producing the client stub file and header file.

❼ Write the client program code. This is the code that will present information to the user and invoke remote procedures.

❽ Use the C compiler on the PC to compile and link the client program, stub file, and header file with the Microsoft RPC runtime library, producing an executable client.

We recommend using *make* or *nmake* with a makefile to simplify compiling.

Once your client and server build successfully you can test and use your distributed application. First, start the server so it's ready to handle incoming remote procedure calls. Then start the client program and use it to interact with the server. Distributed applications can streamline the ways you manage widely-used information. Something as simple as an organization's phone number list can be difficult to manage when it's updated on a regular basis. Someone needs to send it out to everyone, and then each person needs to replace their old list with the new list.

In this book, we take on the little problem of distributing phone numbers and solve it through a client-server application using RPC. Everyone in the organization uses his or her own client application to query the server's phone number list as needed. Now the secretary just updates the central list. No one else really has to do anything.

We call our application *phnbk*. Our server maintains a file that contains a list of organization members and their phone numbers. A single phonebook client can simply browse the file or it can request a specific user's information.

Let's walk through the development steps for this straightforward cross-environment application. First, we'll develop the phonebook application's interface definition file and client ACF, and then we'll complete the files that make up the client side. Finally, we'll develop and build the files that make up the server side. The complete set of files for this simple phonebook application is included in Appendix B. Throughout this book we will build on this program, showing ways to make it more flexible.

Writing the Interface Definition File

Clients and servers must agree on the remote procedure's calling sequences—basically, their names and the arguments that are passed and returned. You write this agreement (it could even be called a contract) in the form of an interface definition file using the IDL or MIDL language. You impart this contract to the client and server when you compile and link the interface definition file with the client and server code.

The main use of an interface definition is to declare each remote procedure offered by the server. Each procedure declaration specifies the name of the procedure, the order and data types of any parameters, and the data type of any return value. Each interface definition must also be unique so that clients can distinguish interfaces from one another. Uniqueness is provided by the interface definition file header that includes a UUID and version number.

You can generate a UUID and optionally create a template for an IDL file by using a *uuidgen* utility, which is provided with both DCE and Microsoft RPC. Generate a template *.idl* file for the *phnbk* application by typing the *uuidgen* command. Some non-UNIX systems might use a command syntax other than that shown here:

```
uuidgen -i > phnbk.idl
```

The *phnbk.idl* file template looks like the sample output in Example 2-1.

Example 2-1: IDL File Template

```
[
 uuid(F2FE85A0-0C28-1068-A726-AA0004007EFF),          ❶
 version(1.0),                                         ❷
]
interface INTERFACENAME                                ❸
{
                                                       ❹
}
```

❶ Universal Unique Identifier (UUID). This number, along with the version number (see the second callout), distinguishes this particular interface from any other interface.

❷ Interface version number. This number allows you to change an interface in minor ways without changing the interface number. For instance, you can add new features for new clients while maintaining compatibility between the server and earlier versions of clients.

❸ Interface name. You will replace INTERFACENAME with the name of the interface.

❹ Delimiters for procedure declarations.

Use your favorite editor to complete the IDL file. Example 2-2 shows the completed *phnbk.idl* file.

Example 2-2: phnbk.idl File

```
/*
**   Interface Definition File for simple phnbk client
*/
[
 uuid(F2FE85A0-0C28-1068-A726-AA0004007EFF),
 version(1.0),
 pointer_default(ref)]                                       ❶
interface phnbk                                              ❷
{
/*
** Constant for maximum line size
*/
const long LINESIZE = 100;                                   ❸
/*
** Flag for hitting end of phonebook file
*/
const short END = -1;
/*
** Flag for normal completion of operation
*/
const short NORMAL = 0;
/*
** Define all possible operations on phonebook file
*/
typedef enum                                                 ❹
           {
            FIRSTMATCH,
            NEXTMATCH,
            BROWSE,
            RESET,
            BROWSE_RESET
           } operations;
/*
** Perform some operation on the phonebook
*/
short lookup                                                 ❺
     (
     [in]         short operation,
     [in,string]  char  search_string[LINESIZE],
     [out,string] char  return_string[LINESIZE]
     );
}
```

❶ Pointer default. This default is used by some distributed applications to ensure that pointer data is efficiently transmitted. Although our application does not use pointers, we include the pointer default line because the MIDL compiler complains when the line is missing.

❷ Name the interface. The interface name is usually something easy to remember because users put it in environment variables and commands. For DOS-based clients, limit interface names to six or fewer characters because the MIDL compiler adds two characters to the interface name when naming the resulting stub files.

❸ Constants *LINESIZE, END,* and *NORMAL* are defined for use in client and server.

❹ The enumerated type maps *phnbk* operations to integers that will be used by the remote procedure.

❺ This remote procedure performs a user-specified action on the phonebook data file.

Writing the Attribute Configuration File

Clients and servers need to agree on each procedure's arguments and how they are passed over the network, so these are defined in the IDL file. But some things can change from client to client, or from server to server, and each side never has to know what choices you make for the other side. Since you don't want these things set in stone, DCE and Microsoft RPC provide ACFs as a way to change the behavior of individual clients and servers.

Here, we'll use an ACF to change the way a client finds a server. RPC offers several ways for a client to find and to start communication with (bind to) the server. For the purposes of this chapter, we'll use a method called *implicit binding* because it doesn't require the use of the directory service. Using the directory service would add some steps to the application that we don't want to discuss yet.

Instead of a directory service, the user has to get involved in binding. The server prints its binding information on the screen. Users pass this binding information to the client as a parameter when they start the client program.

We might want future clients to use another binding method to find servers, so we'll put the binding instructions in an ACF. This approach allows us to change the binding method later without modifying the actual client program or server remote procedures. Use your editor to create the *phnbk.acf* file as shown in Example 2-3.

Example 2-3: phnbk.acf File

```
[
implicit_handle (handle_t xhandle)                        ❶
]
interface phnbk                                           ❷
{                                                         ❸
}
```

❶ Use the `implicit_handle` attribute and the IDL data type `handle_t` to declare a global binding handle named *xhandle*.

❷ Make the interface name (*phnbk*) match the interface name in the corresponding IDL file.

❸ The braces can hold other attributes to control compilation, but in this application there is nothing we need to do.

Developing the Client Program

Our simple phonebook client program provides three functions for its users. First, it presents a user interface (a menu) which lets users interact with the phonebook application. Second, the client sends requests to the phonebook server. Third, it interprets and returns server responses to users.

The client code runs on Microsoft Windows NT, Microsoft Windows, and Microsoft DOS system. For simplicity, we've made the user interface rather primitive; the client program simply prints a menu of possible user commands onto the screen as shown in Example 2-4. Users then enter the information needed for each action.

Example 2-4: Phonebook Application User Interface

```
Valid commands are:
(b)rowse          - List next entry
(r)eset           - Reset to beginning of file
(f)ind <string>   - Find a substring
(f)ind            - Find next occurrence of <string>
(q)uit            - Exit program
```

The user can either search the phonebook for a particular string, or browse sequentially. One possibility is to request a search for a name, then start browsing at that point to see all the following entries. Other options include searching for the same string, returning to the beginning of the list, or quitting.

The client provides these commands by entering an infinite loop in which it accepts simple keyboard input and interprets it as a command. Every command except "quit" requires some action with the remote database, either to get a line of information or to reset the pointer to the beginning. Thus, each of these commands generates a call to a remote procedure.

Preprocessor Directives

The client application contains several preprocessor directives required for Microsoft RPC client and server program code. We've also included condition statements that allow the client code to be used on a DCE platform. Example 2-5 shows the portion of client code with preprocessor directives.

Example 2-5: Phonebook Client Preprocessor Directives

```
/*
**
**
** MODULE:    client.c
**
**
** PROGRAM:   Portable PHNBK Application (OpenVMS,DOS,NT,OSF/1,ULTRIX)
**
**
** ABSTRACT:  PHNBK is a sample RPC application intended to illustrate
**            the basics of RPC interoperation between DCE platforms
**            and Microsoft platforms.
**
**
**
**
*/
#include <stdio.h>
#include <string.h>
#include <stdlib.h>
#include <malloc.h>
#include "phnbk.h"                                                    ❶
#if defined(MSDOS) || defined(WIN32)
#include "dceport.h"                                                  ❷
#endif
#ifdef WIN32
#define MAIN_DECL _CRTAPI1                                            ❸
#else
#define MAIN_DECL
#endif
```

❶ *phnbk.h* is generated by MIDL (or IDL). It defines the IDL data type idl_char used by the *lookup* remote procedure, the remote procedure function prototypes, and all the requisite constants needed by the application.

❷ The *dceport.h* header file redefines Microsoft RPC calls to take the form of DCE RPC calls.

❸ On Windows NT, `_CRTAPI1` provides a hardware-platform-independent way to declare "main" so that the proper function calling types are used.

Declaring Data Types

Example 2-6 shows the portion of client code that declares data types used in the program. `MAINDECL` is necessary in Windows NT but is stripped out by the C preprocessor on other systems.

Example 2-6: Phonebook Client Data Type Declarations

```
int
MAIN_DECL main
              (
                  ac,
                  av
              )
int    ac;
char *av[];
{
    int                i;
    int                lookup_status;      /* lookup return status */
    error_status_t     status;             /* rpc status */
    idl_char           input[LINESIZE];    /* 'find' search string */
    idl_char           output[LINESIZE];   /* string returned from database*/
    idl_char           oldmatch[LINESIZE]; /* previous 'find' string */
    char               command;            /* lookup command */
    unsigned char      server[80];         /* string binding for server */
```

Initializing the Client

Before the client interacts with the server, we need to set some starting parameters, construct a server binding, and print a menu of user commands on the screen. Example 2-7 includes the portion of code that initializes the client application.

Example 2-7: Phonebook Client Initialization

```
/*
** Initialize some strings
*/
oldmatch[0] = '\0';
server[0]   = '\0';
```

Example 2-7: Phonebook Client Initialization (continued)

```
if (ac < 2)
    {
    /*
    ** With this version of phonebook, the user must specify the
    **    server's binding as a string on the command line.  If the
    **    user hasn't done that, then tell them about the error and
    **    exit the program so they can try again.
    **
    */
    printf("\nPlease specify a server hostname on command line:\n");
    printf("\n\tphnbk myhost\n\n");

    exit (EXIT_FAILURE);
    }
else
    {
    /*
    ** The user has specified a string binding
    */
    strcat (server,"ncacn_ip_tcp:");                              ❶
    strcat (server,av[1]);
    }
/*
** Display the server in use
*/
printf("\n\t(Selected server binding: %s)\n\n",server);
/*
** Convert the character string binding into an RPC handle
*/
rpc_binding_from_string_binding                                  ❷
            (
             server,
             &xhandle,
             &status
            );
if (status)
    {
    printf("Invalid string binding\n");
    exit (EXIT_FAILURE);
    }
/*
** Usage -- present user with a list of valid commands              ❸
*/
printf("Valid commands are:\n");
printf(" (b)rowse        - List next entry\n");
printf(" (r)eset         - Reset to beginning of file\n");
printf(" (f)ind <string> - Find a substring\n");
printf(" (f)ind          - Find next occurrence of <string>\n");
printf(" (q)uit          - Exit program\n\n");
```

❶ This client and server use TCP/IP only, because that protocol is available on both Microsoft and DCE systems. Users enter a server's hostname on the command line and a bind server provides the address.

❷ The program constructs a binding handle (*xhandle*) from the string binding the user entered on the client command line.

❸ The Usage section prints the menu of user commands shown earlier.

The Main Client Loop

The main client loop is the part of the program that waits for user input, sends requests to the phonebook server, and returns server responses to users. It consists of an infinite loop. Example 2-8 shows some essential elements of the main loop in the client program code.

Notice that even though the client code relies on Microsoft RPC, the client RPC calls follow the DCE RPC API naming convention. We've redefined the Microsoft calls using the header file *dceport.h*.

Example 2-8: Phonebook Client Program Main Loop

```
/*
** Keep looking for further commands until the user issues the
**      (q)uit command...
*/
while(1)
    {
    /*
    ** Initialize input and output strings
    */
    input[0]  = '\0';
    output[0] = '\0';
    /*
    ** Wait for user input
    */
    command = getchar();                                          ❶
    /*
    ** Select on user input
    */
    switch(command)
        {
        .
        .                                                        ❷
        .
        /*
        ** Command "b" means just return the next entry
        **      in the phonebook file.
        */
```

Example 2-8: Phonebook Client Program Main Loop (continued)

```
case 'b' :                                                        ❸

    /*
    ** Display next entry from wherever we happen to be
    **    positioned in the phonebook
    */
    lookup_status = lookup                                        ❹
                       (
                       BROWSE,
                       input,
                       output
                       );
    /*
    ** Echo entry or rewind database if we're at the end
    **    of the phonebook
    */
    if (lookup_status != END)
        printf("Entry is: %s\n", output);
    else
        printf("Resetting...\n");
    break;
```

❶ The program waits for a user to enter a character. The *getchar* function usually line-buffers the input so you'll likely have to press ENTER or RETURN.

❷ We've omitted several cases (f, f<string>, and r) from this sample client program. The entire program is contained in Appendix B.

❸ If the user enters a "b", look up the next entry in the phonebook file on the server system. The server maintains a file pointer for the client.

❹ The lookup function initiates a remote procedure on the server.

Client Program Termination

Example 2-9 shows how the client program terminates. Users invoke this part of the program by choosing the quit option from the menu in the main client loop.

Example 2-9: Phonebook Client Program Exit

```
/*
** Command "q" means exit the program
*/
case 'q' :                                                        ❶
```

Example 2-9: Phonebook Client Program Exit (continued)

```
                    /*
                    ** Free binding handle
                    */
                    rpc_binding_free                                    ❷
                            (
                            &xhandle,
                            &status
                            );
                    /*
                    ** Exit program
                    */
                    printf("Exiting...\n");
                    exit(EXIT_SUCCESS);
            default :
                break;
            /*
            ** End of "switch" block
            */
            }

        /*
        ** End of "while" block
        */
        }
}
#if defined(MSDOS) || defined(WIN32)                                    ❸
/**********************************************************************/
/***              MIDL_user_allocate / MIDL_user_free             ***/
/**********************************************************************/
void * __RPC_API
MIDL_user_allocate
            (
            size
            )
size_t size;
{
    unsigned char * ptr;
    ptr = malloc( size );
    return ( (void *)ptr );
}
void __RPC_API
MIDL_user_free
            (
            object
            )
void * object;
{
    free (object);
}
#endif
```

❶ Case q in the main loop terminates the client program. The server is not affected by client program termination.

❷ Initialization code created a binding handle that was used on each call to the server. Now, this RPC routine frees the memory used by the binding handle.

❸ Microsoft RPC client stub code allocates and frees memory using the *MIDL_user_allocate* and *MIDL_user_free* functions. The program never calls these functions directly, but defines them for internal use by the Microsoft libraries.

Compiling the Client Program

Compiling the client program is similar to compiling any application except that one preprocessor step is added: you need to run MIDL. This accepts the interface definition and attribute configuration files as input and produces the stub files and header files. Then you compile and link the resulting stub and header files with the client program in the usual manner.

The build process, and the files involved in it, are illustrated by Figure 2-2 with these features noted:

❶ On the Microsoft platform, the MIDL compiler produces client stubs and header files from the interface definition files and attribute configuration files.

❷ The C compiler and linker produces the executable client from the application source files, client stub and header files, and *dceport.h* header file. Intermediate object files are not shown.

When you are developing an application, we strongly encourage you to use a build tool like *nmake* to automate repetitive building tasks. Makefiles also release you from platform dependencies. Makefile scripts used by *nmake* rely on a file such as Windows NT's <*ntwin32.mak*> to translate commonly-named variables like $(cc), $(cdebug), and $(cflags) into platform-appropriate compiler and linker commands and switches. Appendix B, *The Simple Phonebook Application*, includes various makefiles you can use to build this chapter's program on different platforms. On a Windows NT system you can build the phonebook client (and server) using an *nmake* command like:

```
nmake -f makefile.nt
```

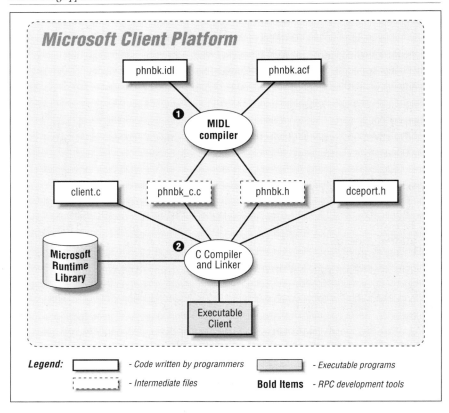

Figure 2-2: Building the executable client application

Developing the Server Program

Our phonebook server's main task is to perform various operations on a local text file in response to remote procedure calls from clients. To provide constant service, it needs to be ready and waiting for incoming remote procedure calls. So we'll divide the server program into two main files: the server initialization code which prepares the server to accept client calls, and the remote procedure which performs various operations requested by the client. We'll examine the server code in the order of its execution: first the initialization code, then the remote procedure.

Writing the Server Initialization Code

The phonebook initialization code places the server in a waiting state where it can receive incoming remote procedure calls from a client. The initialization code in our example follows standard DCE coding practices; the code doesn't need anything special to enable operation with a Microsoft RPC client. Example 2-10 shows the preprocessor directives, and Example 2-11 shows the rest of the initialization code.

Example 2-10: Phonebook Server Preprocessor Directives

```
/*
**
**
** MODULE:    server.c
**
**
** PROGRAM:   Portable PHNBK Application (OpenVMS,DOS,NT,OSF/1,ULTRIX)
**
**
** ABSTRACT:  PHNBK is a sample RPC application intended to illustrate
**            the basics of RPC interoperation between DCE platforms
**            and Microsoft platforms.
**
**
**
**
*/
#include <stdio.h>
#include <string.h>
#include <stdlib.h>
#include <malloc.h>
#include "phnbk.h"                                              ❶
#ifdef WIN32
#include "dceport.h"                                            ❷
#define MAIN_DECL _CRTAPI1
#define IFSPEC phnbk_ServerIfHandle                             ❸
#else
#define MAIN_DECL
#define IFSPEC phnbk_v1_0_s_ifspec                              ❹
#endif
```

❶ The IDL-generated *phnbk.h* header file contains definitions needed by the server program.

❷ The *dceport.h* header file redefines Microsoft RPC calls to take the form of DCE RPC calls. Even though we're building this on a DCE system, the source code can also be built on a Microsoft Windows NT server system.

❸ Microsoft RPC MIDL-generated interface specifications look like this.

❹ DCE IDL-generated interface specifications look like this.

Example 2-11: Phonebook Server Initialization Code

```
FILE * filehandle;        /* File handle used for phonebook file */
short previous_operation; /* Keeps track of previous phonebook operation */
int
MAIN_DECL main
            (
                ac,
                av
            )
int    ac;
char *av[];
{
    unsigned int            i;
    error_status_t          status;
    unsigned_char_t         *string_binding;
    rpc_binding_vector_p_t   bvec;
    /*
    **
    ** Specify TCP/IP as a protocol sequences
    */
    rpc_server_use_protseq                                                 ❶
            (
                "ncacn_ip_tcp",
                rpc_c_protseq_max_reqs_default,
                &status
            );
    if (status != error_status_ok)
        {
        printf("No available protocol sequences\n");
        exit(EXIT_FAILURE);
        }
    /*
    ** register the server interface
    */
    rpc_server_register_if                                                 ❷
            (
                IFSPEC,
                NULL,
                NULL,
                &status
            );
    if (status != error_status_ok)
        {
        printf("Can't register interface \n");
        exit(EXIT_FAILURE);
        }
    /*
    ** find out what binding information is actually available
    */
```

Example 2-11: Phonebook Server Initialization Code (continued)

```
rpc_server_inq_bindings                                          ❸
        (
        &bvec,
        &status
        );
if (status != error_status_ok)
    {
    printf("Can't inquire bindings \n");
    exit(EXIT_FAILURE);
    }
/*
** register with endpoint mapper
*/
rpc_ep_register                                                  ❹
        (
        IFSPEC,
        bvec,
        NULL,
        (unsigned_char_t *)"phnbk endpoint",
        &status
        );
if (status != error_status_ok)
    {
    printf("Can't register endpoint\n");
    exit(EXIT_FAILURE);
    }
/*
** Get the string bindings and print them                       ❺
*/
for (i = 0; i < bvec->count; i++)
    {
    /*
    ** For each binding, convert it to a
    **     string representation
    */
    rpc_binding_to_string_binding
            (
            bvec->binding_h[i],
            &string_binding,
            &status
            );
    if (status != error_status_ok)
        {
        printf("Can't get string binding \n");
        exit(EXIT_FAILURE);
        }
    printf("%s\n", string_binding);
    }
```

Example 2-11: Phonebook Server Initialization Code (continued)

```
    /*
    ** Open the phonebook file
    */
    filehandle = fopen("phnbk.txt","r");                              ❻
    /*
    ** Server is all ready to start listening for client
    **    requests...
    */
    rpc_server_listen                                                 ❼
            (
             (long)2,
             &status
            );
    if (status != error_status_ok)
        printf("Error: rpc_server_listen() returned \n");
    return (EXIT_FAILURE);
}
#ifdef WIN32                                                          ❽
/*******************************************************************/
/***                MIDL_user_allocate / MIDL_user_free         ***/
/*******************************************************************/
void * __RPC_API
MIDL_user_allocate
            (
             size
            )
size_t size;
{
    unsigned char * ptr;
    ptr = malloc( size );
    return ( (void *)ptr );
}
void __RPC_API
MIDL_user_free
            (
             object
            )
void * object;
{
    free (object);
}
#endif
```

❶ This call begins the process of registering the server, which will be described in detail by Chapter 6. The goal of *rpc_server_use_protseqs* is to create information that allows a client to bind to this server. Here, we use this call to instruct the DCE or NT runtime library to use the TCP/IP protocol sequence, and to accept the default number of requests from clients.

❷ The *rpc_server_register_if* call registers the interface with the DCE runtime library. This information enables the DCE runtime library to receive and dispatch the incoming RPC to the function defined by IFSPEC.

❸ The *rpc_server_inq_bindings* call returns the vectors of all binding handles for use by the DCE runtime library.

❹ The *rpc_ep_register* call places the server endpoint into the host endpoint map where it can be retrieved by clients.

❺ This part of the program gets the string bindings (using the binding handles pointed to by the vectors returned in step 8) and prints them on the screen.

❻ The program opens the phonebook text file associated with the server and sets the file pointer to the first line in the file.

❼ The program waits for incoming remote procedure calls. The first parameter (2) sets the maximum number of remote procedure calls that can execute concurrently. This allows two clients to use the server at the same time.

❽ Microsoft RPC server stub code allocates and frees memory using the *MIDL_user_allocate* and *MIDL_user_free* functions. The program never calls these functions directly, but defines them for internal use by the Microsoft libraries.

Writing the Server Remote Procedure (Manager Procedure)

The phonebook remote procedure file, *manager.c*, contains one remote procedure that performs various operations on the *phnbk.txt* text file associated with the server. The exact operation performed depends on a parameter passed with the remote procedure call from the client. The remote procedure can return sequential or specified lines of the file to the client as well as reset to the top of the file.

We've divided *manager.c* into two parts. The first part, Example 2-12, includes some preprocessor directives, initializing operations, and a local procedure that returns lines from the phonebook data file. The second part, Example 2-13, is the remote procedure.

Example 2-12: Start of manager.c

```
/*
**
**
** MODULE:    manager.c
**
**
** PROGRAM:   Portable PHNBK Application (OpenVMS,DOS,NT,OSF/1,ULTRIX)
**
```

Example 2-12: Start of manager.c (continued)

```
**
** ABSTRACT: PHNBK is a sample RPC application intended to illustrate
**           the basics of RPC interoperation between DCE platforms
**           and Microsoft platforms.
**
**
*/
#include <stdio.h>
#include <string.h>
#include <malloc.h>
#include <stdlib.h>
#include "phnbk.h"
#ifdef WIN32
#include "dceport.h"
#endif
extern FILE *filehandle;        /* Phonebook file filehandle */
extern short previous_operation; /* Keeps track of previous operation */
/*
**
** FUNCTION:  getfileline
**
** PURPOSE:
**       Retrieve Lines from input file
**
*/
int
getfileline
            (
              line,
              phone
            )
idl_char * line;
FILE * phone;
{
    /*
    ** Each call of this routine returns a line of the
    **    phonebook file.  On EOF, it returns -1.
    */
    char ch;
    while ((ch = fgetc(phone)) != '\n' && ch != EOF)
        {
        /*
        ** Tabs are unpredictable, so substitute
        **    three spaces if you run across a tab...
        */
        if (ch == '\t')
            {
            *line++ = ' ';
            *line++ = ' ';
            *line++ = ' ';
            }
```

❶

❷

❸

Example 2-12: Start of manager.c (continued)

```
        else
            *line++ = ch;

        }
    *line++ = '\0';
    if (ch == EOF)
        return (END);
    else
        return (NORMAL);
}
```

❶ We include *phnbk.h* because it defines the IDL data type `idl_char` used by the *lookup* remote procedure, the remote procedure function prototypes, and all the requisite constants needed by the application.

❷ The *dceport.h* header file redefines Microsoft RPC calls to take the form of DCE RPC calls. Even though we're building this on a DCE system, the source code can also be built on a Microsoft Windows NT server system. The *phnbk* and *phnbk2* server programs in the appendices work on DCE and Microsoft Windows NT platforms.

❸ *getfileline* is a procedure that reads the file a character at a time until it detects the end of a line. It will be called by the remote procedure we'll see next.

The *lookup* remote procedure is shown in Example 2-13.

Example 2-13: Remote Procedure in manager.c

```
/*
**
** FUNCTION:   lookup
**
** PURPOSE:
**       Lookup up entries in database
**
*/
short
lookup
        (
        op,
        stringin,
        stringout
        )
short op;
idl_char stringin[LINESIZE];                              ❶
```

Example 2-13: Remote Procedure in manager.c (continued)

```
idl_char stringout[LINESIZE];
{
    idl_char buf[LINESIZE];
    /*
    ** Switch on requested operation
    */
    switch (op)
        {
        case  RESET:                                              ❷
            /*
            ** Reset context
            */
            printf("Phonbook:\tRESET\n");
            rewind(filehandle);
            previous_operation = FIRSTMATCH;
            return(NORMAL);
            break;
        case  FIRSTMATCH:
            /*
            ** Look for first match of a string, starting at the
            **    beginning of the file...
            */
            printf("Phonbook:\tFIRSTMATCH\n");
            rewind(filehandle);
            break;
        case  NEXTMATCH:
            /*
            ** Nothing special here, fall out and continue search
            */
            printf("Phonbook:\tNEXTMATCH\n");
            break;
        case  BROWSE:
            /*
            ** A BROWSE operation just returns the next entry...
            **
            ** If the last operation was a BROWSE that got an EOF,
            **    then rewind and start cycling through again.
            */
            printf("Phonbook:\tBROWSE\n");                         ❸
            if (previous_operation == BROWSE_RESET)
                rewind (filehandle);

            if ((getfileline(buf,filehandle)) != -1)
                {
                /*
                ** If not EOF, then just return next entry.
                */
                strcpy ((char *)stringout,(char *)buf);
                printf("Phonbook: \tFound %s\n", buf);
                previous_operation = BROWSE;
                return(NORMAL);
                }
```

Example 2-13: Remote Procedure in manager.c (continued)

```
            else
                {
                /*
                **    This allows the client to flag "no more entries"
                **    before cycling through the file again on
                **    another BROWSE request.
                */
                previous_operation = BROWSE_RESET;

                return(END);
                }
        }
    /*
    ** Keep track of previous operation in p_context
    */
    previous_operation = op;                                      ❹
    /*
    **    Either return the line of the file that contains a string
    **    match, or return -1...
    */
    while ((getfileline(buf,filehandle)) != -1)                   ❺
        {
        if ((strstr((char *)buf, (char *)stringin)) != (char *) NULL)
            {
            printf("Phonbook: \tFound %s\n", buf);
            strcpy ((char *)stringout,(char *)buf);
            return(NORMAL);
            }
        }
    return(END);
}
```

❶ The *op* parameter in the *lookup* remote procedure call can't simply be declared as char, because the char defined by the server system's compiler might be different from the char defined by IDL (for instance, in size or in being signed versus unsigned). IDL solves this by defining data types that are usable in C programs and guaranteed to be the same as corresponding IDL types. The C type idl_char corresponds to the IDL type char. So declare the arguments in the lookup remote procedure call as idl_char.

❷ The RESET, FIRSTMATCH, and NEXTMATCH operations aren't shown in the client code example in this chapter. We provide all of the client and server code in the appendices.

❸ The BROWSE operation calls the *getfileline* function and updates the file pointer.

❹ The previous operation is stored for use by the *getfileline* procedure.

❺ The *getfileline* procedure returns lines from the phonebook data file.

Compiling the Server Program

Compiling the DCE server program is similar to compiling the client application. The build process and associated files are shown by Figure 2-3.

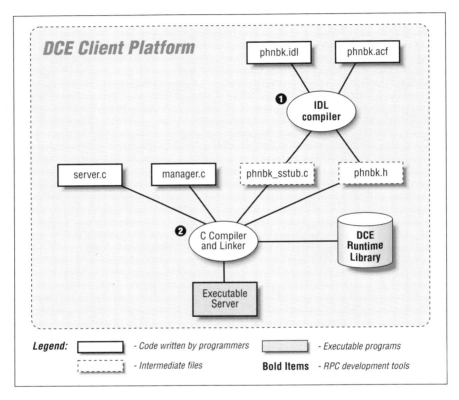

Figure 2-3: The server build process

❶ On the DCE platform, the IDL compiler produces server stubs and header files from the interface definition files and attribute configuration files. The IDL compiler can also invoke the C compiler and linker.

❷ The C compiler and linker produces the executable client from the application source files, client stub and header files, and *dceport.h* header file. Intermediate object files are not shown.

Here too, as in the client build process, we encourage you to use a build tool like *make* to automate repetitive building tasks and free you from platform dependencies. Appendix B includes a makefile called *makefile.unx*, which you can use to build the simple phonebook application on UNIX platforms. You can build the phonebook server (and client) using a *make* command like:

```
% make -f makefile.unx
```

Programming and Debugging Tips

It's obvious by now that compared to writing a local application, there is an extra wrinkle or two involved with writing a distributed version of that application. By following a few guidelines, however, programmers can avoid common pitfalls and reduce the length of the debugging phase to a minimum. The suggestions below that refer to *printf* statements assume that you do not have a good source-level debugger. Such a tool will obviate the need for a *printf* and will significantly cut down on debugging time by allowing you to view your program's execution in real time. Describing these steps in terms of *printf*, however, makes them universally applicable.

- Never ignore the status returned from an RPC runtime API. Proceeding after a failed call is a frequent cause of problems later in the application.

- Without special features that convert exceptions into status values, errors during a remote procedure call are reported via exceptions. While the operating system will give you some information about the exception, you may wish to surround individual remote procedure calls with exception handling constructs (such as TRY and CATCH_ALL) to more clearly identify the site of the problem.

- Use *printf* to record your progress through the client and into the server. This venerable debugging technique has withstood the test of time and still holds value for our purposes. Software developers often place *printf* statements in their code and surround them with conditionals, which allows the code to be disabled when the debugging phase is over. However you may decide to enable them, there are three places where a *printf* can be especially useful:

    – On the server side, translate the server's bindings from their internal format into strings and display them on server startup. Verify that they are what you expect.

    – On the client side also, translate the server binding into a string. Print this binding and make sure it matches one of the server bindings you displayed on the server above.

- Place a *printf* at the very beginning of the server manager procedure being called. If this *printf* works, then you know that the call has made its way into the client stub, through the client RPC runtime, over the network, through the server RPC runtime, into the server stub, and finally into the manager procedure. That's quite an accomplishment. If your application gets this far before failing, then you've proven that there's nothing wrong with the network communications aspect of your distributed application.

A more modern, and sometimes more helpful, variation on this theme is to bring up the client and server under your debugger of choice, setting breakpoints at least at the server manager routines.

If your server manager procedure isn't getting called, even after the server is able to start up using bindings that look reasonable, and the client's binding matches one of the server's bindings, then the parameters in the remote procedure call may not match their description as given in the interface definition file. Error status returns or exception values may help narrow the search for the culprit, but may not be enough.

If you've still not struck gold, you should check into any debugging support that your particular DCE implementation provides. Some vendors' implementations, for example, provide an event logging mechanism that can be turned on within the stubs to signal significant events, and to give details about errors that wouldn't be visible otherwise.

The next step is to examine your IDL files closely and make sure that the same version was fed to IDL and MIDL. Here are some significant things to check for:

- Make sure that the interface UUIDs and version numbers are identical.

- Ensure that the number and types of arguments match.

- Verify that the procedure arguments are properly initialized.

3

Writing Interface Definitions

In monolithic applications, there is no concept of client or server—the application makes calls to procedures that are built into the application. The procedures correctly interpret data passed to them because definitions are available to all parts of the application; the entire application exists in a single address space. Moreover, monolithic applications execute in a single, consistent environment—an environment established by the host architecture and operating system. In this kind of homogeneous environment, data is represented with a fixed byte order and consistent data sizes throughout the application.

Distributed applications do not share the luxury of a single address space and a homogeneous environment. While the client/server division offers the advantages of distribution, programmers must deal with the possibility that clients and servers will run in different address spaces, on differing architectures, and on different operating systems. Clients and servers need a way to share definitions of data types and procedure declarations. They also need a way to handle varying data sizes imposed by architectural differences. Fortunately, DCE and Microsoft RPC provide a convenient mechanism to manage these differences—the interface definition file.

Interface definitions act as a contract between a client and server; both sides use the interface definition so they can interpret each other's data and interact in a compatible manner. We won't belabor every detail of writing interface definition files here; those basics are the subject of other books (including the O'Reilly & Associates book *Guide to Writing DCE Applications*). But in a nutshell, you write interface definition files (or, as we'll call them, IDL files) that contain data type definitions and procedure declarations. Then you use a compiler that generates a header file and client and server stub files. Finally, you produce the executable application client and server by compiling the header file and stub files with the client application and server application files.

As we go through the cross-environment issues regarding the development of IDL files, you'll notice many more similarities than differences. Both environments provide a *uuidgen* utility for generating IDL file templates. The structure and content of DCE and Microsoft IDL files are almost identical. But you have to use each system's native IDL compiler to generate stub and header files.

Let's begin by looking first at compiler differences and then at differences between the DCE and Microsoft IDL languages.

Compiler Differences

DCE and Microsoft RPC use different names for their stub compilers: DCE calls it *idl* while Microsoft calls it *midl*. But the two commands do the same things in their respective environments. You'll need to adjust your makefiles to use the right command in each case, along with the proper options.

The MIDL compiler's default mode of operation is DCE compatibility mode. This mode supports features that are consistent with DCE and must be the mode used for building cross-environment applications. Do not use the Microsoft extensions that the MIDL compiler offers through the */ms_ext* switch. Microsoft's *RPC Programmer's Guide and Reference* identifies keywords and attributes that are Microsoft extensions to DCE IDL.

While the DCE IDL compiler automatically invokes the C compiler to process the generated stub files and application files, the MIDL compiler does not. You'll need to control this manually or in your makefile when building Microsoft clients and servers. Sample makefiles for building Microsoft clients and servers are included with the example applications in the appendices.

IDL and MIDL Languages

Interface definition files are written in an interface definition language or IDL that is very similar to the C programming language. IDL, however, has attributes that support distribution and some additional data types for representing data sizes consistently across different systems.

Although the IDL and MIDL languages are compatible, they differ (in relatively minor ways) in whether and how they support distributed operations. For instance, Microsoft RPC Version 1.0 does not support the use of pipes to transfer large amounts of data. But Microsoft supports the use of the named pipes transport—not to be confused with IDL pipes—while DCE does not. When a distributed capability or service is not equally supported in both environments or is incompatible for some reason, your application must generally avoid its use. Thus, pipes and the named pipes transport should not appear in any application that you plan to distribute between DCE and Microsoft RPC.

Data Type Differences

IDL data types make it possible for programmers to refer to data sizes in a consistent way across different systems. For instance a C char data type might be 16 bits on one system and 8 bits on another. An IDL char data type is always 8 bits. The IDL compiler on the target system performs any necessary translation to the system's native C char data type at client or server build time.

Both environments' interface definition languages support most of the same data types. Some shared data types behave differently as well, and each language contains a few data types not supported by the other language. See Appendix A for a table of differences.

We're going to take just a minute here to show you a very basic interface definition file (Example 3-1). You'll notice it looks a lot like C, but it isn't. The IDL compiler, however, changes many constructs into the right type of C for the host machine. Instructions regarding the use of the network appear as keywords in square brackets.

Example 3-1: Basic Interface Definition File

```
[
 uuid(3871D140-710C-108A-B1D1-08002B281045),          ❶
 version(1.0),
 pointer_default(ref)
]
interface phnbk                                        ❷
{    short lookup (
               [in]            short   operation,      ❸
               [in,string]     char    search_string[100],
               [out,string]    char    return_string[100]
               );
}
```

❶ The interface header comes first, enclosed in brackets. The header includes at least a universal unique identifier (UUID) and version number. These can be automatically generated by a *uuidgen* utility.

❷ The interface name (in this case *phnbk*) comes after the header.

❸ The interface body appears between braces and includes remote procedure declarations. Keywords like [in] and [in,out] aid in efficient use of the network.

Pointers

Any C programmer is familiar with pointers and how to use them. Pointers have provided an efficient way to provide access to large and complex data structures among procedures without passing around the entire structure itself. Until now, that is.

A simple C application that calls another local procedure can pass a pointer to data, rather than the data itself, because the data exists in an address space that is common to both the calling code and the called procedure. With a remote procedure, the calling code and the called procedure exist in different address spaces. Therefore the pointer, as well as what it points to (often referred to as the *target*), must be passed to the callee.

The good news here is that when a distributed application passes a pointer to a complex data structure as a parameter in a remote procedure call, the additional complexity involved with marshalling the target is transparent to the application developer. In fact, the main difference between a local procedure call and a remote procedure call amounts to where you define the data structure. In a local procedure call, you typically describe the data structure in some C header file, then include the file in all source files that refer to the data structure. When writing a distributed application, you describe the data structure in the interface definition file.

When you describe a data structure in the IDL file and write a procedure definition in such a way that a pointer to the data structure is passed, the stub compiler has all of the information it needs to produce client and server stubs that send each other both the pointer and the target.

As an example, here is an IDL fragment that defines a structure, called *pointer_t*, that consists of a 32-bit unsigned integer *x*, and two 16-bit unsigned integers *y* and *z*.

```
typedef struct _pointer_t
    {
    unsigned long x;
    unsigned short y;
    unsigned short z;
    } pointer_t;
```

Consider the following remote procedure definition of *CallIt* within the IDL file. The definition looks like a standard ANSI prototype, showing a function with one argument. IDL simply adds a pair of keywords in square brackets. They indicate that the data must be passed in both directions (into the server and out again).

```
void CallIt ( [in,out] pointer_t * p );
```

In the client stub, this involves marshalling the pointer *p*, and following or "chasing" it in order to marshall the target into its components *x*, *y*, and *z*.

On the server side, the stub reverses this operation as the structure is rebuilt and a pointer to it is passed on to the manager procedure.

To provide the application developer more control over how pointers are used, the DCE architecture definition for the stub compiler defines three kinds of pointers that we will discuss in more detail. In order of increasing capabilities, they are the *reference pointer*, the *unique pointer*, and the *full pointer*.

Reference pointers

When all you need is a pointer that provides a simple level of indirection, and you're sure the value will never be null, use a reference pointer. As the simplest form of pointer, a reference pointer is merely the address of some data. The stubs that are produced by the stub compiler are smaller and simpler when reference pointers are used because they don't have to incur the overhead of probing a reference pointer to ensure the address is valid. As a result, there is a performance advantage to using reference pointers. A reference pointer is denoted by the [ref] attribute.

```
void MyProcedure ( [in,ref] short * x );
```

Reference pointers can never be null. However, some situations demand the use of null pointers. A common case is that of a singly-linked list where a null pointer denotes the end of the list. If you want to use constructs that require null pointers, then you have to use unique pointers or full pointers.

Unique pointers

When you need a pointer that can be null, use a unique pointer instead of a reference pointer. A unique pointer still keeps one of the limitations of a reference pointer: neither of them can be aliased to another pointer in the argument list, nor can they have cycles (cascading pointers that end up pointing to the original data). You'll also need to use unique pointers to operate with a client or server that uses unique pointers.

A unique pointer can be either null or a valid address of some data, so you must initialize a unique pointer to reflect one of these two states.

Because a unique pointer can be null, the stub compiler must produce stub code that protects itself from an access violation by probing unique pointers before they are chased. As a result, unique pointers result in slightly larger client and server stubs. Unique pointers are indicated by the [unique] attribute.

```
void YourProcedure ( [in,unique] unsigned long * y );
```

Unfortunately, many implementations of DCE do not yet support unique pointers. So if you need its capabilities, you must jump all the way to using a full pointer.

Full pointers

If your program has complex data structures with cycles (doubly-linked lists) or aliasing (two pointers point to the same address) in its pointer paths, you'll need to use full pointers. Full pointers are also necessary when pointers might be null but the DCE implementation doesn't support unique pointers.

One of the difficult situations that a stub must deal with is chasing pointers where it can encounter cycles or loops. A simple example of this is a set of data structures hooked together in a doubly-linked list, where there is both a forward pointer to the next element and a backward pointer to the previous element. How can a client stub, in the midst of chasing pointers and marshalling data, determine whether or not it has been here before?

While reference and unique pointers do not handle this situation well, the stubs address this problem with full pointers by assigning each pointer a unique node identification number. When the stub is chasing a pointer, it checks the list of pointers that have already been handled and determines if this path has been followed before. Full pointers have the [ptr] attribute.

```
short OurProcedure ( [in,out,ptr] long * z );
```

Pointer usage guidelines

These three varieties of pointers bring a lot of power and versatility to writing distributed applications. As a rule of thumb though, you should strive to use the simplest pointers you can get by with. While early experience has shown that reference pointers are inadequate for many applications, full pointers provide capabilities that are not frequently used. Unique pointers are a good compromise, by providing reasonable functionality without the overhead of full pointers. It's a simple fact of life that the more situations a stub must deal with, the more code it takes to handle them.

Differences

Of the three pointer types, most DCE implementations currently support only full pointers and reference pointers. Support for unique pointers is planned for a future release.*

Although Microsoft RPC currently supports only reference pointers and unique pointers, the MIDL compiler accepts interface definitions that contain any of the architected pointer types, treating full pointers as though they are unique pointers.

---

*Vendors like Digital Equipment Corporation, whose DCE versions include IDL implementations based on DCE Version 1.0.3 do support the use of unique pointers in their current release.

The Microsoft behavior will not cause problems as long as all you need is something simple like the ability to be null. In other words, if a unique pointer suffices—but you use a full pointer because DCE doesn't provide a unique pointer—the Microsoft and DCE sides work seamlessly together. A singly-linked list illustrates this well.

If you really need the full pointer, such as in the doubly-linked list mentioned above, then the potential for problems exists. The most likely behavior is that multiple copies of what should be the same target may be marshalled and sent to the server. Depending on which instance of the target the server accesses and modifies, the result can be inconsistent versions of the target and lost information. The worst case is that the client stub could get itself into an infinite loop chasing pointers it doesn't recognize having already chased .

However, if a server isn't required to traverse both the forward and backward links in the doubly-linked list, you could mark the unused pointers with the [ignore] attribute. This attribute tells the stub compiler to save its time and avoid chasing pointers that have this attribute. For instance, if the server used only the forward link pointer, then the backward link pointer could be given the [ignore] attribute, and the client stub can process the linked list without getting into trouble by chasing pointers with cycles.

Arrays and Character Strings

Since arrays and strings are similar to pointers—they're addresses of data—they, too, require some hidden magic to work in a distributed application. Each offers a few extra features in IDL or MIDL that you don't find in the C language; we'll discuss these here.

Arrays

There's not a lot of new or complicated material to present on arrays. Assuming you are using one of the pointer types outlined above, most of the rest of the information that the stubs need is straightforward. In order to produce correct stubs, the stub compiler must understand three things about the array:

- The size and type of each element of the array

- Where in the array to begin the marshalling operation

- How many elements to marshall

There are several ways to relate this information to the stub compiler.

Fixed arrays

The most straightforward way to pass an array to a remote procedure is by declaring the array to be of a constant dimension. The array called *z_array* (below) illustrates how to declare and pass a fixed sized array.

```
void TheirProcedure ( [in] long z_array[82] );
```

Conformant arrays, varying arrays, and conformant varying arrays

A *conformant array* is an array whose upper and/or lower bound is determined while a program is running. By way of contrast, the bounds of a fixed array are declared once and forever at compile time.

The size of a *varying array* is fixed at compile time, but the range of elements to be transmitted is determined at run time. The ability to pass only a small range of elements in a larger array is a way to improve performance when only part of the large array is of interest at any one time.

Both the array bounds and the range of elements to be transmitted are determined at run time for a *conformant varying array*.

Because the stub must know where to start marshalling and how many elements to marshall, array attributes relate this information to the IDL compiler. The attributes below apply to the run time bounds of conformant arrays:

- [min_is] specifies the lower bound of the array. For the earlier releases of some DCE products this attribute is unsupported and is assumed to always be 0.

- [max_is] declares the upper bound of the array.

- [size_is] defines the number of elements in the array.

A conformant array declaration does not allow the [max_is] and [size_is] attributes to be used together. Your choice is a matter of personal preference. An example of the declaration and use of a conformant array is shown in the following code.

```
short HisProcedure ( [in] long array_size,
                     [in,size_is(array_size) short y_array[] );
```

With varying arrays, there are further attributes that relate the range of elements to be transmitted for the call:

- [first_is] denotes the first element of the array to start transmitting.

- [last_is] specifies the last element to transmit.

- [length_is] defines the number of elements to transmit.

You can't use both [last_is] and [length_is].

The following code illustrates the use of a varying array:

```
const long ARRSIZE = 128;
        . . .
  short HerProcedure ( [in] long first_element,
                       [in] long last_element,
                       [in,first_is(first_element),
                           last_is(last_element)]
                           long z_array[ARRSIZE] );
```

In *HerProcedure*, *z_array* is a varying array. It is always 128 elements on both the server and client sides, but the number of elements transmitted is determined at run time by the other arguments in the procedure.

This code uses an array that is both conformant and varying:

```
  short ItsProcedure ( [in] long first_element,
                       [in] long array_length,
                       [in] long array_size,
                       [in,first_is(first_element),
                           length_is(array_length),
                           size_is(array_size)] long b_array[]);
```

You could almost lose the name of the last variable, *b_array*, in the list of attributes that accompany it. The [first_is] and [length_is] attributes mark it as a varying array. The [size_is] attribute indicates that it is also conformant (with the first element numbered zero).

All of the above can be extremely confusing to those of us who aren't compiler experts. One way of looking at this information is to think of the conformant array attributes as declaring the run time bounds of the array, allowing the stub compiler to figure out where the array begins and ends. Then you can think of the varying array attributes as specifying the range of elements to be transmitted in the remote procedure call. If you look at it this way, the combination of the attributes makes more sense.

Character strings

Strings are really a special case of arrays, where each individual element is of type char, and the string is terminated by the null character (\0). Indicate parameters you want to manipulate with string semantics by tacking on the [string] attribute to the declaration in the interface.

If a string parameter is allocated and returned by the server side of an application (i.e., an [out] parameter), the stub compiler has to be given some further guidance on how much memory to allocate for the parameter on the client side. This advice can be provided by two of the attributes that we have already discussed, [size_is] or [max_is]. On the other hand, string parameters that are either [in] or [in,out] have memory already allocated for them by the time the remote procedure call is made, so no further information about the size of the string is required.

Sample uses of the string attribute are shown in the following example:

```
void SomeProcedure    ( [in,string] char *name );
void AnotherProcedure ( [in] long string_size,
                        [out,size_is(string_size),string] char * xyz );
```

Combining pointers, arrays, and character strings

Now that we've described a number of the basic capabilities, you can of course take things much further by combining these constructs. You can continue embedding or encapsulating the above types as long as you can stand it (in fact, you can go far beyond the point where you can stand it), just as you might write an application where a set of base types comprise a C structure, which is accessed through a pointer, which is in turn an element of an array of pointers to structs, etc. This is illustrated below:

```
typedef [string,ptr] char *description;
typedef struct _two_values {
    short x;
    long y;
} two_values;
typedef struct _value_record {
    description name;
    two_values  values;
} value_record;
void AnotherProcedure ( [in,ptr] value_record *this_record );
```

Enumerated Types, Structures, and Discriminated Unions

Enumerated types and structures are basic C language features. Use these constructs in IDL and MIDL the same way you use them in standard C programs.

One caution about enumerated types: Microsoft RPC Version 1.0 extensions allow you to assign integer values to enumerators. Do not do this in cross-environment applications.

Unions are a useful feature of the C language that allow a data structure to hold a different collection of objects. For IDL and MIDL to marshall and unmarshall a union properly, there must be additional information that specifies the internal structure of a union that is currently in effect. This is referred to as a *discriminant* and must be part of the union's interface definition, as shown below:

```
typedef enum
    {
    OPEN, READ, WRITE
    } file_operation;
```

```
typedef union switch (file_operation operation) file_union
    {
    case OPEN:    char filename[32];
    case READ:    char inbuffer[100];
    case WRITE:   char outbuffer[100];
    } file_op;
```

A remote call passes both the *operation* variable (the discriminant) and the *file_op* variable. If operation is OPEN, then the server interprets *file_op* as a filename. But if operation is READ or WRITE, then the server interprets *file_op* as the appropriate character buffer.

Pipes

In DCE, applications can use pipes to optimize bulk data transfer when all the data is not necessarily present in memory as a single contiguous array. This enables an application to process the data incrementally rather than all at once after it's all been transferred, possibly requiring it to be paged back into memory.

Microsoft RPC Version 1.0 does not support pipes. Avoid them in cross-environment applications. Possible alternatives include using arrays to transfer large amounts of data when all of the data is present in memory or making multiple remote procedure calls to transfer the data.

Procedure Declarations and Parameter Attributes

To make RPC more efficient, each parameter in a remote procedure has an IDL attribute that specifies whether it is an input (`[in]`), output (`[out]`), or both an input and output (`[in, out]`) parameter. These attributes control the direction in which the parameter is transmitted. For instance, an input parameter is transmitted only from client to server but not in the other direction, saving transmission bandwidth and processing time.

Input parameters can be simple variables, pointers, or arrays. Output parameters and input-output parameters are always arrays or pointers to other data types.

DCE IDL execution semantics consist of `idempotent`, `maybe`, `broadcast`, and `at-most-once` to specify whether a remote procedure call can be safely retried if it fails for some reason before or during execution. These semantics help programmers protect the validity of data.

Microsoft RPC supports only `at-most-once` semantics. It doesn't support the use of `idempotent` semantics, and it doesn't recognize `maybe` or `broadcast` semantics because these apply only to datagram RPC (UDP/IP), which is not supported in Microsoft RPC Version 1.0. Do not use these keywords in cross-environment applications.

Well-known Endpoints

After the client finds the server's host, it communicates with the server through an endpoint. An endpoint is a number such as a TCP/IP port number. A server's RPC runtime library can pick a random (dynamic) endpoint for use each time the server runs. Alternatively, the server initialization code can specify a specific (well-known) endpoint that is used every time the server runs. Chapter 6 discusses the pros and cons of using dynamic and well-known endpoints, including the need to register well-known endpoints with the official authority responsible for a given transport. For this reason, most developers use well-known endpoints just for debugging purposes.

If you use a well-known endpoint, clients can get the endpoint from users who type it in or from a configuration file maintained by the server. But the easiest way is to include the endpoint in the interface definition file.

In IDL files, you specify an endpoint as part of the interface attribute list; for example, `endpoint("ncacn_ip_tcp:[1044]")`. In the next example, we use the protocol sequence for the TCP/IP transport protocol. Although other transport protocols may exist between Microsoft and DCE clients and servers, the TCP/IP transport is the most widely supported, common transport.

```
[
  uuid(F2FE85A0-0C28-1068-A726-AA0004007EFF),
  version(1.0),
  pointer_default(ref),
  endpoint("ncacn_ip_tcp:[1044]")
]
interface phnbk
{    short lookup (
                   [in]          short   operation,
                   [in,string]   char    search_string[100],
                   [out,string]  char    return_string[100]
                   );
}
```

Defining Context Handles

Normally, each client remote procedure call is a single event that is unrelated to previous or subsequent remote procedure calls. Once a server executes a client's remote procedure call, the server returns to the state that was in effect at the time the remote procedure call started. Although this is sufficient for single operations like calculating the standard deviation of a set of numbers, it's not enough when you want to perform a series of related operations such as searching sequentially through a set of files or records. In this case, the server must maintain the state (or context) achieved by one RPC (for instance, recording which record was last searched) so the next RPC can succeed.

If a single client uses a server, the server could simply hold onto the context and wait for the next client call. But in a distributed environment, servers perform RPCs from multiple clients, making it difficult for servers to track each client's individual context. The phonebook server we showed in Chapter 2 works best when it's used by a single client. A client's BROWSE operation returns a line of a file and advances the file pointer to the next line. The next BROWSE operation returns that line and again advances the file pointer. But intervening BROWSE operations from other clients also advance the file pointer, leaving it in an unknown state when the first client needs to rely on the pointer again.

DCE and Microsoft RPC solve this problem using context handles. A context handle is a structure that you declare in the interface definition file for use by clients and servers. A client passes this structure to the server along with an RPC for which the context must be maintained. The server executes the RPC, storing the client's context in a structure in memory. The server then stores a pointer to the structure in the context handle which it passes to the client. The client simply stores the context handle, passing it back to the server with the next related RPC. Clients don't modify data stored in a context handle—the client stub and runtime library just maintain it. Clients can use many different context handles by defining them in the interface definition file.

Figure 3-1 conceptualizes how a server can see, and thus modify, a context handle while a client treats it as an opaque (non-modifiable) data structure. Adding context handles means clients and servers must perform a few extra operations. Servers must establish the context handle for use by remote procedure calls. When the context handle is no longer needed, the servers need to remove the context handle, freeing the resources it uses. Servers rely on extra remote procedure calls from clients to establish and remove context handles, so these extra calls must be declared in the interface definition file.

In Example 3-2, we use the phonebook application's IDL file that we saw in Chapter 2, adding declarations for remote procedure calls that establish and remove context handles. The first time a context handle is needed, the server creates it and passes it back. Thus, the client needs to declare an [out] argument in the relevant procedure. Each subsequent call that needs the context passes a handle as an argument. When the server is done, it assigns zero to the pointer that represents the context handle.

In Chapter 5, we'll see how the client side manages a context handle, and in Chapter 6, we'll see the remote procedures that establish, use, and remove context handles.

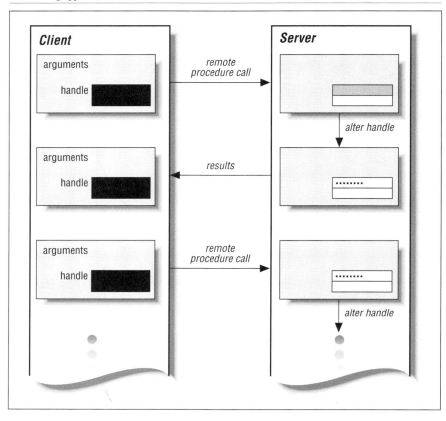

Figure 3-1: Context handles

Example 3-2: Declaring a Context Handle in an IDL File

```
/*
** IDL File for phnbk client
** using context handles
*/
[
 uuid(65C6918A-667E-11CC-BAF0-08002B24389A),
 version(1.0),
 pointer_default(ref)]
interface phnbk2
{
/*
** Constant for maximum line size
*/
const long LINESIZE = 100;
/*
** Flag for hitting end of phonebook file
*/
```

Example 3-2: Declaring a Context Handle in an IDL File (continued)

```
const short END = -1;
/*
** Flag for normal completion of operation
*/
const short NORMAL = 0;
/*
** Define all possible operations on phonebook file
*/
typedef enum
            {
              FIRSTMATCH,
              NEXTMATCH,
              BROWSE,
              RESET,
              BROWSE_RESET
            } operations;
/*
** Context handle definition
*/
typedef [context_handle] void * phonebook_handle;          ❶
/*
** Establish context handle
*/
void
open_phonebook_file                                        ❷
            (
              [out] phonebook_handle *ph
            );
/*
** Clean up context handle
*/
void
close_phonebook_file                                       ❸
            (
              [in,out] phonebook_handle *ph
            );
/*
** Perform some operation on the phonebook
*/
short
lookup
        (
          [in]         phonebook_handle ph,                ❹
          [in]         short            operation,
          [in,string]  char             search_string[LINESIZE],
          [out,string] char             return_string[LINESIZE]
        );
}
```

❶ The [context_handle] attribute is applied to a void * type.

❷ This remote procedure opens the server's phonebook file, creates the context handle and returns it to the client. The [out] parameter enables the client to free its copy of the context handle later on.

❸ This procedure closes the server's phonebook data file, releases the resources associated with the context handle, and zeroes the pointer to the context handle. Inactive context handles are indicated by a null pointer.

❹ This remote procedure performs a user-specified action on the phone-book data file, causing an update to the information kept in the context handle.

Using an ACF

An attribute configuration file allows you to change the behavior of particular clients or servers without affecting other clients or servers that use the same interface. Because the ACFs change the way that the IDL compiler produces stub and header files, you can also think of an ACF as an easier way to specify some IDL compiler command-line options.

The behaviors you can modify using an ACF include:

- Choosing a binding method
- Controlling errors and exceptions
- Placement of marshalling code
- Suppressing stub code and header generation for unused procedures.

Specifying Binding Methods

Clients find servers by acquiring and using the servers' address (binding) information. Client applications can leave binding activity entirely up to the stub code (automatic binding), or the application can control the binding activity using implicit or explicit binding. Each binding method is fully described in Chapter 5. So we won't go into those details here, we'll just introduce the three types and show how to specify each in an ACF. The ways you can specify binding methods apply equally to Microsoft and DCE systems.

Automatic binding is the default method and is used whenever another binding method is not specified. You can also use the [auto_handle] attribute in the ACF as shown in Example 3-3.

Example 3-3: Automatic Client ACF

```
[
auto_handle
]
interface phnbk
{
}
```

Implicit binding is similar to automatic binding in that it applies to all procedures in an interface. It names a global variable that is used as a handle for every procedure. Use the [`implicit_handle`] attribute to specify that the application uses implicit bindings.

Example 3-4 uses the IDL data type `handle_t` to define a global variable named *xhandle* that is used as a handle for all of the procedures in the interface.

Example 3-4: Implicit Client ACF

```
[
implicit_handle (handle_t xhandle)
]
interface phnbk
{
}
```

Explicit binding applies to individual remote procedures in an interface. This allows your client application to select different servers for particular remote procedure calls in an interface.

You can force explicit binding for selected procedures by including a binding handle as the first parameter of a procedure in the IDL file, as shown in Example 3-5. You might do this, for example, to force all clients to use specific servers when servers have varying charges for use.

Example 3-5: Forcing Explicit Binding on All Clients and Servers

```
[
 uuid(F2FE85A0-0C28-1068-A726-AA0004007EFF),
 version(1.0),
 pointer_default(ref)]
interface phnbk
{    short lookup (
                  [in]           handle_t binding_handle,
                  [in]           short    operation,
                  [in,string]    char     search_string[100],
                  [out,string]   char     return_string[100]
                  );
```

DCE, but not Microsoft RPC, also allows an [explicit_handle] attribute in the ACF file. You can apply it to the entire interface or to individual procedures. The attribute causes the stub compiler to generate procedure declarations that have a binding handle as the first parameter. When you specify the use of explicit binding in this manner, your application code must manage the binding for remote procedure calls—but because the attribute is in an ACF file, one side can manage the bindings without forcing the other side to do so.

Example 3-6 uses the [explicit_handle] attribute for all procedures in the interface. If you use this ACF file for your DCE server, then the server can manipulate the binding handle without forcing the client to use explicit binding.

Example 3-6: Explicit Client ACF

```
[
explicit_handle
]
interface phnbk
{
}
```

In DCE, you can override automatic or implicit binding by including the [explicit_handle] attribute with a particular procedure. Example 3-7 requires that *lookup* use explicit binding.

Example 3-7: Overriding Auto and Implicit Binding

```
interface phnbk
{
[explicit_handle] lookup():
}
```

Controlling Errors and Exceptions

In DCE, server and communication errors are raised to clients as exceptions during remote procedure calls. An exception is a software state or condition caused by an event that the normal flow of control in the code cannot handle. Your program will exit unless you design it to handle exceptions.

You can avoid writing extra exception handling code by using the [comm_status] and [fault_status] attributes in your client ACF. These attributes cause communication errors and server errors to be returned as values in the named parameters rather than be raised as exceptions. You can then use the DCE RPC procedure *dce_error_inq_text* to interpret the error code.

Although Microsoft RPC does not provide the [comm_status] and [fault_status] ACF attributes, it does provide the capabilities offered by these attributes. You must declare a variable of the type error_status_t as a parameter in your remote procedure. When MIDL notices this error_status_t parameter, it assumes that the stub should catch all exceptions and return them as a status value through this variable. In a sense, you can think of this as an implicit [comm_status] and [fault_status] declaration. When writing a distributed application, you should describe the data structure in the interface definition file from which you'll generate a C header file.

Appendix D, *The Remote Search Application,* contains a cross-environment application called *searchit* that searches a remote file for a string. The IDL file for the *searchit* application declares its error-handling variable like this:

```
short searchit
        (
        [in]            search_spec     custom_handle,
        [in,string]     char            search_string[LINESIZE],
        [out,string]    char            return_string[LINESIZE],
        [out]           error_status_t  *error
        );
```

In the ACF, you can declare the variable shown in the following ACF code example. MIDL will warn that [comm_status] and [fault_status] are ignored. Nevertheless, the MIDL compiler will continue and treat the variables correctly because of the error_status_t parameter.

```
interface search
{
searchit ([comm_status,fault_status] error);
}
```

The client code declares the variable along with the rest of the variables, as shown below:

```
char *av[];
{
    short            search_status;    /* status from search      */
    error_status_t   rpc_status;       /* comm/fault status code   */
    idl_char         result[LINESIZE]; /* string that matched      */
    idl_char         match[LINESIZE];  /* string to look for       */
    search_spec      custom_handle;    /* search customized handle */
```

A client remote procedure call then includes the variable named *rpc_status* as a parameter:

```
search_status = searchit
                    (
                    custom_handle,
                    match,
```

```
    result,
    &rpc_status
  );
```

Marshalling

Clients and servers communicate through RPC by using some kind of transport mechanism, usually network protocols. Potentially complex procedure parameters aren't naturally suited for transmission over transports which treat data as a linear string. Consequently, the transmitting side must reorganize these parameters into some kind of linear string of bytes that can be passed to the transport mechanism as a message buffer. This process of reorganization is called *marshalling*.

Of course, the receiving side must receive this message buffer and put the data back into the form of procedure parameters. This mirror-image operation is referred to as, amazingly enough, *unmarshalling*. Both the client and the server are a sender and a receiver, and thus both must do marshalling and unmarshalling.

IDL and MIDL generate the code that controls data marshalling for clients and servers. When many procedures marshall data inline (in the direct flow of stub code), the size of the stub can grow appreciably. In DCE, you can reduce the size of stub code by using the ACF attribute [out_of_line]. This causes the IDL stub compiler to place the marshalling code into separate auxiliary stub files. When multiple procedures use arguments of the same data type, a single marshalling procedure can be called repeatedly, eliminating the redundancy of inline marshalling code in multiple procedures.

Microsoft RPC chooses whether data is marshalled inline or out-of-line. Complex data types like pointers and arrays are always marshalled out-of-line. Consequently, Microsoft RPC does not provide the [in_line] and [out_of_line] ACF attributes.

Supressing Stub Code Generation for Unused Procedures

Some clients of a server might not need to perform all of the procedures defined in an interface. So DCE and Microsoft RPC provide [code] and [nocode] ACF attributes that control the stub compiler generation of stub code for selected procedures.

You can control stub code generation for all procedures in an interface by using the [code] and [nocode] ACF attributes in the ACF header. You can control client stub code generation for individual procedures by applying the attributes to individual procedures. This saves space when an interface contains many procedures and you want your client to use just a few. Use [nocode] in the header and then use [code] to enable just those you want to use.

4

Administration

Most of the work of a cross-environment application goes on inside the client and server. But the name service lies outside the application, and thus requires some attention from an administrator. As we said in Chapter 1, *Building Bridges,* both sides of a cross-environment application have to use the DCE name service, which is the Cell Directory Service (CDS).

Both client systems and server systems include all of the software they need to use CDS. When a DCE application makes a call that uses CDS, it actually calls an RPC routine that, in turn, calls the local CDS clerk API. The clerk interacts with CDS, leaving the application free from the overhead of querying multiple clearinghouses and caching retrieved bindings.

The default name service of Microsoft RPC systems is the Microsoft Locator. The Locator is a simpler mechanism than CDS and doesn't use an intermediary like the CDS clerk. When a Microsoft RPC application makes a call that uses the Locator, the called RPC routine makes a remote procedure call directly to the Locator name service.

To enable Microsoft RPC systems to use CDS, we need two things.

- First, we need software that can interact with CDS on behalf of Microsoft RPC systems. This software is provided in a special daemon called the name service interface daemon (*nsid*) that runs on a DCE system.

- Second, we must redirect Microsoft RPC name service calls so they go to the *nsid* rather than the Microsoft Locator.

This chapter discusses the administration steps you might need to take so that Microsoft RPC systems can use CDS. But before we begin the administration steps, let's look a little more closely at how the *nsid* fulfills its critical role.

nsid: A Gateway to CDS

In Figure 4-1, we've reprinted a view of how the name service works from Chapter 1. An *nsid* is the intermediary between a Microsoft RPC client and a DCE CDS server. On the Microsoft RPC side, the *nsid* looks like a Microsoft Locator, while on the DCE side, it looks and behaves much like a DCE client application; it interacts with CDS by making calls to the DCE RPC name service interface, thereby invoking the CDS clerk.

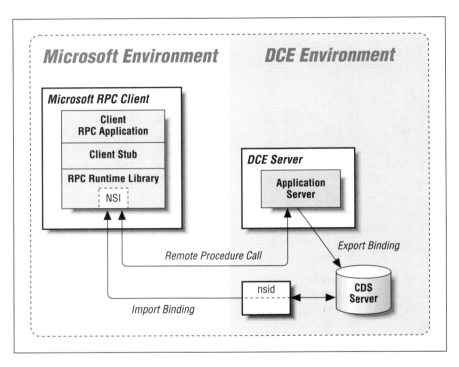

Figure 4-1: The nsid uses CDS on behalf of Microsoft RPC systems

*nsid*s **Can Handle Large Configurations.** Figure 4-1 shows the basic configuration with an *nsid* as an intermediary between Microsoft systems and a DCE CDS server. If your site contains many PCs that will use DCE CDS for relaying server binding information, you may want to avoid bottlenecks by installing multiple *nsid*s.

The number of PCs that an *nsid* can support really depends on how frequently PCs make name service requests. For instance, all PCs might import bindings from CDS in the morning to initalize some handle, or perhaps each PC might refresh a list of handles hourly, creating periodic bottlenecks. If you don't expect much simultaneous traffic, you could probably get by with 100 or more PCs per *nsid*.

An *nsid* Provides Some DCE Security for Microsoft RPC. Some DCE vendors ship DCE with the default level of security set to a minimum level. When DCE environments employ the minimum level of security, all clients, including Microsoft RPC clients, can probably access most DCE resources without restrictions. Resources that fall into this category include:

- CDS servers and directories (except for root)

- DCE endpoint map services

- Application servers and the resources they offer

When DCE environments need more than minimum security, DCE administrators will probably need to take extra steps to configure and operate the environment. Higher security levels enable servers, including CDS servers, to filter client requests based on an authenticated identity associated with each request.

The *nsid* enables Microsoft RPC clients and servers to write and read information into and out of CDS. However, when security is enforced, Microsoft clients and servers cannot be authenticated, and unrestrained access to CDS resources would pose a security risk. So CDS needs a way to restrict Microsoft client and server access to directories that are designated for their use. DCE provides this control by authenticating the *nsid*s through which Microsoft servers and clients access CDS. In this role, an *nsid* is a proxy server, performing authenticated CDS lookups on behalf of untrusted Microsoft systems.

Individual Accounts Provide Needed *nsid* Flexibility. The *nsid*s in an environment can start at different times, causing their DCE security credentials to expire at different times. To give *nsid*s the necessary ability to renew their security credentials independently of one another, each *nsid* in an environment has a unique principal name and a security account name based on its executor host name.

A Group Name Controls *nsid* Access to CDS. CDS directories are protected by access control lists (ACLs) that specify which operations can be performed by which principal. It's relatively easy to add principal names to provide CDS access for one or two *nsid*s. But it becomes impractical to add principal names of many more. So we recommend assigning all *nsid*s to a security group and controlling access based on the group name rather than by each *nsid*'s principal name. This allows the addition or removal of *nsid*s from a cell without changing any access control lists. Instead, the security administrator just adds or removes the affected principal's name and group ID from the DCE Security Service's registry database.

Installing and Configuring an nsid

Some DCE vendors may automate the task of installing and configuring the *nsid* in a cell. For example, the DCE installation procedure provided by Digital Equipment Corporation with their DCE kit automates the following operations:

- It installs an *nsid* on hosts where you install a CDS server. If you choose, you can install an *nsid* on any DCE machine. But for security reasons, a single host can run only a single *nsid*.

- For each *nsid* being installed, it adds a principal name and an account name to the DCE Security Service registry database. The principal and account names are based on the hostname for uniqueness.

- It registers a security group for *nsid*s named */.:/subsys/DEC/pc-user-servers*.

- It creates a CDS directory named */.:/subsys/DEC/pc*. The script then adds an ACL group entry for the group name */.:/subsys/DEC/pc-user-servers* to the CDS directory. The ACL allows *nsid*s read, write, and insert access (`r`, `w`, `i`) to the created directory and its contents, as well as to all descendents of the directory. By default, all DCE principals have read access to every object in every CDS directory.

If the installation script supplied by your vendor automates *nsid* installation and configuration, all you need to do is tell your Microsoft systems to use an *nsid* rather than the Microsoft Locator for name service operations (described later in the section "Redirecting Microsoft Systems to Use the nsid"). Otherwise, here are some steps you can take:

1. Set up an account for an *nsid*

2. Assign membership in a group to an *nsid*

3. Establish a CDS directory for *nsid* use

4. Set permissions on the directory

Possibly, your organization assigns separate people to manage the locations of Microsoft RPC applications and DCE applications. Perhaps a LAN Manager expert handles the Microsoft side, while a UNIX networking guru manages CDS on the DCE side. Anyway, the CDS administrator and the Microsoft administrator will need to decide which CDS directories will be used by Microsoft RPC clients and servers. The CDS administrator then creates an ACL group entry for */.:/subsys/COMPANY/pc-user-servers*, associating it with the designated directories. The *COMPANY* part of the ACL entry is typically something like "DEC."

The following steps use names and directories specified in the installation script provided with one of Digital Equipment Corporation's DCE kits. You can use names like those recommended here or you can use names of your own. If you use Digital Equipment Corporation's *dcesetup* procedure to set up your DCE environment, these six steps have already been done for you.

You should log into DCE as *cell_admin* before issuing the following commands. For step 6 below, you should be logged in as root or as the superuser.

1. Use the CDS control program *cdscp* to create a directory in CDS that can be used by Microsoft RPC servers and clients. (Note that the following command assumes that the directory */.:/subsys/COMPANY* already exists. If it doesn't, you can create it by issuing the *cdscp* command create dir /.:/subsys/*COMPANY*.)

   ```
   cdscp> create dir /.:/subsys/COMPANY/pc
   ```

2. Use the *acl_edit* program to modify the ACLs on the */.:/subsys/COM-PANY/pc* CDS directory (issue the following commands directly from the operating system prompt).

   ```
   % acl_edit /.:/subsys/COMPANY/pc -ic \
    -m group:subsys/COMPANY/pc-user-servers:rwi
   % acl_edit /.:/subsys/COMPANY/pc -io \
    -m group:subsys/COMPANY/pc-user-servers:rw
   % acl_edit /.:/subsys/COMPANY/pc \
    -m group:subsys/COMPANY/pc-user-servers:rwi
   ```

3. Use the *rgy_edit* program to add the *nsid* principal name to the registry.

   ```
   rgy_edit=> domain principal
   Domain changed to: principal
   rgy_edit=> add hosts/hostname/pc-user
   ```

4. Add the group *subsys/COMPANY/pc-user-servers* to the registry database.

   ```
   rgy_edit=> domain group
   Domain changed to: group
   rgy_edit=> add subsys/COMPANY/pc-user-servers
   ```

5. Next, add the *nsid* account to the registry.

   ```
   rgy_edit=> domain account
   Domain changed to: account
   rgy_edit=> add hosts/hostname/pc-user \
    -g subsys/COMPANY/pc-user-servers -o none \
    -pw cell password -mp cell password
   ```

6. Finally, create a password for the *nsid* and add it to the *nsid* account in the registry.

```
rgy_edit=> ktadd -p hosts/hostname/pc-user -pw password
rgy_edit=> ktadd -p hosts/hostname/pc-user -a -r
```

Redirecting Microsoft Systems to Use the nsid

The *nsid* helps you find servers—but how do you find the *nsid*? This regression problem can be solved through a small administrative task: specify the binding information for the *nsid* in the appropriate configuration file on each Microsoft system. On NT machines, you store and modify name service binding information in the NT Registry. On Windows or DOS machines, you store and modify name service binding information in a configuration file called RPCREG.DAT that normally appears in the root directory (C:\RPCREG.DAT).

Like any server, an *nsid*'s binding consists of a transport protocol, a host, and an endpoint. But the information you store consists of just the transport and hostname. The client obtains the endpoint from the *nsid* server machine's endpoint map. This allows flexibility in the event that the *nsid* needs to be restarted for any reason. Whenever the *nsid* starts, it writes its dynamically assigned endpoint into the local endpoint map where it can be retrieved by clients.

Users can modify or change the name service binding whenever necessary. For instance, a user might need to access an *nsid* on another machine if the first *nsid* machine is unavailable for some reason.

To get the *nsid* binding information from a DCE system where an *nsid* is installed, run the *rpccp* program on the DCE system and enter the *show mapping* command. The *nsid* bindings are those with the annotation "NSID: PC Nameserver Proxy Agent V1.0." Select the appropriate protocol sequence and host address from among these bindings.

Modifying the Windows NT registry

Clients and servers on Microsoft Windows NT systems find an *nsid* using the NT Registry, which sets system configuration data. You use the *regedt32.exe* program to modify entries in the registry.

Use the following steps to include *nsid* binding information in the NT Registry. The goal is to find the pointer to the name service in your system's configuration information for RPC and to put in it the necessary protocol, network address, and default syntax for using an *nsid*. The following procedure works on our current Beta version of Windows NT. You shouldn't have much trouble adapting it if the procedure changes for the released version.

1. Invoke the registry editor by double-clicking on the REGEDT32 icon in the Applications group. Alternatively, you can type *regedt32* from a command prompt.

   The *regedt32* program displays four windows:

   HKEY_LOCAL_MACHINE on Local Machine
   HKEY_USERS on Local Machine
   HKEY_CLASSES_ROOT on Local Machine
   HKEY_CURRENT_USERS on Local Machine

2. Maximize the HKEY_LOCAL_MACHINE on Local Machine window.

3. In the left portion of the window, find and double click on SOFTWARE. The SOFTWARE subclass of entries appears in the left portion of the window.

4. In the SOFTWARE subclass, find and double click on Microsoft. The Microsoft subclass of entries appears in the left portion of the window.

5. In the Microsoft subclass, find and double click on Rpc. The Rpc subclass of entries appears in the left portion of the window.

6. In the Rpc subclass, find and double click on NameService. The Name-Service entries appear in the right portion of the window. Just after installation, the first four lines appear as:

   ```
   Protocol:REG_SZ:
   NetworkAddress:REG_SZ:Locator
   ServerNetworkAddress:REG_SZ:
   Endpoint:REG_SZ:
   DefaultSyntax:REG_SZ:1
   ```

7. Double click on each entry and enter the *nsid* binding information into the dialog box that corresponds to each entry. The person who installed and configured DCE CDS server software can provide you with that system's *nsid* binding information.

   a. Set the Protocol variable to be `ncacn_ip_tcp`. TCP/IP is the only transport currently available to both Microsoft Windows NT systems and DCE systems.

   b. Set the NetworkAddress to be the hostname or host address where an *nsid* is running.

   c. Set the DefaultSyntax to 0.

   When you are done, the entries will look similar to the following:

   ```
   Protocol:REG_SZ:ncacn_ip_tcp
   NetworkAddress:REG_SZ:wardr
   ServerNetworkAddress:REG_SZ:
   ```

```
Endpoint:REG_SZ:
DefaultSyntax:REG_SZ:0
```

8. Save your changes by pulling down the Registry menu and clicking on Exit.

Modifying the RPCREG.DAT Configuration File

Clients on Microsoft DOS and Microsoft Windows find an *nsid* through binding information that you include in the RPCREG.DAT configuration file. The RPC installation procedure places this file in the PC's root directory.

Edit the RPCREG.DAT file so it contains the *nsid* binding information. The first four lines of this file must specify the location of the *nsid*. Just after installation, the first four lines appear as:

```
\Root\Software\Microsoft\Rpc\NameService\Protocol=ncacn_np
\Root\Software\Microsoft\Rpc\NameService\NetworkAddress=\
\Root\Software\Microsoft\Rpc\NameService\Endpoint=\pipe\locator
\Root\Software\Microsoft\Rpc\NameService\DefaultSyntax=1
```

Edit these lines to specify the binding of an *nsid* in the cell with which your RPC applications will operate. You can use a regular text editor. The person who installed and configured DCE CDS server software can provide you with that system's *nsid* binding information.

1. Change the Protocol variable to `ncacn_ip_tcp`. Make sure the *nsid* is available over TCP/IP. Alternatively, you can specify any other mutually supported protocol.

2. Change the NetworkAddress variable to be the host name where you started the *nsid*. Replace everything to the right of the "=" sign with the *nsid*'s network hostname.

3. Delete everything to the right of the "=" sign on the Endpoint parameter.

4. Set DefaultSyntax to 0.

The following sample lines in the RPCREG.DAT file define a TCP/IP binding for an *nsid* on network host *wardr*.

```
\Root\Software\Microsoft\Rpc\NameService\Protocol=ncacn_ip_tcp
\Root\Software\Microsoft\Rpc\NameService\NetworkAddress=wardr
\Root\Software\Microsoft\Rpc\NameService\Endpoint=
\Root\Software\Microsoft\Rpc\NameService\DefaultSyntax=0
   ⋮
```

Example 4-1 shows a sample RPCREG.DAT configuration file.

Example 4-1: Sample RPCREG.DAT Configuration File

```
# RPCREG.DAT
\Root\Software\Microsoft\Rpc\NameService\Protocol=ncacn_ip_tcp
\Root\Software\Microsoft\Rpc\NameService\NetworkAddress=wardr
\Root\Software\Microsoft\Rpc\NameService\Endpoint=
\Root\Software\Microsoft\Rpc\NameService\DefaultSyntax=0
\Root\Software\Microsoft\Rpc\ClientProtocols\ncacn_np=rpcltc1
\Root\Software\Microsoft\Rpc\ClientProtocols\ncacn_ip_tcp=rpcltc3
\Root\Software\Microsoft\Rpc\ClientProtocols\ncacn_nb_nb=rpcltc5
\Root\Software\Microsoft\Rpc\ClientProtocols\ncacn_nb_tcpip=rpcltc5
\Root\Software\Microsoft\Rpc\ClientProtocols\ncacn_nb_xns=rpcltc5
\Root\Software\Microsoft\Rpc\ClientProtocols\ncacn_dnet_nsp=rpcltc4
\Root\Software\Microsoft\Rpc\NetBios\ncacn_nb_nb0=0
\Root\Software\Microsoft\Rpc\NetBios\ncacn_nb_tcpip0=0
\Root\Software\Microsoft\Rpc\NetBios\ncacn_nb_xns0=0
```

DOS and Windows Might Support One Transport at a Time

MS-DOS and Windows-based PCs typically have fewer resources than larger DCE machines and, therefore, generally use a single network protocol at any one time. Consequently, users might need to reboot their PCs to use a different network protocol. For instance, a PC client that has been using a DCE server over TCP/IP might need to reboot to use an NT server over named pipes (or any other Microsoft-only protocol). You might need to consider this when you're planning software for use in a network LAN or WAN environment.

Setting the Search Path Starting Point

Whenever a client uses a name service to find binding information, the stub code begins the search for the right interface, protocol sequence, and host. Either the user or the client code has to specify a CDS entry where the search starts. Usually this will be a group or profile entry in CDS, but it can also be a server entry. Group and profile entries help establish the order in which CDS returns server entries to clients, and are explained in detail in Chapter 6.

You can specify a starting entry name in one of several ways:

- On DCE: the RPC_DEFAULT_ENTRY environment variable, in a start-up file like *.profile* or *.login*.

- On DOS and Windows 3.x: the C:\RPCREG.DAT configuration file.

- On Windows NT: the NT Registry.

- On all systems: the *rpc_ns_binding_import_begin* and *rpc_ns_binding_lookup_begin* routines in the client code. An entry name specified in this manner overrides any setting at the user level.

Setting the Starting Point on DCE Clients and Servers

On DCE clients you can specify the starting entry name with the RPC supplied environment variable RPC_DEFAULT_ENTRY.

For the Bourne or Korn shell, set and export the variable in *.profile*:

```
RPC_DEFAULT_ENTRY=/.:/calendar_grp
export RPC_DEFAULT_ENTRY
```

For the C shell, set the variable in the *.login* file or at any time before running the client:

```
setenv RPC_DEFAULT_ENTRY /.:/calendar_grp
```

If your process will run other client applications that use another starting entry in CDS, you could pass the RPC_DEFAULT_ENTRY environment variable as an argument on the client command line.

Setting the Starting Point on DOS and Windows 3.x Clients

On DOS and Windows RPC clients, you can add your starting entry as the DefaultEntry to the C:\RPCREG.DAT configuration file.

Edit the RPCREG.DAT file, adding a line similar to the following:

```
\Root\Software\Microsoft\Rpc\NameService\DefaultEntry=/.:/calendar_grp
```

Setting the starting point on NT clients and servers

On NT RPC clients and servers you can add your starting entry as the DefaultEntry to the NT Registry.

1. Invoke the *regedt32* program and go to the NameService entries of the NT Registry (refer to the previous section called "Modifying the NT Registry").

2. Pull down the Edit menu and click on Add Value. An Add Value dialog box appears.

3. In the Value Name field, type in DefaultEntry, then click on OK. A string editor dialog box appears.

4. Type in the name of the default entry, then click on OK. When you are done, the entries will look similar to the following:

    ```
    Protocol:REG_SZ:ncacn_ip_tcp
    NetworkAddress:REG_SZ:wardr
    ServerNetworkAddress:REG_SZ:
    Endpoint:REG_SZ:
    DefaultSyntax:REG_SZ:0
    DefaultEntry:REG_SZ:/.:/calendar_grp
    ```

5. Save your changes by pulling down the Registry menu and clicking on Exit.

5

Writing Clients

In Chapter 2, *Developing a Cross-Environment Application*, we saw what RPC client code looks like—it just issues function calls like a traditional, non-distributed application. As much as possible, the RPC activities are hidden in the interface definition file and the server. If all clients could be this simple, you would not have to do anything to adapt the C code for RPC, and of course there would be no difference between DCE client code and Microsoft RPC client code. But clients usually cannot be so simple.

The implementation of remote procedure calls sometimes has to leak into the client code. Major areas that client programmers have to address include:

- Choosing a particular server from many. This requires your code to manipulate binding handles.

- Recovering gracefully from a failure on the network or server system. This involves the manipulation of binding handles and code to trap and recover from errors.

Because the Microsoft RPC and DCE implementations are very similar, clients will behave largely the same in both environments. Moreover, Microsoft client code will look very much like DCE client code with a few fairly minor exceptions. So we'll walk through client activities, pointing out differences as we run into them.

The most obvious differences we'll encounter in this chapter relate to security. We'll see how unauthenticated Microsoft clients differ from authenticated DCE clients and what steps a secure client takes to communicate with a secure server.

Writing Consistent Code

Although Microsoft RPC and DCE RPC are compatible, differences in naming conventions and other superficial details can cause coding problems. The differences make it hard to move client code between DCE and Microsoft environments because you'd need to use the other environment's conventions.

We've captured most of the RPC implementation differences in a file called *dceport.h* that redefines Microsoft RPC API to match the DCE API. We chose to make everything look like the DCE API because DCE is the standard API, and its availability preceded the Microsoft API.

By including *dceport.h* with your Microsoft client code, you can write Microsoft clients and servers using the standard DCE API coding conventions. Consistent coding conventions will greatly aid application portability. The functions defined in *dceport.h* won't require changing if your client or server gets ported to another environment that supports the DCE API.

We've included various parts of *dceport.h* in Example 5-1 to show how it resolves differences between DCE RPC and Microsoft RPC. A complete copy of the file is included in Appendix E.

Example 5-1: DCEPORT.H maps DCE RPC to Microsoft RPC

```
⋮
#ifndef DCEPORT_H
#define DCEPORT_H
/*
** Define various idl types
*/
#define idl_char        unsigned char                         ❶
#define idl_boolean     unsigned char
#define idl_byte        unsigned char
#define idl_usmall_int  unsigned char
⋮
#ifndef _ERROR_STATUS_T_DEFINED
typedef unsigned long error_status_t;                         ❷
#define _ERROR_STATUS_T_DEFINED
#endif
⋮
typedef struct                                                ❸
{
    unsigned long           count;
    handle_t                binding_h[1];
} rpc_binding_vector_t, *rpc_binding_vector_p_t;
⋮
```

Example 5-1: DCEPORT.H maps DCE RPC to Microsoft RPC (continued)

```
#define rpc_endpoint_vector_elt_t    RPC_PROTSEQ_ENDPOINT          ❹
#define rpc_endpoint_vector_elt_p_t PRPC_PROTSEQ_ENDPOINT
#define rpc_endpoint_vector_t        RPC_IF_ID_VECTOR
⋮
#define rpc_ns_binding_import_done(import_context,status) \
  *status = RpcNsBindingImportDone(import_context)                 ❺
⋮
#if defined (__RPC_WIN16__) || defined (__RPC_DOS__)               ❻
#define TRY \
     {           \
     int _mODE_fINALLY_;                           \
     int _exception_code;                          \
     ExceptionBuff exception;                      \
     _exception_code = RpcSetException(&exception); \
     if (!_exception_code)                         \
       {

#define CATCH_ALL                                  \
       _mODE_fINALLY_ = false;                     \
       RpcLeaveException();                        \
       }                                           \
     else                                          \
       {
/*
 * #define CATCH(X)                \
 *     }else if ((unsigned long)RpcExceptionCode()==(unsigned long)X) {
 */
#define FINALLY                                    \
     _mODE_fINALLY_ = true;                        \
     RpcLeaveException();                          \
     } {
#define ENDTRY                                     \
     }                                             \
     if (_mODE_fINALLY_ && _exception_code)        \
          RpcRaiseException(_exception_code);      \
     }
#endif /* WIN16 or DOS */
#if defined (__RPC_WIN32__)                                        ❼
#define TRY           try {
/* #define CATCH(X)         \
 *                  } except (GetExceptionCode() == X ? \
 *                  EXCEPTION_EXECUTE_HANDLER : \
 *                  EXCEPTION_CONTINUE_SEARCH) {
 */
#define CATCH_ALL     } except (EXCEPTION_EXECUTE_HANDLER) {
#define FINALLY       } finally {
#define ENDTRY        }
#endif /* WIN32 */
```

Example 5-1: DCEPORT.H maps DCE RPC to Microsoft RPC (continued)

```
/*****************************************************************
 * DCE Status code mappings
 ****************************************************************/
#define rpc_s_ok                      RPC_S_OK
#define rpc_s_no_more_bindings        RPC_S_NO_MORE_BINDINGS
#define error_status_ok               RPC_S_OK
#define rpc_s_invalid_arg             RPC_S_INVALID_ARG
/*****************************************************************
 * DCE Exception mappings
 ****************************************************************/
#define rpc_x_ss_char_trans_open_fail   RPC_X_SS_CHAR_TRANS_OPEN_FAIL
#define rpc_x_ss_char_trans_short_file  RPC_X_SS_CHAR_TRANS_SHORT_FILE
#define rpc_x_ss_in_null_context        RPC_X_SS_IN_NULL_CONTEXT
   ⋮
```

❶ Defines some frequently used DCE data types not defined by Microsoft RPC.

❷ Defines the common DCE error status type.

❸ Redefines internal components of the Microsoft RPC data type `RPC_BINDING_VECTOR`. The data structures are of identical composition, but the individual components of the structure are named differently.

❹ Redefines RPC data types so programmers can follow DCE coding conventions.

❺ One example of redefining a Microsoft RPC API to a DCE RPC API.

❻ On Microsoft DOS or Microsoft Windows, define exception handling macros this way.

❼ On Microsoft WIN32 or Microsoft Windows NT, define exception handling macros this way.

Binding Methods

The process of finding a server and requesting a network connection to it is called *binding.* A potentially complex process, it can be completely hidden from the client, or exposed so that the client programmer can affect it to some degree. When hidden, the process is called *automatic binding.* To expose and manipulate the process, use either implicit or explicit binding.

The underlying activities in binding to a server are always the same, regardless of the method you use. The three binding methods just offer you some trade-offs between convenience and flexibility.

Even with automatic binding, you need to give your application a starting point for finding information. So let's look at what binding really is.

Unless you severely restrict your options, binding is a two-step process:

1. Get compatible bindings. A compatible binding means simply that the client can potentially establish communications with the server. A binding is compatible when the client and server share a common transport and RPC protocol such as TCP/IP. Client application calls such as *rpc_ns_binding_import_next* and *rpc_ns_binding_lookup_next* get compatible bindings from CDS. Later in this chapter we provide code that gets a binding from CDS.

2. Select compatible servers from the compatible bindings. A compatible server can perform remote procedure calls invoked by a client. This level of compatibility requires more than compatible binding information. A compatible server must offer the requested RPC interface. Advanced applications permit an additional criterion called an RPC object. Later, in the section titled "Implicit Binding," we'll look at some client application code that calls *rpc_binding_to_string_binding* and *rpc_string_binding_parse* to help clients select compatible servers.

Once a compatible server binding has been found, the client stub and RPC runtime library do the work of actually connecting to the server, of marshalling, transmitting, receiving, and unmarshalling RPC data, and of returning RPC output parameters to the calling client application code.

Automatic Binding

For client programmers, the automatic binding method is the simplest way to manage binding information because all of the binding management activity is performed by the client stub code. The client stub gets the server transport and host address information from CDS (or a compatible name service), making the use of a name service mandatory. If necessary, the client stub then gets the server endpoint from the server host endpoint map. Now equipped with the necessary parameters, the client stubs communicate directly with the server.

Another significant advantage of automatic binding is hidden error recovery. When several servers offer identical services, automatic binding can find alternative servers if the one in current use fails. The client application is notified only if all attempts to find a new server fail.

While the automatic method is the easiest for client applications to implement, it doesn't allow clients to perform intervening actions. This method doesn't allow the client to choose a specific server when necessary, to log a server failure, or to notify the user of the change in service. Implicit and explicit binding offer these subtleties to client applications.

Because automatic binding is the default binding method for both DCE and Microsoft clients, you can use the automatic method by simply not specifiying alternative (implicit or explicit) methods. If you choose, you can use the [auto_handle] attribute in an ACF. Automatic binding can be selectively overridden by explicit bindings.

For ease of development, we recommend that you use automatic binding whenever possible. Automatic binding relies on CDS (or some other compatible name service). If your client server configuration does not use CDS to pass binding information to clients, you must use the implicit or explicit binding method. In the sections that follow, we provide some other reasons to use these manual binding methods.

Implicit Binding

The implicit binding method offers clients greater control in selecting a server. Implicit binding information is referenced by a global handle so every remote procedure call in the interface can use the same server.

As the client programmer, you have to do some work to find and choose the right binding handle. But the client stub then stores the handle internally and reuses it on each remote procedure call.

Implicit binding brings with it a restriction. All calls by the same client image must be to the same server, unless you override the implicit handle with explicit binding as discussed in the next section. To be more exact, for each interface description (IDL or MIDL file), the implicit handle you choose applies to all calls unless you override it. However, if you use different interfaces—for instance, one to query a database and one to print a report—you can use a separate implicit binding handle for each interface.

Implicit binding gives you more control than automatic binding, but also more responsibility. If a server fails, your client code must be able to trap the error and bind to another server.

Here are some situations that can benefit from implicit binding:

- A set of database servers consists of a primary database where the most up-to-date information resides and secondary databases that contain copies of the primary database. Automatic binding works fine for most read-only users who are satisfied by using any database. However, the few users who perform data entry must consistently access the primary server. Implicit binding can ensure that these users consistently access the primary server.

- You're converting a standalone application to a distributed model by writing RPC wrapper routines for various API functions. You've decided against using automatic binding because you want your application to select which server it uses. Explicit binding is too expensive in terms of maintenance because it requires code changes to each function call and risks introducing bugs into the program. So you choose implicit binding, where you set the binding handle only once for all calls.

The mechanics of using implicit binding in Microsoft RPC are identical to those used in DCE. Include the [implicit_handle] attribute in the ACF to define a data type and global handle. The sample client ACF in Example 5-2 specifies the use of implicit binding. The handle_t data type is recognized by both IDL and MIDL. This example chooses the name *xhandle* to refer to the binding handle.

Example 5-2: Implicit Client ACF

```
[
implicit_handle (handle_t xhandle)
]
interface book
{
}
```

Your client needs to create the binding handle, using information obtained from CDS. Example 5-3 shows one way to do this. The actual code of *find_servers* appears later in Example 5-7.

Example 5-3: Client Use of Implicit Binding

```
    /*
    ** Call the find_servers procedure to locate a suitable
    **     phonebook server using the nameservice...
    */
    if (find_servers(server))                                      ❶
        {
        printf("\nServer lookup failed:\n\n\t %s\n",server);
        exit (EXIT_FAILURE);
        }
    /*
    ** Display the server in use
    */
    printf("\n\t(Selected server binding: %s)\n\n", server);
    /*
    ** Convert the character string binding into an RPC handle
    */
    rpc_binding_from_string_binding                               ❷
            (
            server,
            &xhandle,
            &status
            );
```

Example 5-3: Client Use of Implicit Binding (continued)

```
if (status)
    {
    printf("Invalid string binding\n");
    exit (EXIT_FAILURE);
    }
```

❶ The local *find_servers* procedure gets a binding by searching a CDS entry.

❷ Now use the *rpc_binding_from_string_binding* function to convert the server string binding into an implicit binding handle named *xhandle*.

Be careful when using implicit binding in multithreaded client applications. When different client threads share a binding handle, make sure the binding handle is protected so it is available to the client threads to read when needed. For instance, don't use *rpc_binding_free* when other client threads have not finished using the binding handle.

Explicit Binding

Like implicit binding, explicit binding requires the client code to manage binding information. But explicit binding offers clients even more precise control in selecting servers. While an implicit binding applies to all remote procedures in an interface, an explicit binding applies to an individual procedure. Explicit bindings override implicit bindings and automatic bindings.

The situations that benefit from the use of explicit bindings are similar to those that benefit from implicit binding. In addition, explicit bindings make it easy to use multiple servers—for instance, to get data from different data bases on different systems—because you pass the binding handle you want to each call.

In multithreaded applications, clients can use explicit bindings to make concurrent RPCs to different servers. This is a traditional technique for parallel, divide-and-conquer algorithms.

Explicit bindings can have an advantage over implicit bindings in a case like our database server, in which read-only secondary servers copy updated information from a primary database server. Most read-only RPCs can be dispatched to any server, but the handful of RPCs performing data entry must go to the primary server. In this case, the interface as a whole could use automatic or implicit binding, and those remote procedures requiring the primary server could use explicit binding.

Some ways of specifying the binding method require all clients to use explicit binding, while others permit a choice.

- You can force explicit binding for selected procedures for all clients of this interface by including a binding handle as the first parameter of a procedure in a MIDL or IDL file, as shown in Example 5-4. This method might be useful in a multi-site application where you want clients to access site-specific servers for selected activities. This technique (shown below) forces all clients to use explicit binding for the *lookup* procedure. In Microsoft RPC, this method is the only way to achieve explicit binding.

Example 5-4: Forcing Explicit Binding on All Clients

```
[
 uuid(3871D140-710C-108A-B1D1-08002B281045),
 version(1.0),
 pointer_default(ref)]
interface phnbk2
{    short lookup (
                    [in]            handle_t binding_handle,
                    [in]            short    operation,
                    [in,string]     char     search_string[100],
                    [out,string]    char     return_string[100]
                    );
```

- In DCE, you can specify explicit binding by using the [explicit_handle] attribute in an ACF as shown in Example 5-5. This method causes the stub compiler to generate header files whose procedure declarations have a binding handle as the first parameter. Consequently, all procedures in this interface on this client must use explicit binding. Since you choose an ACF when building a client, this method does not force other clients to use explicit bindings.

Example 5-5: Explicit Binding in an ACF

```
[
explicit_handle
]
interface phnbk2
{
}
```

- Also in DCE, you can override automatic or implicit binding in an ACF by including the [explicit_handle] attribute with those operations for which you want to use explicit binding. Your application code must manage the binding for each call to a procedure that uses explicit binding. Example 5-6 uses [explicit_handle] to override automatic or implicit binding used for other procedures in the interface.

Example 5-6: Overriding Automatic or Implicit Binding

```
[
]
interface phnbk2
{
[explicit_handle] lookup():
}
```

Whenever an explicit binding is specified, the client code must decide which server it wants and generate a binding for each remote procedure call. The next section deals with how a client gets server bindings and selects one of these for use in an RPC.

Finding Servers Through the CDS Name Service

Now that we've seen ways to manage binding handles in client code, let's look at some ways a client can find a compatible server.

While you may feel that finding and choosing binding information is complex enough, yet another level of complexity remains. A network-wide database must exist to furnish the binding information. Suppose you notified users what binding information to use, stored it in batch files, and so forth—but then the server system came down and the server had to be moved. Instead of giving users the information directly, you should let it be put in the network-wide database by the server itself upon startup, and then let clients retrieve it when they run. In this section, we explain how to do that using DCE's Cell Directory Service (CDS).

We mentioned previously that binding information consists of a transport (used by both client and server), the server host's network address, and the server endpoint. While these are structured into a binary format for actual communication, they also have a string format in which the program can examine their contents and even show them to the user. Here's an example of a string binding that could be displayed by a client or manually entered by the user. The example includes an endpoint and is known as a complete binding:

```
ncacn_ip_tcp:mrbig.bos.goodcompany.com[1113]
```

Probably, you'd rather not force a user or even an administrator to deal with such strings. It is more convenient for the server and client to deal with the binding themselves, using the name service as a repository.

RPC applications interact with the name service through a set of calls that are standard, and therefore fairly portable. They are called name-service independent calls (NSI) because they can be implemented by different name services. Therefore, you can compile your application for either DCE or Microsoft RPC with only trivial changes to the calls, particularly if you hide syntax differences through our DCEPORT.H file. Even better, when you run the program on a Microsoft system, it can use either the Locator or CDS with only a minor change in system administration. The binary doesn't have to change.

The NSI routines in DCE begin with the sequence `rpc_ns_`. Corresponding Microsoft RPC NSI routines begin with the sequence `RpcNs`. If you are using the DCEPORT.H file, you can use the DCE function names (`rpc_ns_`) in your code.

Use of a name service is mandatory when clients use the automatic binding method (see the section "Automatic Binding," in this chapter). Name service use is optional when clients use implicit or explicit binding methods. If you have a special reason for string bindings, you can use them instead of using the name service.

Cross-Environment Clients and Servers Use CDS

CDS is the common service tying together Microsoft and DCE. If an RPC client runs on a Microsoft-only network, it can use the Microsoft Locator, as described in the Locator documentation. But it's also easy to redirect Microsoft RPC systems to use the DCE Cell Directory Service. Chapter 4, *Writing Clients*, shows how.

But DCE systems are not easily redirected from their reliance on CDS to pass binding information. Rather than use information in a file to find the name service, the DCE software listens for network advertisements that contain a location for the directory service. Consequently, the Microsoft environment is the one that must adapt. Cross-environment applications use CDS.

Searching for entries in a name service is complicated, so DCE applications interact with CDS through an intermediary called the CDS clerk. The clerk manages all the overhead of using CDS on behalf of the application. The NSI routines in DCE RPC and Microsoft RPC provide a relatively simple and portable way to interact with these clerks.

Although the CDS clerk process does not overburden DCE machines, it consumes enough resources so that it could be a burden on PCs, which generally have less disk space and less memory than typical DCE machines. So the clerk functions for Microsoft RPC clients and servers reside in a process called the name service interface daemon (*nsid*) that runs on a DCE machine. Microsoft applications interact with the *nsid* (and consequently, with CDS) by making function calls to the name service independent (NSI) interface.

Chapter 4 explains the steps you need to take to enable Microsoft RPC systems to use CDS.

Importing a Binding from CDS

This section is for programmers who decide to use implicit or explicit binding. We show a simple sequence for finding and specifying the binding information. You have to get bindings—a process called importing—from CDS, and then examine them to decide which one you want to use.

Once you have redirected Microsoft clients to use CDS (refer to Chapter 4), you can write client code exactly like DCE code. The Microsoft NSI routines and DCE NSI routines behave in the same manner.

Example 5-7 is a user-supplied procedure we'll call *find_servers* that imports a binding from CDS and returns it as a parameter. This procedure works for both Microsoft clients and DCE clients. In the procedure, we interpret the bindings, selecting one that has a TCP/IP protocol sequence. You can use other critera for selecting a server binding as well. For instance, you can look for a binding that contains a specific network host name or object UUID.

Example 5-7: A Procedure that Imports a Binding from CDS

```
#if defined(MSDOS) || defined(WIN32)
#include "dceport.h"
#define IFSPEC phnbk2_ClientIfHandle                          ❶
#else
#include <pthread_exc.h>
#define IFSPEC phnbk2_v1_0_c_ifspec
#endif
#define SERVER_ENTRY_NAME   "/.:/phnbk2_srv_"
/*
** The find_servers() routine retrieves a phnbk2
**      server binding from the default CDS server
**      and returns it as a parameter.
*/
static int
find_servers
            (
              server
            )
unsigned char *server;
{
    unsigned char    *string_binding;
    unsigned char    *protseq;
    handle_t          handle;
    rpc_ns_handle_t   import_context;
    int               found=0;
    error_status_t    status;
    error_status_t    status2;
    /*
    ** Get ready to import bindings that match the
    **      given entry name
    */
```

Example 5-7: A Procedure that Imports a Binding from CDS (continued)

```
rpc_ns_binding_import_begin                                          ❷
            (
            rpc_c_ns_syntax_default,
            SERVER_ENTRY_NAME,
            IFSPEC,
            NULL,
            &import_context,
            &status
            );
if (status)
    {
    strcpy(server, "rpc_ns_binding_import_begin failure");
    return (1);
    }
/*
** search for TCP binding
*/
while (!found)
    {
    /*
    ** Get next binding
    */
    rpc_ns_binding_import_next                                       ❸
                (
                import_context,
                &handle,
                &status
                );
    if (status)
        {
        strcpy(server, "server not found");
        return (1);
        }
    /*
    ** Convert binding to string binding
    */
    rpc_binding_to_string_binding                                   ❹
                (
                handle,
                &string_binding,
                &status
                );
    if (status)
        {
        strcpy(server, "rpc_binding_to_string_binding failure");
        return (1);
        }
    else
        {
        /*
        ** Parse the binding into its individual components...
```

Example 5-7: A Procedure that Imports a Binding from CDS (continued)

```
**      actually all we care about here is the protocol
**      sequence...
*/
rpc_string_binding_parse                                             ❺
              (
              string_binding,
              NULL,
              &protseq,
              NULL,
              NULL,
              NULL,
              &status
              );


if (status)
    {
    strcpy(server, "rpc_string_binding_parse failure");
    return(1);
    }
else
    {
    /*
    ** Check for a TCP/IP protocol sequence
    */
    if (!(strcmp((char *)protseq, "ncacn_ip_tcp")))                  ❻
        /*
        ** Got one!
        */
        {
        strcpy(server, (char *)string_binding);
        /*
        ** Free the string binding
        */
        rpc_string_free
                  (
                  &string_binding,
                  &status2
                  );
        found = 1;
        /*
        ** finish the search
        */
        rpc_ns_binding_import_done                                   ❼
                  (
                  &import_context,
                  &status
                  );
        }
```

Example 5-7: A Procedure that Imports a Binding from CDS (continued)

```
                else
                    rpc_string_free                                    ❽
                        (
                        &string_binding,
                        &status2
                        );
                }
            }
        /*
        ** End of while block
        */
        }
    /*
    ** Only way to return successfully
    */
    return (0);
}
```

❶ The conventions for building an interface specification differ in DCE IDL and Microsoft IDL. We assign the proper string to IFSPEC in preprocessor directives.

❷ The *rpc_ns_binding_import_begin* routine creates an import context for importing compatible binding handles from CDS. In the preprocessor definitions, we supply a starting server entry name (.:/phnbk_srv_), so RPC doesn't use the RPC_DEFAULT_ENTRY as the search path starting point in CDS.

❸ The *rpc_ns_binding_import_next* routine actually imports a binding from CDS. This RPC routine returns only those bindings whose protocol sequences are supported on the host that the process is running on.

❹ The *rpc_binding_to_string_binding* routine converts the binding handle to a string binding so it can be manipulated by the client application code.

❺ The *rpc_string_binding_parse* routine separates the binding into its component parts so we can look for a specific protocol.

❻ Here we compare the protocol in the binding to the protocol we need to use (TCP/IP).

❼ If the entry has the TCP/IP protocol, we use *rpc_ns_binding_import_done* to end the import process.

❽ Otherwise, we free the memory used by the binding and report the problem.

Constructing Binding Handles from Strings

If you don't use CDS to obtain binding information, your application must be able to construct binding handles. Example 5-8 shows how you can construct a binding handle from a string binding using a string passed as an argument on the client command line. Here, we use a partial binding consisting of the server transport and host name only. The RPC runtime library obtains the endpoint when the client uses the binding handle.

Example 5-8: Converting a String Binding to a Binding Handle

```
{
  /*
  ** The user has specified a string binding in a format
  ** such as "ncacn_ip_tcp:mrbig.bos.goodcompany.com"
  */
  strcpy((char *)server, av[1]);
}
/*
** Convert the character string binding into an RPC handle
*/
rpc_binding_from_string_binding(server, &xhandle, &status);
if (status)
{
    printf("Invalid string binding\n");
    return(1);
}
```

Client Management of Context Handles

You may remember from Chapter 3, *Writing Interface Definitions*, that context handles provide an optional way for servers to maintain a client's state when a client executes multiple remote procedure calls on the same server. For instance, a server can maintain individual file pointers for separate clients by using context handles.

Context handles are declared in the IDL file for use by clients and servers. A client passes it with each remote procedure call it makes to a server. The server performs the operation, updates the handle with the new state, and returns the handle to the client. The client just stores the handle and returns it to the server with the next call.

Although clients can test a context handle for null, clients cannot manipulate the data the handle contains; only the server can modify context handle data. The client stub and runtime library manage the context handle on behalf of the server.

In Chapter 3, we looked at an interface definition file that declared a context handle for the phonebook application. We'll build on that concept here, showing how the client code declares the context handle variable and then controls its establishment and removal on the server using remote procedure calls. Although we're just showing the pertinent code fragments from the client program, we include a complete phonebook application with context handles in Appendix C.

1. In your client code, you need to declare a variable for your context handle.

   ```
   phonebook_handle    ph;
   ```

2. To use the context handle you need to initialize it to null and then issue a remote procedure that establishes the context handle on the server. The *open_phonebook_file* remote procedure was defined in the IDL file in Chapter 3.

   ```
   /*
   ** Initialize the phonebook context handle to NULL
   */
   ph = NULL;
   /*
   ** Establish the phonebook context handle
   */
   open_phonebook_file(&ph);
   ```

3. Once the context handle is established on the server, remote procedures can use it. Here, the phonebook client's BROWSE operation passes the context handle to the server.

   ```
   /*
   ** select on user input
   */
   switch(command)
   {
   case 'b' :

      /*
      ** Display next entry from wherever we happen to be
      **     positioned in the phonebook
      */
      st = lookup(ph,BROWSE, input, output);
      /*
      ** echo entry or rewind database if we're at the end
      **     of the phonebook
      */
      if (st != -1)
      {
      printf("Entry is: %s\n", output);
      }
   ```

```
        else
        {
    printf("resetting...\n");
        }
        break;
```

4. When the client is finished using the handle, it needs to remove it from the server. Here, the phonebook client's QUIT operation issues a *close_phonebook_file* remote procedure call. In that call, the server closes the phonebook data file and frees all resources associated with the context handle. The pointer to the context handle will be NULL on return from *close_phonebook_file*.

```
    case 'q' :

        /*
        ** Clean up phonebook context
        */
        close_phonebook_file (&ph);
        /*
        ** Free handle and exit program
        */

        printf("Exiting...\n");
        rpc_binding_free(&xhandle,&status);
        exit(0);
    default :
        break;

    } /* case */
```

Using Customized Binding Handles

In DCE and Microsoft RPC, a basic (primitive) binding handle refers to binding information that clients use to find servers. DCE and Microsoft client programs can also use customized binding handles that allow you to do more, like specify a particular file for a server to use.

Let's say you're a user on a PC and you want to quickly check a file on a UNIX system for a certain character string. Rather than log into the UNIX system, you could use a distributed application that searches remote files for strings. We've created such an application here that uses a customized binding handle to name a file on a remote host. The complete code for this application, called *searchit*, is in Appendix D.

The customized handle contains the binding information and the filename. Thus, it is a structure with two members, looking like this in the MIDL file:

```
typedef [handle] struct
    {
        unsigned char binding[BINDING_SIZE];
        unsigned char filename[FILENAME_SIZE];
    } search_spec;
```

The first member is a string binding, which the program converts to internal format before contacting the server. The second member is a character string that contains a filename.

Our client takes three arguments from the user: a host name, a filename, and a string to match. The client inserts the host name into its proper place in the string binding, loads the filename into its member of the data structure, and passes the string as an argument to the remote procedure call. A more complex client application could use customized binding handles to use multiple files on one or more servers.

In our experience, customized binding handles are one-shot affairs. That is, you probably want just one operation from the server—in contrast to context handles, where you want to build a long term relationship between the client and server. The reason that a customized handle is suited for a single operation is that each operation requires it to contain different information.

Because your client code does more with a customized binding handle, these handles are managed differently from explicit or implicit handles. Implicit handles reside in a global variable, while your application supplies an explicit handle as a parameter in the RPC. But customized binding handles are managed by the stub. You just have to write binding and unbinding routines, which the stub calls as needed. These routines are where you do the work of setting up the information you need in the binding handle.

Declare a customized binding handle by applying the [handle] attribute to a type definition in an IDL file. Example 5-9 is an IDL file for our cross-environment *searchit* application.

Example 5-9: Defining a Customized Binding Handle

```
/*
** Interface Definition File for Search program
*/
[
 uuid(2450F730-5170-101A-9A93-08002B2BC829),
 version(1.0),
 pointer_default(ref)]
interface search
{
/*
** Constant for maximum line size
*/
const long LINESIZE = 100;
```

Example 5-9: Defining a Customized Binding Handle (continued)

```
/*
** Constant for file name length
*/
const long FILENAME_SIZE = 100;
/*
** Constant for host name size
*/
const long BINDING_SIZE = 32;
/*
** Status for search file error
*/
const short FILE_ERROR = -1;
/*
** Status for no match found
*/
const short NO_MATCH = 0;
/*
** Customized binding handle definition -- it
**     contains the file name and the string
**     binding to use.
*/
typedef [handle] struct                                                ❶
                    {
                        unsigned char binding[BINDING_SIZE];
                        unsigned char filename[FILENAME_SIZE];
                    } search_spec;                                      ❷
/*
** Search for a string match on the file specified
**     in the customized binding handle above.
*/
short
searchit
        (
        [in]          search_spec    custom_handle,                    ❸
        [in,string]   char           search_string[LINESIZE],
        [out,string]  char           return_string[LINESIZE],
        [out]         error_status_t *error
        );
}
```

❶ Declare the customized binding handle to be of the type *search_spec*.

❷ Initialize the customized binding handle with its two components: a string binding and a filename. Client users will enter some of these components (hostname and filename) on the client command line.

❸ The customized binding handle is the first parameter of a procedure declaration.

Although you use a customized binding handle just like a primitive binding handle, you must write special bind and unbind procedures that are called by the client stub during each remote procedure call. These special procedures obtain the primitive binding handle and perform cleanup after the client finishes using the handle. Example 5-10 shows the bind and unbind procedures used in the *searchit* application. These routines are included in the client code shown in Example 5-11.

Example 5-10: Search Program Bind and Unbind Procedures

```
handle_t __RPC_API
/*
**
** search_spec_bind is called by the client stub
**     to establish a customized binding handle used
**     by the search() remote procedure call.
*/
search_spec_bind
          (
            custom_handle
          )
search_spec custom_handle;
{
    rpc_binding_handle_t xhandle;
    error_status_t        status;
    /*
    ** Display the server in use
    */
    printf("\n\t(Selecting server binding: %s)\n\n",
          custom_handle.binding);
    /*
    ** Convert the character string binding into an RPC handle
    */
    rpc_binding_from_string_binding
              (
                custom_handle.binding,
                &xhandle,
                &status
              );
    if (status)
        {
        printf("Invalid string binding\n");
        exit (EXIT_FAILURE);
        }

    return ( xhandle );
}
/*
**
** search_spec_unbind is called by the client stub
**     to free the customized binding handle used
**     by the search() remote procedure call.
```

Example 5-10: Search Program Bind and Unbind Procedures (continued)

```
*/
void __RPC_API
search_spec_unbind
            (
                custom_handle,
                xhandle
            )
search_spec custom_handle;
handle_t   xhandle;
{
    error_status_t status;
    /*
    ** Free the binding handle
    */
    rpc_binding_free
                (
                    &xhandle,
                    &status
                );
    return;
}
```

Customized binding handles are managed in the client stub. But it expects you to provide procedures for binding and unbinding the handle. The names and parameter types for these procedures must follow the right conventions.

The binding procedure in your client should look like:

```
handle_t handle-datatype_bind ( customized handle )
```

The binding procedure is called from the stub before it executes the RPC. The stub passes in the customized binding handle to our _*bind* procedure. Our procedure creates a primitive binding handle and returns it to the stub.

The unbinding procedure in your client should look like:

```
void handle-datatype_unbind ( customized handle, handle_t )
```

The unbinding procedure is also called from the stub, but after the RPC. The stub gives us the original, customized binding handle and the primitive binding handle, which we subsequently free.

In our example, the customized binding handle data structure is called a *search_spec,* so we have to supply functions named *search_spec_bind* and *search_spec_unbind.*

How our application chooses to establish a binding handle and to unbind it later is completely up to us. We've chosen to include a string binding as part of the customized handle and to use that to construct the handle for this RPC. Therefore, we'll be using the *rpc_binding_from_string_binding* in the *search_spec_bind* procedure.

Example 5-11 shows how the client search program uses customized binding handles.

Example 5-11: Searchit Program with Customized Binding Handles

```
#include <stdio.h>
#include <string.h>
#include <stdlib.h>
#include <malloc.h>
#include "search.h"
#if defined(MSDOS) || defined(WIN32)
#include "dceport.h"
#else
#define __RPC_API
#endif
#ifdef WIN32
#define MAIN_DECL _CRTAPI1
#else
#define MAIN_DECL
#endif
int
MAIN_DECL main
              (
                ac,
                av
              )
int    ac;
char *av[];
{
    short          search_status;     /* status from search        */
    error_status_t rpc_status;        /* comm/fault status code    */
    idl_char       result[LINESIZE];  /* string that matched       */
    idl_char       match[LINESIZE];   /* string to look for        */
    search_spec    custom_handle;     /* search customized handle  */  ❶

    /*
    ** Initialize some strings
    */
    match[0]  = '\0';
    custom_handle.binding[0]  = '\0';
    custom_handle.filename[0] = '\0';
    /*
    ** There should be 4 parameters to searchit:
    **
    **      searchit <hostname> <filename> <matchstring>
    **
    ** where
    **
    **      <hostname> is the hostname where the file to be searched
    **                    exists.
```

Example 5-11: Searchit Program with Customized Binding Handles (continued)

```
**
**       <filename> is the name of the file to be searched.
**
**       <matchstring> is the string to search <filename> for.
**
*/
if (ac != 4)
  {
  /*
  ** Not the right number of parameters
  */
  printf("\t\nUsage: searchit <hostname> <filename> <matchstring>\n\n");
  exit(EXIT_FAILURE);
  }
/*
** Set up the string binding, the filename, and the
**     match string from the command line.
*/
strcpy (custom_handle.binding,  "ncacn_ip_tcp:");          ❷
strcat (custom_handle.binding,  av[1]);
strcpy (custom_handle.filename, av[2]);
strcpy (match, av[3]);
/*
** Search the given file on the given host for the
**     given string...
*/
search_status = searchit
                        (
                        custom_handle,                     ❸
                        match,
                        result,
                        &rpc_status
                        );
```

❶ The client allocates the customized binding handle.

❷ The client sets up the customized binding handle using the TCP/IP transport along with parameters passed on the command line.

❸ The customized binding handle is the first parameter in the remote procedure call.

Using Exception Handling Macros

When a client or server program encounters an exception (an error in the program, OS, or network), only rudimentary information is given to the user about the problem. By default, no provision is made to intercept the exception so that the application can attempt to recover, or offer more detailed information about the cause of the problem.

We can direct programs to catch and report errors by including some
exception handling macros around the region of program code in which
stub code and remote procedures execute.

The DCE exception macros TRY, CATCH, CATCH_ALL, FINALLY, and
ENDTRY are (or attempt to be) platform independent constructs for handling exceptions in a way that makes sense for the local operating system.
For example, UNIX systems typically implement these constructs as macros
that use *setjmp* and *longjmp*. On Windows NT, *try*, *finally*, and *except* are
Microsoft C keywords. Here, the platform independent exception handling
constructs are implemented in terms of these native C keywords. Our API
mapping file DCEPORT.H maps correspondence between these similar
macro sets.

Example 5-12 shows ways that you could use some of those macros (TRY,
CATCH_ALL, RERAISE, and ENDTRY) to trap exceptions in the
find_servers routine we used earlier to get server bindings from CDS.

Example 5-12: A Routine Using Exception Handling Macros

```
/*
** The find_servers() routine retrieves a phnbk2
**      server binding from the default CDS server
**      and returns it as a parameter.
**
*/
static int
find_servers
        (
            server
        )
unsigned char *server;
{
    unsigned char    *string_binding;
    unsigned char    *protseq;
    handle_t          handle;
    long              entry_name_syntax=3;
    rpc_ns_handle_t   import_context;
    int               found=0;
    error_status_t    status;
    error_status_t    status2;
  TRY                                                            ❶
    /*
    ** Get ready to import bindings that match the
    **      given entry name
    */
    rpc_ns_binding_import_begin
                (
                    rpc_c_ns_syntax_default,
                    SERVER_ENTRY_NAME,
                    IFSPEC,
                    NULL,
```

Example 5-12: A Routine Using Exception Handling Macros (continued)

```
                &import_context,
                &status
              );
    if (status)
        {
        strcpy(server, "rpc_ns_binding_import_begin failure");
        return (1);
        }
:
:
                        /*
                        ** finish the search
                        */
                        rpc_ns_binding_import_done
                                (
                                &import_context,
                                &status
                                );
                }
                else
                    rpc_string_free
                            (
                              &string_binding,
                              &status2
                            );
            }
        }
    /*
    ** End of while block
    */
    }
CATCH_ALL
#if defined (WIN32) || defined (MSDOS)
    /*
    ** If MSDOS or Windows NT, print the specific error code
    **     and exit
    */
    unsigned long Exception;
    Exception = RpcExceptionCode();
    printf("\n\tException # %d in find_servers...exiting\n",Exception);
#else
    /*
    ** Else, with a "native" DCE platform, let the operating system
    **     take care of printing the exception
    */
    RERAISE;
#endif
    exit (EXIT_FAILURE);
```

❷

❸

❹

Example 5-12: A Routine Using Exception Handling Macros (continued)

```
ENDTRY                                                              ❺
    /*
    ** Only way to return successfully
    */
    return (0);
}
```

❶ The TRY macro begins the region of code where we want to trap exceptions.

❷ We've omitted intervening code so we can focus on the macros rather than what's going on in the code.

❸ CATCH_ALL traps exceptions so they can be reported. The Microsoft DOS, Windows, and Windows NT operating systems can print the error when you call the *RpcExceptionCode* function. Windows and Windows NT print the error in a dialog box. Microsoft DOS prints the error as a line on the screen.

❹ The operating systems of most DCE platforms can print the exceptions. Issue the RERAISE macro to pass exceptions to the operating system on a DCE platform when the operating system will print them.

❺ ENDTRY ends the region of code over which exceptions are to be trapped.

Security and Client Development

Microsoft RPC and DCE security mechanisms differ. Microsoft RPC Version 1.0 does not provide its own security mechanism, but rather depends on security that is built into the named pipes transport. Thus, Microsoft applications that use named pipes are secure; those that use other transports are not secure. The DCE Security Service is transport-independent and applies to a higher level of the application; it is built into the remote procedure call architecture and it also provides a security API for general use by DCE applications.

Since Microsoft security does not apply directly to remote procedure calls, DCE servers can always accept Microsoft RPCs; DCE servers just treat them as unauthenticated clients. But DCE security affects the remote procedures themselves, encrypting parts or all of the call depending on the security mode chosen. A Microsoft server cannot interpret and therefore, cannot accept authenticated DCE RPCs. A Microsoft server can accept RPCs only from DCE clients that are not using security.

Consequently, the security differences between Microsoft and DCE can affect how you develop clients and servers of cross-environment applications:

- Don't use security in DCE clients of Microsoft RPC servers.

- Allow DCE servers to accept RPCs from unauthenticated clients. Chapter 6 discusses security and server development in detail.

Recently, Microsoft said they would provide an authenticated RPC with the first release of Microsoft Windows NT. This authentication method will not be compatible with DCE security. Unfortunately, we haven't seen the authentication software, and thus are not able to give practical advice on its use.

Differences Between Microsoft RPC and DCE

While some differences between Microsoft RPC and DCE limit the capabilities you can build into a cross-environment application, other differences simply restrict code portability across the DCE and Microsoft RPC platforms.

Client Memory Management

In monolithic C applications, memory is allocated and deallocated using *malloc* and *free* routines. But distributed application clients and servers execute in different address spaces, requiring alternative ways to control memory allocation. Both Microsoft and DCE provide ways to manage memory for clients and servers, delegating the messy implementation to client and server stubs. But the models used by Microsoft and DCE differ in the way client applications allocate and deallocate memory.

In DCE clients, calls to *malloc* and *free* are sufficient to control memory allocation and deallocation. Servers use special calls, as we'll see in Chapter 6.

Microsoft RPC clients require you to provide memory management functions. Client and server stubs produced by Microsoft's MIDL stub compiler depend on the existence of two procedures for allocating and deallocating memory, called *MIDL_user_allocate* and *MIDL_user_free*. They must be supplied by the application developer, and frequently are no more than "wrapper" routines around calls to *malloc* and *free*, respectively, as illustrated below.

```
void * MIDL_user_allocate (size_t length)
    {
        return (malloc (length));
    }
```

```
void MIDL_user_free (void * pointer)
    {
            free (pointer);
    }
```

You can choose whatever memory management techniques you prefer and code it inside these two procedures.

Freeing Idle Client Resources

When a DCE server has not heard from a client after a default timeout period of 20 seconds, servers dispatch an asynchronous shutdown message instructing DCE clients to free any resources used by the call. This behavior ensures that client resources are freed up on a regular basis.

Microsoft RPC clients ignore this shutdown message, relying instead on the client programmer to include a call to the *RpcMgmtEnableIdleCleanup* function. Include this call to make your Windows NT client application periodically release client resources.

The different approaches to freeing idle client resources affect portability of client code. You'll need to remove this function (or `ifdef` around it) when porting a Microsoft client to a DCE platform.

API and Macro Differences

Microsoft RPC supports most of the 97 DCE API functions. Microsoft RPC function names are shorter than corresponding DCE function names because the underscore character is removed. Appendix A shows the correspondence between the Microsoft RPC and DCE RPC APIs.

Microsoft RPC has several macros to handle exceptions. These are defined by the Microsoft RPC runtime library.

```
RpcAbnormalTermination (Microsoft extension)
RpcEndExcept
RpcEndFinally
RpcExcept
RpcExceptionCode
RpcFinally
RpcRaiseException
RpcTryExcept
RpcTryFinally
```

Error Code Differences

Although DCE and Microsoft RPC differ in the some of the error codes they support, you can use the API mapping file *dceport.h* to manage most differences. Appendix A lists the error codes the environments have in common.

Handling Other Differences

There are some other fairly minor differences between the DCE and Microsoft APIs that can be resolved by using the DCEPORT.H API mapping file in cross-environment applications. Appendix A identifies these API differences.

Compiling and Linking Clients

Modern development environments provide tools that automate the tasks of compiling and linking. While these tools differ slightly among different systems, they all generally rely on a command file (called a makefile) that orders the commands and options needed to compile and link your program. On UNIX systems, this utility is called *make*. For MS-DOS, Windows, and Windows NT, Microsoft provides a utility called *nmake*.

Although you could enter all of the compiler and linker commands on the command line, as a general practice, you should use a makefile and *make* or *nmake* utilities to build client (and server) executables.

The appendices include makefiles that you can use to build the examples we've discussed in this chapter.

6

Writing a Server

In Chapter 1, *Building Bridges*, we said that the most viable cross-environment applications would build upon the dominant strengths of the Microsoft and DCE environments. Typical configurations consist of many Microsoft Windows clients tapping into the rich variety of DCE servers. In this chapter, that's the model we'll use to demonstrate how to write a server. Since our server examples are fairly portable, they'll run on either DCE or Microsoft RPC systems. Where they're not portable, we'll point out any changes you'll need to make.

We've minimized many of the obvious differences between DCE and Microsoft RPC code examples by including the *dceport.h* file which redefines the Microsoft RPC API to match the DCE API. Chapter 5, *Writing Clients*, discusses this file in some detail.

Servers still need to manage some differences between the two environments, however. As we go through this chapter, we'll walk through server initialization procedures and remote manager procedures, highlighting API differences you'll need to deal with. We'll also see how CDS and other DCE servers can maintain security while allowing access to untrusted Microsoft RPC systems. And along the way, we'll provide some tips about using DCE services to provide functions that Microsoft has not included in their Version 1.0 RPC.

The appendices include makefiles that you can use to build the examples we discuss in this chapter.

Writing Server Initialization Code

There are several relatively minor differences in the way that DCE servers and Microsoft RPC servers carry out their respective server initialization steps. These differences stem primarily from Microsoft's use of the TCP/IP transport as the sole DCE transport and from Microsoft RPC's reliance on the *nsid* for CDS access. Briefly, the initialization steps are:

1. Register the interfaces with the RPC runtime library

2. Create server bindings by selecting protocol sequence(s)

3. Optionally advertise server in CDS

4. Manage endpoints

5. Listen for incoming calls

Register Server Interfaces

Your server has to register its interfaces using strict conventions, so that they can be found by clients using the same original interface definition files. Use the *rpc_server_register_if* routine to register each interface.

DCE servers construct an interface handle by concatenating the interface name, the major and minor version numbers, the letter s or c depending on whether the handle is for a server or client, and the word `ifspec`. The interface name and version numbers are specified in the IDL file. Here's an example:

```
phnbk_v1_0_s_ifspec
```

For Microsoft RPC, construct the interface handle by concatenating the interface name, the word `Server` or `Client` depending on whether the handle is for a server or client, and the word `IfHandle`. The interface name is specified in the IDL file. Here's an example of a Microsoft RPC interface handle:

```
phnbk_ServerIfHandle
```

In Example 6-1, the two NULL arguments in the *rpc_server_register_if* routine are the manager type UUID and the manager_epv. These are advanced topics beyond the scope of this book.

Example 6-1: Registering a Server Interface

```
/*
** register the server interface
*/
rpc_server_register_if
```

Example 6-1: Registering a Server Interface (continued)

```
                (
                phnbk2_v1_0_s_ifspec,  /* IDL-generated handle */
                NULL,
                NULL,
                &status
                );
    if (status != error_status_ok)
        {
        printf("Can't register interface \n");
        exit(EXIT_FAILURE);
        }
```

Create Server Binding

A binding is a collection of information that clients need in order to reach your server: a host, a protocol sequence, and an endpoint. The host is always inserted automatically by the runtime library, but you have control over the protocol sequence and the endpoint.

A protocol sequence is a valid combination of communication protocols that clients and servers use to communicate. For example, `ncacn_ip_tcp` is a combination of strings representing the Network Communication Architecture connection-oriented protocol (`ncacn`) over a network using the internet address format (`ip`) and the Transmission Control Protocol transport (`tcp`). Although DCE and Microsoft RPC systems might support several protocol sequences, the only one that both DCE and Microsoft support is TCP/IP.

Therefore, to make your applications run between the two environments, always include `ncacn_ip_tcp` among the supported protocols. For DCE servers, one easy way to do this is to specify in your server that you use all the protocols supported by your system. For now, Microsoft RPC servers that use CDS to relay binding information to clients should limit the protocol sequences they support to `ncacn_ip_tcp`. That's because the *nsid*, which relays binding information between Microsoft systems and CDS, cannot currently handle protocols that use NetBIOS, or named pipes. There are plans to fix this in a future release of the *nsid*.

An endpoint is a generic term referring to a number through which one program can be reached by programs running on other hosts. For instance, when you communicate via TCP/IP, the endpoint corresponds to a port number maintained by the TCP protocol. When you communicate via named pipes on MS-DOS, the endpoint is the name of the pipe. The software for each protocol on each host maintains its own set of endpoints. Once a client gets to your system, all it needs to know is the endpoint where you have registered in order to get a call to your server.

Before you create a server binding, you need to decide whether you will use a dynamic endpoint or a well-known endpoint. Dynamic endpoints are randomly selected by RPC runtime library functions and generally vary from one invocation of the server to the next. When the server stops running, the endpoint is released for use by another process.

A well-known endpoint is a fixed endpoint that is used every time the server runs. Well-known endpoints are generally reserved for widely used or persistent applications such as daemons and are usually assigned by the authority responsible for a given transport protocol. If you use well-known endpoints, you need to include the endpoint in the IDL file as an *endpoint* attribute in the interface header so it's available to clients (see Chapter 3).

DCE and Microsoft RPC provide several routines for creating server bindings. The routine you use depends on whether you want to select a specific protocol sequence or all available protocol sequences, and whether you want to use dynamic or well-known endpoints. Remember that Microsoft RPC servers using CDS to relay binding information to clients should limit the protocol sequences they support to `ncacn_ip_tcp`.

- *rpc_server_use_protseq* selects a specific protocol sequence for use with a dynamic endpoint.

- *rpc_server_use_protseq_ep* selects a specific protocol sequence and a well-known (specific) endpoint.

- *rpc_server_use_all_protseqs* selects all available protocol sequences, using dynamic endpoints.

- *rpc_server_use_all_protseqs_if* selects all available protocol sequences, associating them with well-known endpoints that are defined in the interface definition file where clients can find them.

For now, Microsoft RPC servers should not use the *rpc_server_use_all_protseqs* or *rpc_server_use_all_protseqs_if* routines, because you need to stick to TCP/IP.

Example 6-2 shows how to use *rpc_server_use_protseq* to select a dynamic endpoint for the TCP/IP protocol sequence. The argument `rpc_c_protseq_max_reqs_default` specifies to use the default number of concurrent calls that the server can accept.

If you want to allow more than one protocol sequence but you don't want to support all of them, you can call `rpc_server_use_protseq` or `rpc_server_use_protseq_ep` repeatedly. In order to get cross-environment applications working, you can choose `ncacn_ip_tcp`, or a combination of protocols that includes `ncacn_ip_tcp`, or for a DCE server, just specify all protocol sequences.

Example 6-2: Creating a Server Binding with a Dynamic Endpoint

```
/*
** tell the server to use the TCP/IP protocol sequence
*/
  rpc_server_use_protseq
      (
        "ncacn_ip_tcp",
        rpc_c_protseq_max_reqs_default,
        &status
      );

if (status != error_status_ok)
{
  printf("No available protocol sequences\n");
  exit(1);
}
```

Example 6-3 shows how to use a specific protocol sequence and a well-known endpoint.

Example 6-3: Creating a Server Binding that Uses a Well-Known Endpoint

```
/*
** tell the server to use a well-known endpoint
*/
rpc_server_use_protseq_ep
      (
        "ncacn_ip_tcp",
        rpc_c_protseq_max_reqs_default,
        "1014",
        &status
      );

if (status != error_status_ok)
{
    printf("No available protocol sequences\n");
    exit(1);
}
```

Advertise the Server

Now that you've created binding information, you have to put it someplace where clients can find it. Several methods are available, though production-ready applications almost always use a name service.

Print or display the binding information for clients

This method is useful in limited situations such as when testing an application or when a name service is unavailable for some reason. In practice, this method can be tedious and prone to errors because users must type in binding information for each server they use.

DCE servers can print their complete binding information (protocol sequence, host network address, and endpoint) using the *rpc_binding_to_string_binding* function, as shown in Example 6-4.

Example 6-4: DCE Servers Can Print Complete Binding Information

```
/*
** Get the string bindings and print them
*/
for (i = 0; i < bvec->count; i++)
{
    unsigned char *string_binding;
    rpc_binding_to_string_binding(
                        bvec->binding_h[i],
                        &string_binding,
                        &st);
if (st != error_status_ok)
    {
      printf("Can't get string binding \n");
      exit(1);
    }
    printf("%s\n", string_binding);
}
```

Microsoft RPC Version 1.0 does not document a means to display the endpoint portion of the server binding information. Thus, clients of Microsoft servers must rely on the server host's endpoint map to obtain the endpoint.

Place the full or partial binding in an application specific file

It is possible to take the previous method of printing binding information one step farther. After you get the string binding through *rpc_binding_to_string_binding* (as shown in Example 6-4), you could manually enter the binding into a central file that all clients read when they start up.

While this method offers complete control over how binding information is managed, you are responsible for keeping the files with binding information up-to-date. For instance, if you move a server, you'll have to update the application specific file with the server's new location.

Export the binding to a name service database

Using a name service database is the recommended way to pass server binding information to clients. You use RPC name service interface (NSI) functions that take care of most low-level details involved in communicating with and using the name service.

Cross-environment applications use CDS as the name service. DCE servers and clients use CDS by default when it's installed, but Microsoft RPC clients and servers must be redirected to use CDS rather than the default Microsoft Locator name service. In Chapter 4, we described how to redirect Microsoft DOS, Windows, and Windows NT systems to use CDS. Once you've done this, you can use the Microsoft NSI functions to export server bindings to CDS. In short, the same NSI functions that work for Microsoft's Locator also work when you redirect the application at run time to use CDS; your program does not have to change.

If the server will run on Microsoft RPC, the *nsid* and CDS administrators must have agreed upon a CDS directory that Microsoft servers can use (also described in Chapter 4). This directory, and all of its subsequently created descendents, are then available to Microsoft servers for storing binding information. Some DCE implementations create a default CDS directory for use by Microsoft clients and servers. This directory can be defined in configuration scripts that install and start the *nsid* on a DCE system.

Example 6-5 shows the portion of the initialization code that advertises a server in CDS.

Example 6-5: Advertising a Server in CDS

```
/*
** register endpoint with the name server
*/
rpc_ns_binding_export
            (
            rpc_c_ns_syntax_default,                      ❶
            (unsigned_char_t *)"/.:/phnbk2_srv_",         ❷
            phnbk2_v1_0_s_ifspec,                         ❸
            bvec,
            NULL,
            &status
            );
if (status != error_status_ok)
    {
    printf("Can't register entry with name service\n");
    exit(EXIT_FAILURE);
    }
```

❶ The *rpc_ns_binding_export* function exports the server binding information to CDS. The `rpc_c_ns_syntax_default` constant specifies to use the default syntax (the only syntax currently supported by DCE and Microsoft RPC) for interpreting an entry name.

❷ Define the server entry name. DCE server entry names are unique and take forms like */.:/phbk2_srv_* or */.:/subsys/DEC/examples/phnbk_srv_*. Microsoft servers can't write into either of these CDS directories. They need an entry name like */.:/subsys/DEC/pc_users_servers/phnbk2_srv_* in the directory allocated to them by the CDS administrator (see Chapter 4).

This example has another limitation: CDS cannot maintain multiple entries that have the same entry name. Because our example here doesn't distinguish server entry names, only one of these servers can exist in a DCE cell. Later in this chapter, in the section "Using CDS to Organize Servers," we'll show you how to use a server system's hostname to create unique server entry names.

❸ The example uses a DCE server interface specification. For Microsoft servers, the interface specification would be `phnbk2_Server-IfHandle`.

Manage Endpoints

CDS is good for general-purpose storage—why not just use it to store endpoints as well as binding handles? First, endpoints are meaningful only on the hosts where they are generated; putting them in CDS is a waste of the network's storage capacity. Second, a dynamic endpoint changes every time a server restarts. So putting it in CDS simply increases the chance that clients would get outdated information. For these reasons, we place endpoint information into the server host endpoint map where it can be more easily managed by the server.

Dynamic endpoints must be in the endpoint map. But for well-known endpoints, you have a choice. You can put them into the endpoint map by issuing the *rpc_server_use_protseq_ep* routine, or you can write them directly into the interface definition file, in which case clients know them automatically (see Chapter 3). However, if you do this, you cannot change the endpoint without revising the interface definition file, thus changing the application significantly.

RPC provides two routines that place server endpoint information into the endpoint map:

- *rpc_ep_register* replaces any existing entries remaining from earlier instances of the same server. That is, it replaces entries having the same interface specification, interface UUID, and optional object UUID. Use this routine when a single instance of a server is running at any given time.

- *rpc_ep_register_noreplace* adds server endpoint information to the endpoint map, without replacing any existing entries remaining from other instances of the same server. Use this routine when more than one instance of a server is running an any given time on your host.

  If you use *rpc_ep_register_noreplace*, the server also has to issue *rpc_ep_unregister* when it stops in order to clean up the endpoint map. Otherwise, obsolete endpoints accumulate each time a server stops running. A system crash wipes out the endpoint map so you needn't worry about old information lying around when the system reboots.

On DCE machines, you can manually manage endpoint map information using the *rpccp* program. Microsoft RPC, however, does not provide such a program.

Example 6-6 uses the *rpc_ep_register* routine to place endpoint information in the endpoint map.

Example 6-6: Managing Server Endpoints

```
/*
** register endpoint in the endpoint map
*/
rpc_ep_register ( phnbk_v1_0_s_ifspec,      /* IDL-generated handle  ❶
*/
                 bvec,
                 NULL,
                 "phonebk endpoint",
                 &st);
if (st != error_status_ok)
{
    printf("Can't register endpoint\n");
    exit(1);
}
rpc_binding_vector_free(                  /* free server binding handles  ❷
*/
    &binding_vector,
    &status);

{
    printf("Can't free server binding handles:\n");
    exit(1);
}
```

❶ For Microsoft servers the interface handle would be `phoneb_Server-IfHandle` (see Example 6-1).

❷ Frees the memory used for storing the binding handle because we're finished using it.

Listen for Incoming Remote Procedure Calls

As the final step in server initialization, you need to issue the *rpc_server_listen* routine, which places the server in a wait state for incoming remote procedure calls.

rpc_server_listen monitors established endpoints and passes incoming calls to the correct interface in the server stub code. This routine performs another function: it specifies the maximum number of threads a server can use to handle incoming calls. Once called, *rpc_server_listen* does not return until the server stops running (see Example 6-7).

Example 6-7: Listening for Incoming Remote Procedure Calls

```
    /*
    ** Server is ready to start listening for client requests.
    */
    rpc_server_listen
            (
             (long)2,                                                ❶
             &status
            );
    if (status != error_status_ok)
        printf("Error: rpc_server_listen() returned \n");
    return (EXIT_FAILURE);
}
```

❶ The first argument to *rpc_server_listen* specifies to use two threads. This enables the server to handle two remote procedure calls concurrently.

Recapping Differences

Here are some differences between DCE and Microsoft RPC that we've encountered along the way:

* Microsoft systems must be redirected to use CDS.

* CDS might restrict Microsoft servers to a particular CDS directory.

* Microsoft systems can't print endpoint data on the display.

* Microsoft systems don't have a service like *rpccp* to manage or display endpoints.

* The interface specification names generated by IDL and MIDL differ.

* TCP/IP is the only protocol in common between both environments at this time.

Using CDS to Organize Servers

In Chapter 5, we showed how clients can interpret a server's binding information and select an appropriate server based on specific client needs. A client might need a server for a particular object such as a particular set of data files. Another group of clients might seek servers based on proximity. For instance, users would want to use print servers for printers located nearby, rather than in another building. And other high priority clients of other applications might seek servers based on speed and be charged accordingly, while low priority clients use any available server.

RPC clients can use just about any criteria in selecting servers. Each server (or, more precisely, each interface that a server registers) has its own entry in CDS, which is called a server entry. Group and profile entries gather related servers together under descriptive names, offering clients a variety of ways to import server bindings.

Clients begin their CDS search with the entry specified in the user's RPC_DEFAULT_ENTRY environment variable, or by specifying an entry as a parameter to the *rpc_ns_binding_import** or *rpc_ns_binding_lookup** functions. The entry that this variable or parameter points to can be very specific or very inclusive; it can point to a server entry, a group entry, or a profile entry.

Server Entries

Server entries provide the binding information for a specific server. Clients rarely use a server entry for RPC_DEFAULT_ENTRY; it's useful only if there is just one server that will satisfy all a client's needs (for example, when only one server has access to a particular data file). When an RPC_DEFAULT_ENTRY points to a specific server entry, it offers the client no alternatives. A client's search begins and ends with this one entry. If the server isn't available, the client can only wait and try the server again later. Furthermore, every client that you run has to use that same server, unless you change RPC_DEFAULT_ENTRY between runs.

Although you can use a server entry as the RPC_DEFAULT_ENTRY variable for automatic or implicit binding, it's more likely to be used for clients that use explicit binding. You might also use a server entry while testing or debugging an application. This lets you temporarily streamline your application, avoiding use of CDS group or profile functions so you can test client-server interaction with minimal use of CDS.

Groups

Group entries offer more server choices to clients because groups can collect many individual servers (or even other groups of servers) under a common descriptive group name. Set your RPC_DEFAULT_ENTRY to a group entry when any of multiple servers will satisfy a client's needs, as in the case of several print servers offering identical printers nearby.

When clients use automatic or implicit binding, CDS returns a server entry at random from those in the group entry. If the server isn't available for some reason, CDS can often provide another random server for use from the group. Random selection is an essential part of a group entry's ability to help balance the workload among similar servers. When group entries contain other group entries, CDS traverses entries until a server entry is found and returned.

A random choice assumes that all group entries are equally valid; this in turn means that your group should include entries for a single application, where they offer the same procedures but differ either in the systems where they are located or the transport over which they are available.

Figure 6-1 shows how group entries identify related servers, any of which will satisfy a client's needs. The group entry related_servers_sales includes another group, related_servers_service. Nesting such as this allows you to fine-tune the load balance across your available servers. Clients specifying related_servers_sales as the RPC_DEFAULT_ENTRY can use any of the seven available servers. Clients that use related_servers_service as the RPC_DEFAULT_ENTRY are limited to using servers 4 through 7.

Example 6-8 adds the server entry name to a group entry in CDS. The group name gathers identical services under a common name we'll call */.:/phnbk2_group.* You can add the entry name to multiple groups by repeating the call with different group names.

Example 6-8: Example Using rpc_ns_group_mbr_add

```
rpc_ns_group_mbr_add(
     rpc_c_ns_syntax_default,
     (unsigned_char_t *) "/.:/phnbk2_group",
     rpc_c_ns_syntax_default,
     (unsigned_char_t *)entry_name,
     &status);
if (status != error_status_ok)
{
    printf("Can't add member to name service group\n");
    exit(1);
}
```

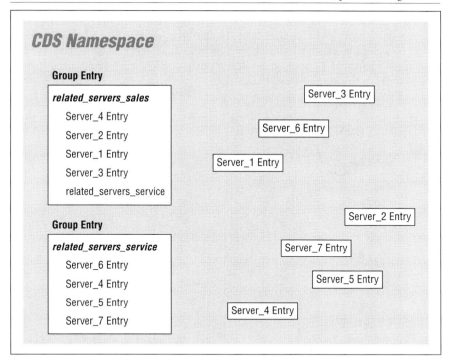

Figure 6-1: Groups gather related service together

Profiles

Profile entries offer the most choice to the user; they can provide entirely different information to different clients. A profile entry can contain entries for servers, groups, and even other profiles, but its most important advantage is a priority value attached to each embedded entry. (Actually, the term *element* is applied to what's inside a profile, because the element contains this priority value and other information that an entry does not contain.) The priority value controls the client's search order.

For instance, consider a company in a building with several floors. For convenience, each floor has several laser and dot matrix printers. Each floor maintains a profile that prioritizes print servers based on how near they are to clients. Print servers on the client's floor are tried first, while print servers on other floors are tried later. Each client or group of clients can use custom tailored profiles to control the order in which they import bindings from CDS.

You should set an RPC_DEFAULT_ENTRY variable to a profile entry when you want to control the order in which servers are used.

Figure 6-2 shows how a profile's priority values direct a search. Clients on floor 2 use direct print requests to the `Print_servers_floor2` profile entry. The first printers tried reside in the `Floor2_printers` group entry. The next group of printers tried reside in the `Floor3_printers` group entry. Floor 1 printers are tried last.

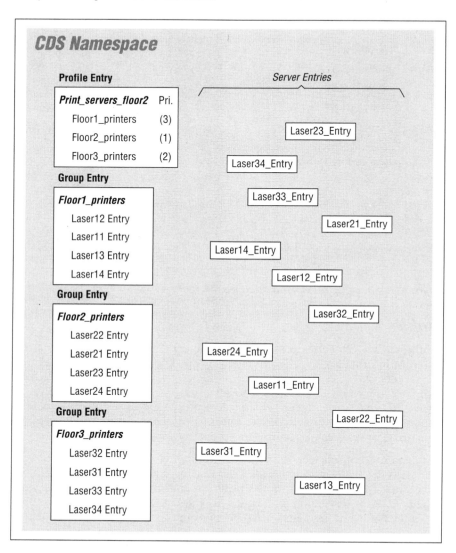

Figure 6-2: Profiles direct the search for servers

Although you can use a program to create and manage profiles, we expect that users customizing their environments will most often perform profile-related tasks manually, using *rpccp* commands from a DCE machine. Microsoft RPC Version 1.0 does not provide a command interface. If you want to perform profile operations from a Microsoft RPC system you need to create a program that includes the *rpc_ns_profile_elt_add* RPC runtime API. The structure and use of this API closely resembles the group function *rpc_ns_group_mbr_add* shown in Example 6-8.

Balance Server Use by Including Groups in Profiles

Profiles provide a convenient way to control the order in which CDS returns server bindings to clients through the use of priority attributes associated with each element in the profile. But when profiles are used exclusively (that is, profiles don't include any groups), they can create bottlenecks. Because the same search order is used every time the profile is accessed, the same server binding is likely to be returned to every client request.

In distributed environments offering many similar and identical services, you need to provide each client with the most appropriate server while balancing the load across all of the available servers. You can achieve this balance by including groups in the profile search order. While profiles can direct the overall approach, groups can provide a level of randomness that tends to distribute the workload across available servers.

Unique Server Entry Names

Some DCE cells might have multiple servers offering the same functions. To avoid problems, you should follow some convention that lets each server have a unique name.

The first server to export a binding under a given name creates an entry in CDS. Later servers just add to the same entry. CDS treats the first server as the owner, which gives it additional privileges—the owner can modify as well as remove (unexport) the entry. These functions enable servers to keep CDS free of unused server entries. For example, a server entry name exported by our phnbk2 server is */.:/phnbk2_srv_*. When the server is terminating (permanently), it can issue an *rpc_ns_binding_unexport* routine to remove its entry.

Problems can occur when more than one server uses the same entry name. Let's assume one server is running and has exported its binding to CDS. A second server starts and adds its binding to the entry that already exists in CDS. When the first server terminates, it unexports the entry along with the second server's binding. Now clients cannot find the second server even though it's up and running normally.

Therefore, we need a way for servers to export unique server entry names. It's impractical to hardcode different entry names into each server, and it's equally impractical to generate unique names each time a server starts. One practical way to create a unique name is to use the server's hostname in some way to distinguish server entry names. DCE offers two ways to do this. You can export the server name to a host specific directory in CDS such as */.:/subsys/HOSTS/topdog/servers/phnbk2_srv_* (where *topdog* is the hostname used in this example). Alternatively, you can append the hostname to the server entry name and export the entry to any suitable directory in CDS, like */.:/subsys/servers/phnbk2_srv_topdog*. By the way, the underscore we've been appending to the server name (*phnbk2_srv_*) just makes the modified name more readable.

DCE servers can use either method since they can export the entry to any suitable directory, but security restrictions might prevent Microsoft RPC servers from writing into a host-specific CDS directory. In this case, we recommend that Microsoft servers append the hostname to the server entry name. Microsoft servers then export the entry name to a CDS directory designated for their use. The DCE configuration script provided by Digital Equipment Corporation with one of their DCE kits creates a CDS directory named */.:/subsys/DEC/pc_users_servers* for use by Microsoft servers.

Example 6-9 shows one way for a DCE server to embed a hostname in a server entry name. Example 6-10 shows how a Windows NT server could append a hostname to a server entry name.

Example 6-9: Creating a Unique DCE Server Name

```
/*
** Construct entry name using hostname...
*/
strcpy(entry_name, "/.:/subsys/HOSTS/");
gethostname(hostname, STRINGLEN);
strcat(entry_name, hostname);
strcat(entry_name,"/servers/phnbk2_srv_");
/*
** Now export these bindings using an entry name of the form:
**
**     "/.:/subsys/HOSTS/<hostname>/servers/phnbk2_srv_"
*/
rpc_ns_binding_export
            (
            rpc_c_ns_syntax_default,
            (unsigned_char_t *)entry_name,
            phnbk2_v1_0_s_ifspec,
            bvec,
            NULL,
            &status);
if (status != error_status_ok)
    {
    printf("Can't register entry with name service\n");
    exit(1);
    }
```

Example 6-10: Creating a Unique Windows NT Server Name

```
/*
** Construct entry name using GetComputerName, which
**     is a better choice for a Windows NT system...
*/
strcpy(entry_name, "/.:/subsys/DEC/pc_users_servers/phnbk2_srv_");
GetComputerName(computername, &computernamelength);
strcat(entry_name, computername);
/*
** Now export these bindings using an entry name of the form:
**
** "/.:/subsys/DEC/pc_users_servers/phnbk2_srv_<computername>"
*/
rpc_ns_binding_export
            (
                rpc_c_ns_syntax_default,
                (unsigned_char_t *)entry_name,
                phnbk2_ServerIfHandle,    .
                bvec,
                NULL,
                &status);
if (status != error_status_ok)
        {
        printf("Can't register entry with name service\n");
        exit(1);
        }
```

We use hostnames to distinguish entry names when servers run on different hosts, but what happens when identical servers run on the same host? Our advise here is to avoid running identical servers on the same host. That's not because it's hard to do, but rather because it's usually unnecessary. Instead, you can enable servers to handle more calls concurrently by setting the *max_call_requests* argument in any of the *rpc_server_use_protseq* or *rpc_server_use_all_protseq* routines. You'll also need to set the *max_calls_exec* argument in the *rpc_server_listen* routine.

If it's necessary to run two or more identical servers on a host, you could distinguish names by picking from a small set of names that you use each time you start a server. You could pass the name (like *jims_server*) as an argument on the server command line. Avoid using random strings like process IDs to distinguish server entry names. These are hard to track and can result in stale entries cluttering up the CDS namespace.

With hostnames appended to server entry names, clients that invoke a server using its entry name now need to know which host a server is running on. To free your clients from having to know a server's hostname, your server should also export its server entry name to a group or profile entry. Earlier, we mentioned several good uses for groups and profiles. Avoiding hostname dependency is another good reason for using them.

Writing Manager Procedures

Manager procedures are implementations of the server remote procedures. In most ways, these are just like local procedures in monolithic applications, but each procedure is defined in the IDL file and called through the RPC stubs, rather than being called directly from a main part of the program.

There are many similarities between remote and local procedures. However, when you're developing remote procedures, you'll probably need to deal with several factors related to the distributed nature of the application: threads, memory management, and optionally, context handles.

Threads and Different Threads Implementations

Your server or client code may have to deal with the effects of running multiple underlying threads. Although the correct and careful use of a threaded environment is an important factor in creating DCE and Microsoft RPC servers, we don't discuss threads in detail in this book. The topic is too big to cover here, and in addition, its effects are limited to a single system; it isn't really a topic in distributed computing. Still, threads play an important role in DCE programming, and the differences between NT threads and DCE threads (based on the POSIX 1003.4a standard) inhibit the portability of code between the two environments.

You've probably noticed that the example phonebook server in this book uses two threads. This example works because clients aren't modifying server information—they're only reading it. Threads becomes more of an issue when data is being changed.

Significant differences exist between DCE threads and the threads implementation on Microsoft Windows NT. Nevertheless, the kinds of functions provided by each implementation are very similar. If you understand one threads implementation you can understand the other one. And if your application uses threads, be prepared to make changes if you port across environments.

Managing Memory

In the typical C language programming environment, applications call *malloc* to allocate memory and use *free* to deallocate or release memory. Once again, this simple model of memory allocation isn't sufficient for writing distributed applications because the client and the server part of the application execute in different address spaces. This requires a lot more thought on the developer's part about where the memory should be allocated and where it should be deallocated.

Remote procedure call parameters with the [in] or the [in,out] attributes are not usually too troublesome because storage for the parameters, by definition, already exists on the client side at the time the call is made. The parameter is passed to the server, and after the server uses it, the parameter is either discarded or returned to the client.

Parameters with the [out] parameter, however, pose an interesting paradox for the distributed application developer. Because memory for the parameter is allocated within the server manager procedure, and the memory can't be deallocated before the server stub returns to the client, when can the server manager procedure ever deallocate the memory associated with the parameter?

For the answer to this question, we must begin a discussion of how memory allocation approaches differ between OSF-derived DCE implementations and the Microsoft DCE RPC implementation. Two of the most important areas of difference are the method by which distributed applications allocate and deallocate memory, and the treatment of memory allocated for [out] parameters.

Memory allocation and deallocation

Client and server stubs produced by Microsoft's MIDL stub compiler depend on the existence of two procedures for allocating and deallocating memory. These procedures, *MIDL_user_allocate* and *MIDL_user_free*, must be supplied by the application developer. Simple versions based on *malloc* and *free* are shown below:

```
void __RPC_FAR * __RPC_API MIDL_user_allocate (size_t length)
{
      return (malloc (length) );
}

void __RPC_API MIDL_user_free (void __RPC_FAR * pointer)
{
      free (pointer);
}
```

The definitions __RPC_API and __RPC_FAR, which reside in the RPC.H header file, allow Microsoft to specify additional attributes to the C compiler that may be required on the various operating system platforms that Microsoft supports. For example, the C compiler on DOS and Windows translates __RPC_FAR to __far which means that this is a "far" pointer, or a four byte address. On Windows NT, all pointers are four bytes, so the compiler just ignores __RPC_FAR.

Server memory allocation for [out] parameters

Server stubs produced by MIDL address the [out] parameter paradox by taking the simple approach that all memory used for parameters is freed after the parameters are sent back to the client.

DCE provides more special stub support routines for allocating and deallocating memory. Any memory allocated by a server manager procedure using *rpc_ss_allocate*, described below, will be freed after the parameters have been returned to the client. You must use this routine to allocate memory for [out] parameters:

```
void * rpc_ss_allocate ( size_t size )
```

The following routine is the counterpart of *rpc_ss_allocate* and should be used for freeing memory allocated by *rpc_ss_allocate*:

```
void rpc_ss_free ( char * ptr )
```

Using Context Handles

Earlier in this book, we talked about how your program can use context handles to maintain a client's state across multiple remote procedure calls. After completing a remote procedure call, the server stores the client's state in a context handle, which it passes back to the client. The client simply holds onto the handle, passing it back to the server with the next relevant RPC.

In Chapter 3, we saw how you can declare context handles in the IDL file, and in Chapter 5 we saw how to program clients to manage context handles they receive from servers. Now we'll see how servers use context handles to maintain a client's state between remote procedure calls.

For servers, the addition of context handles usually adds two extra procedures to the manager code. First you need to allocate resources for the context handle. When you're done using the handle, you must free up the resources so they're available to other processes. These extra procedures are invoked by client remote procedure calls. It makes sense to do it that way—for instance, in our phonebook application, only the client knows when the user is ready to quit.

Once the context handle is established, the server can update the handle as dictated by the remote procedures. The phonebook application stores the last operation (whether the operation was a BROWSE, RESET, and so on) and the file pointer. The server maintains the context handle until one of the following happens:

- The client calls a remote procedure that frees the context.

- The client-server communication breaks.

If the client terminates while the context is being maintained or the client-server communication breaks, a context rundown procedure frees the context handle. But before we look at an example of a context rundown procedure, let's look at some remote procedures that establish and remove context handles on a server. Example 6-11 shows a remote procedure, *open_phonebook_file*, that opens the phonebook data file and establishes the context handle. Example 6-12 shows a second remote procedure, *close_phonebook_file*, that closes the phonebook data file and frees the context handle.

Example 6-11: Establishing Context Handles in a Server

```
void
open_phonebook_file
            (
             ph
            )
phonebook_handle *ph;
{
    /*
    ** This structure is defined in phnbk2.idl and contains both
    **    a filehandle and a short that keeps track of the previous
    **    phonebook operation.
    */
    p_context *pc_p;
    /*
    ** Allocate the required amount of memory for a p_context
    **     structure
    */
    pc_p = (p_context *) malloc ( sizeof (p_context) );
    /*
    ** Allocate a file handle for this client's operations
    */
    pc_p->filehandle = fopen ("phnbk.txt","r");
    /*
    ** Initialize the p_context...
    **
    ** The previous operation is 0 (no previous operation yet)
    */
    pc_p->previous_operation = 0;
    /*
    ** Return the context handle
    */
    *ph = (phonebook_handle) pc_p;

    return ;
}
```

Example 6-12: Freeing Context Handles in a Server

```
void
close_phonebook_file
            (
             ph
            )
phonebook_handle *ph;
{
    /*
    ** Effect a context handle cleanup by calling on the
    **     rundown routine -- it already does what we want
    **     to do
    */
    phonebook_handle_rundown
                (
                 *ph
                );
    /*
    ** Reset the context handle to NULL
    */
    *ph = NULL;
    return;
}
```

Servers also need to be prepared to free resources when a client connection is lost or the client terminates before freeing the context handle resources. When this happens, the server RPC runtime library automatically calls a context rundown procedure. In our case, we want to close the phonebook file and free the memory for the context handle. This is shown in Example 6-13.

To let the runtime library find the procedure, you need to construct its name according to strict conventions. Append *_rundown* to the data type (in this case, *phonebook_handle*) to construct the name *phonebook_ handle_rundown*.

Example 6-13: A Context Handle Rundown Procedure in a Server

```
void
phonebook_handle_rundown
            (
             ph
            )
phonebook_handle ph;
{
    p_context *pc_p;
    pc_p = (p_context *)ph;
    /*
    ** Close the file associated with the filehandle
    */
    fclose (pc_p->filehandle);
```

Example 6-13: A Context Handle Rundown Procedure in a Server (continued)

```
    /*
    ** ...and free the memory associated with this p_context struct
    */
    free(pc_p);
    return;
}
```

Once the context handle is established on the server, remote procedures can modify the handle as needed. Example 6-14 shows how the phonebook application's *lookup* remote procedure uses the context handle.

Example 6-14: A Remote Procedure that Uses a Context Handle

```
short
lookup                                                                ❶
     (
      phone,
      op,
      stringin,
      stringout
     )
phonebook_handle phone;
short op;
idl_char stringin[LINESIZE];                                          ❷
idl_char stringout[LINESIZE];
{
    idl_char buf[LINESIZE];
    p_context *pc_p;                                                  ❸
    /*
    ** Remember that our context handle is a pointer to a
    **     p_context structure
    */
    pc_p = (p_context *)phone;
    /*
    ** Switch on requested operation
    */
    switch (op)
        {
        case  RESET:                                                 ❹
            /*
            **   Reset context
            */
            printf("Phonbook:\tRESET\n");
            rewind(pc_p->filehandle);
            pc_p->previous_operation = FIRSTMATCH;
            return(NORMAL);
            break;
        case  FIRSTMATCH:
            /*
            **   Look for first match of a string, starting at the
```

Example 6-14: A Remote Procedure that Uses a Context Handle (continued)

```
        **      beginning of the file...
        */
        printf("Phonbook:\tFIRSTMATCH\n");
        rewind(pc_p->filehandle);
        break;
    case  NEXTMATCH:
        /*
        ** Nothing special here, fall out and continue search
        */
        printf("Phonbook:\tNEXTMATCH\n");
        break;
    case  BROWSE:                                                   ➎
        /*
        ** A BROWSE operation just returns the next entry...
        **
        ** If the last operation was a BROWSE that got an EOF,
        **      then rewind and start cycling through again.
        */
        printf("Phonbook:\tBROWSE\n");
        if (pc_p->previous_operation == BROWSE_RESET)
            rewind (pc_p->filehandle);

        if ((getfileline(buf,pc_p->filehandle)) != -1)
            {
            /*
            ** If not EOF, then just return next entry.
            */
            strcpy ((char *)stringout,(char *)buf);
            printf("Phonbook: \tFound %s\n", buf);
            pc_p->previous_operation = BROWSE;
            return(NORMAL);
            }
        else
            {
            /*
            ** This allows the client to flag "no more entries"
            ** before cycling through the file again on
            ** another BROWSE request.
            */
            pc_p->previous_operation = BROWSE_RESET;

            return(END);
            }
    }
    /*
    ** Keep track of previous operation in p_context
    */
    pc_p->previous_operation = op;                                  ➏
    /*
    ** Either return the line of the file that contains a string
    ** match, or return -1...
```

Example 6-14: A Remote Procedure that Uses a Context Handle (continued)

```
*/
while ((getfileline(buf,pc_p->filehandle)) != -1)
    {
    if ((strstr((char *)buf, (char *)stringin)) != (char *) NULL)
        {
        printf("Phonbook: \tFound %s\n", buf);
        strcpy ((char *)stringout,(char *)buf);
        return(NORMAL);
        }
    }
return(END);
}
```

❶ The *lookup* function is a remote procedure call.

❷ We cannot simply declare these parameters as char, because the char defined by the server system's compiler might be different from the char defined by IDL (for instance, in size or in being signed versus unsigned). IDL solves this by defining data types that are usable in C programs and guaranteed to be the same as corresponding IDL types. The C type idl_char corresponds to the IDL type char. So declare the arguments in the lookup remote procedure call as idl_char.

❸ The context handle is cast into the *p_context* structure that is defined in the interface definition. This allows the program to more easily access the different components of this client's context information.

❹ The RESET, FIRSTMATCH, and NEXTMATCH operations aren't shown in the client code example in Chapter 5, but we're constantly updating the context handle after each operation.

❺ The BROWSE operation calls the *getfileline* function, which simply reads and formats a line from the phonebook file. It automatically updates the position of the file pointer stored in the context handle (the main reason for creating the context handle in the first place).

❻ Store the previous operation in the context handle (*p_context*).

Security Programming

In Chapter 4, we discussed how to set up CDS so that it's protected while still accepting Microsoft server binding information exported to it. When DCE environments employ the minimum level of security, all clients, including Microsoft RPC clients, can probably access most DCE resources without restrictions. Higher security levels enable servers to filter client requests based on an authenticated identity associated with each request.

When DCE servers enforce security, they expect clients to send information about themselves. Since Microsoft RPC doesn't support DCE security yet, Microsoft RPC calls have no identity at all. So your DCE server treats them as "unauthenticated." Consequently, when your DCE server enforces security, it must make provisions to handle this special category of call.

Microsoft RPC servers and clients rely on a form of security that is built into the named pipes transport. Because the named pipes transport is a secure channel, Microsoft clients and servers needn't (and don't) perform any security functions at all. This means, though, that Microsoft clients and servers are not secure when other transports like TCP/IP are used. Because DCE and Microsoft systems typically interact over something like TCP/IP (as opposed to named pipes), cross-environment applications cannot rely on either environment's security mechanism. Moreover, Microsoft RPC Version 1.0 servers cannot interpret remote procedure calls from DCE clients that are using DCE security. So when cross-environment application servers run on DCE and Microsoft systems, avoid using DCE security.

As we saw in Chapter 4, CDS relies on the *nsid* group name to restrict Microsoft clients and servers to specific regions of CDS. But other DCE servers cannot identify incoming RPCs from Microsoft clients—there's no authentication information included with their incoming RPCs because they don't arrive through a proxy server like the *nsid*. Fortunately, the DCE Security Service provides a way to allow unauthenticated Microsoft clients (or any other unauthenticated client) to use a secure server; DCE access control lists (ACLs) can contain entries that grant permissions to unauthenticated clients. Let's start by looking at how secure DCE servers handle the authentication of clients.

DCE Security involves a series of tasks that all servers go through every time a client tries to connect. The server has to:

1. Extract binding information about the client from the incoming call.

2. Extract any authentication information—the privilege attribute certificate (PAC),—from the binding handle, and check the PAC with the DCE Security Service.

3. Compare the client's authentication information with the access control list (ACL) on the data or other object that the server is offering. This is normally written into the server as a self-contained module called an ACL manager.

For Microsoft RPC clients, the server still goes through all the steps. In the second step, the code must create a null pointer when it doesn't find authentication information. In the third step, it just treats the client's call as a special type of call—an unauthenticated one.

Client binding handles provide client authentication information

In Chapter 5, we discussed how clients use the server's binding information; now we can discuss the flip side. Servers also have to use the client's
binding information, particularly to enforce security.

Clients always pass a binding handle as the first parameter of a remote procedure call, but servers (as distinguished from stub code) can't manipulate
the handle unless it's declared as the first parameter to remote procedures
in either the IDL file or in the server's ACF.

This gives programmers a choice. They can just list the binding handle in
the interface definition file. But this forces all clients to declare and manipulate the binding handle, so they cannot use automatic or implicit binding if
they choose. A gentler method—available for DCE servers but not for
Microsoft RPC—is to leave the binding handles out of the interface definition, but to put the [explicit_handle] attribute into the server's ACF
file. Now the client can use whatever type of binding its programmer
wants, while your server can manipulate the binding handle as if it were
declared explicitly.

Now we know how to get the binding handle, so we can continue with
step 2 of the process—extracting the authorization information.

DCE clients that call *rpc_binding_set_auth_info* can include their authentication information as part of the binding information passed to servers.
Microsoft RPC clients and servers do not support DCE security functions
and cannot include any authentication information as part of the binding
information passed to servers.

When a secure DCE server receives an incoming RPC, it issues the call
rpc_binding_inq_auth_client. Normally, with properly secured DCE clients, this call extracts the client's authorization information and performs
other security functions to check whether the client is authentic.

If the call is from a DCE client and includes valid authentication information, the *rpc_binding_inq_auth_client* call returns a status of *rpc_s_ok* and
along with other client authorization information like the PAC that will be
used by the server to determine client privileges.

If the call is from a Microsoft client, it does not include any authentication
or authorization information. *The rpc_binding_inq_auth_client* call returns
a status of *rpc_s_binding_has_no_auth* and creates a client binding handle
that points to the client's binding information. The binding information consists of the Microsoft client's protocol sequence, network address, and
object UUID. In place of a PAC, the Microsoft RPC binding information has
a null pointer.

An ACL manager procedure grants permissions

We are ready for the final step in security: examining the ACLs on the protected objects and determining what the client is allowed to do. Once the client is authenticated and a client binding handle is established, servers that enforce authorization checks use an ACL manager to determine whether the client can perform the operation requested in the remote procedure call. The server calls an ACL manager procedure such as *sec_acl_mgr_is_authorized*, passing the client credentials as a parameter to the call.* The credentials are either a DCE client's PAC or the Microsoft client's null pointer.

For a normal, authenticated DCE client, the ACL manager checks first for an ACL entry matching the client's principal name (usually the name of the user running the client program). If that fails, it looks for ACL entries matching group names in the PAC and assigns the union of all permissions granted to all matching groups. (We'll see an example soon.) If no matching group names are found, the ACL manager checks for an entry matching the principal's cell name. Finally, if the client does not match any user, group, or cell name ACL entry, DCE provides an ACL type called *any_other*. You can set default permissions there (naturally, it would make sense for them to be more restrictive than the permissions you grant to known users and groups).

The ACLs are set by administrators outside the server program. But before granting permissions, the ACL manager passes the set of permissions granted by the ACL entries through a mask specified within the ACL, which provides a last-ditch chance to deny access. The *mask_obj* mask is applied to all users whose group names or principal names appear in the ACL.

Incidentally, *mask_obj* is not applied to the ACL entries called *user_obj* and *other_obj*. These entries grant permissions to the object's owner and the owner's cell, respectively. This model assumes that you want to permit all operations by the owner. For our purposes, the exception is not important.

Now we get to the heart of the matter. What happens to Microsoft clients who do not furnish an identity at all and therefore cannot have user, group, or cell name ACL entries? First of all, they fall under the default *any_other* ACL entry type, so you can define there the privileges you want to give them. In addition, DCE provides a second mask with the name

---

*DCE does not include a working ACL manager API because each ACL manager must be custom designed to meet the needs of the resource it protects. For instance, one resource, say a file, needs read or write access control while another kind of resource, let's say a specialized remote procedure, needs to control who can execute the procedure. The ACLs for these resources differ too because they control different permissions. Consequently, programmers who want to include ACL checking (and ACL editing) in their program must write their own ACL manager, implementing a set of *rdacl_** and *sec_acl_** routines provided with the Open Software Foundation's DCE source code. The use of these procedures is outside the scope of this book.

unauthenticated. A Microsoft client passes through the *unauthenticated* mask so you can filter its access independently from other principals or groups explicitly named in the ACL. Ordinarily, the *unauthenticated* mask is more restrictive than the *mask_obj* mask.

For instance, you might grant insert and read permissions to authenticated DCE users, while granting only read permission to unauthenticated users. In that case, Microsoft users could query the database for information, but they'd have to get an account on a DCE machine to enter information. You might do this to prevent a malicious or confused user from anonymously inserting bogus information into the database. Remember, since Microsoft RPC clients are unauthenticated, you can't reliably identify who is making the remote procedure call. He or she may be a legitimate user but there's no way to tell for certain.

The following sample ACL demonstrates how the use of masks filters permissions.

```
# SEC_ACL for .:/subsys/DEC/examples/event_srv_:
# Default cell = /.../car.admin.col.edu
mask_obj:               rwxci-t
unauthenticated:        r------
user_obj:               rwxcidt
group_obj:              rwx---t
mask_obj:               rwx---t
user:john:              rwxcidt
user:will:              rwxcidt
group:professors:       rwx---t
group:grad_assistants:  r-x---t
group:administrators:   rwx-i-t
group:students:         r-x----
any_other:              r-x----
```

The ACL (permissions aligned for readability) uses the following permissions:

r - read
w - write
x - execute
c - control
i - insert
d - delete
t - test

The ACL manager determines client permissions as follows:

- User Will, a professor, gets his rwxcidt permissions filtered by the *mask_obj* mask to yield an effective permission set of rwxci-t.

- User Linda's principal name is not listed in the ACL, but Linda's groups—professors and administrators—create a total set of rwxci-t permissions (the union of these sets). It is filtered by the *mask_obj* mask to yield an effective permission set of `rwxci-t`.

- An authenticated user whose PAC doesn't appear here gets the `r-x----` permissions for *any_other*, filtered by the *mask_obj* mask to yield an effective permission set of `r-x----`.

- An unauthenticated user with no PAC gets the `r-x----` permissions for *any_other*, filtered by the *unauthenticated* mask to yield an effective permission set of `r------`.

The ACL editor sets permissions

The ACL manager grants permissions contained in the ACL, but unless the default permissions are sufficient, you'll need to modify them using the ACL editor called *acl_edit*.

Use *acl_edit* to set permissions for the entry type *any_other* and for the *unauthenticated* mask. While ensuring that the permissions you set are sufficient to allow your Microsoft clients to do everything they need to do with the server, be aware that all other unauthenticated clients, even hostile ones, will have the same permissions.

7

A Remodeling Handbook for Existing Local Applications

Because distributed computing can benefit many existing applications, it is worthwhile to take a look at these programs in the light of the distributed programming model discussed in this book. For instance, if you could take a mathematics library written as an RPC server and install it on a high-powered mainframe with a vector processor, all your PC client would have to do is send over the initial parameters of an equation and collect the results when the server is done. A Windows NT client could be doing other work while the server is performing the task, and even an MS-DOS client would show better response time because the task is so much better suited to the server's architecture.

Most adopters of DCE technology today plan to use DCE for designing and developing a brand new application or an integrated system of applications. It is much easier to write a distributed application from scratch, with the capabilities of RPC in mind, than to visualize how an older local or monolithic (in the sense of not being distributed) application would take advantage of the new RPC features.

Still, certain classes of local applications don't require an army of software engineers and two years of effort before they can be made more useful in a distributed computing environment. We're going to show you some steps that describe a kind of distributed "remodeling job" of your existing local application to convert it to a distributed application with a minimal amount of effort. It's your decision as to whether you are satisfied with the result of your remodeled application, or whether this is just an interim step toward a much more substantial "restoration" project.

What Kind of Application Makes a Good Candidate for Remodeling?

As we alluded to earlier, not all existing local applications are suited to this remodeling process. And some programs may technically meet the criteria for being good candidates for remodeling, but ought to be rewritten anyway. A good example of this would be code that has devolved into spaghetti over the years after being handed from one programmer to another, each adding their own spices. There is obviously lots of room for judgment here.

The first step is to identify whether there are one or more "API sets" in the application that can be translated to the RPC model. An API set can be described as a set of functions that performs some operation with each function having a single entry point and a well-defined set of input and output parameters. These operations don't necessarily have to be closely related. A good example of one of these API sets is the DCE Name Service Interface (NSI) API. These calls are the ones that begin with *rpc_ns*. The Name Service Interface Daemon (*nsid*) was in fact written using many of the techniques we will discuss below.

The following sections discuss properties of API sets that facilitate easier conversion to remote procedures.

The API set can be easily separated from the calling code. It is difficult to identify the API sets when a program was written according to extremes of either structured or unstructured programming. When a program is written as one large block, it won't fit our guidelines at all. On the other hand, if every sequence of three lines of code is stashed away in its own procedure, it will also be difficult to define a reasonable API set, but it will still be easier than with a single-block program.

The API set reflects a significant amount of the work done by the program. The parts of the program that you want to separate and implement in a server should be those procedures where the bulk of the real work is done. It doesn't make sense to solve complicated differential equations in the client but then write a server manager procedure that performs the simpler calculations.

The NSI API, for example, fits this criterion for distribution. A lot of work is done behind the scenes by the naming components of the DCE. By providing a remote interface to this code, a PC client can get all of the functionality of the NSI, but rely on the server machine to do the hard work.

The functions in the API set will be safe, or can be made safe, when called by multiple clients simultaneously. This is an important concept, and is worthy of the numerous books that have been written on the subject. It will do you little good to build a server full of useful remote procedures if the multiple threads don't respect each other's rights. Because stack space is per-thread storage, and that's where the manager procedure arguments are stored, this problem isn't as bad as it might seem at first glance. But be sure to consider things like file I/O or network operations that may be performed on behalf of your manager procedure.

The approach to this consideration depends heavily on your operating system implementation. Some operating systems, such as Windows NT, have been designed from the ground up to be thread-aware, but on other operating systems a thread may be no more than a user-level emulation.

Two possible solutions here are:

1. Restricting the server from running with more than one thread at a time (by specifying "1" as the first parameter to *rpc_server_listen*).

2. Using some kind of synchronization primitive that protects those resources that are not thread safe.

The functions in the API set depend on arguments for procedure input and output rather than external, or global, variables. Many of us who are, shall we say, "experienced" programmers have worked with programs where data is largely accessed using global variables. While programmers use this approach more frequently in languages such as Fortran, it is still something to take into account for our purposes with the C language. Applications that use a few global variables can be remodeled safely by protecting them with synchronization primitives. However, any application that makes heavy use of global variables will be unsuitable for multiple threads because adding protective locks is difficult, and the result might be hidden errors or lots of wasted time waiting for locks to be released. Unfortunately, the amount of work required by the true solution—rewriting the application to use procedure arguments and non-global data—is closer to a restoration than a remodeling anyway.

The functions make use of datatypes that are supported by the stub compiler. This is an obvious consideration. Even if the base data types you need may be supported by the compiler, the structures may be complex, or may be constructed in ways that make them difficult to describe as a remote procedure parameter. A good example of an API that is unsuitable for converting into a remote procedure call is one that makes heavy use of void * parameters. Because the stub compilers must know what is being sent over the network, this notion of a "pointer to anything" is completely foreign unless the data behind the void * is truly opaque to the client. In this case context handles can often be used successfully.

Lots of applications meet the criteria for easy distribution. Many in-house software packages will be found to match well with the above criteria, and several third-party software products have an API set that fits well within these guidelines; database products, CAD applications, and mathematical and statistics packages are just a few of the kinds of applications that can offer real value as distributed applications. (Note: be sure to check your licensing agreement for the legality of a situation where you make the functionality of a product on a single system available to multiple clients via a remote API. In cases where it isn't clear, it is best to play it safe, and we'd recommend you not push your luck.)

Remodeling Guidelines

Once you have determined that a particular API set matches well enough with the above criteria, the next step is to take a closer look into the API set you have identified. Is it an API to code you have no control over? For instance, maybe the API is that of an old application library to which the sources have long since disappeared. If this is the case, the recommended course of action is to define a server manager procedure that serves as a remote wrapper around this API. This manager procedure accepts input arguments from the client and merely passes them on to the API by calling it within the manager routine. After control returns from the API, the return arguments are passed back to the client.

Example 7-1 is a manager routine that is an excerpt from the *nsid* and is implemented as a remote wrapper routine around a procedure in the NSI API set. The procedure can be called from a Windows NT system and will remove a set of server bindings from the CDS name service on a DCE host system. Before making the *rpc_ns_binding_unexport* call that does the real work, this example does some preparation: a check for a valid binding and some character conversion.

Example 7-1: Wrapper Routine

```
void nsi_binding_unexport
    (
    UNSIGNED32                      entry_name_syntax,
    STRING_T                        entry_name,
    NSI_INTERFACE_ID_T              *if_spec,
    NSI_UUID_VECTOR_P_T             object_uuid_vec,
    UNSIGNED16                      *status
    )
{
    error_status_t st;
    homespun_rpc_if_rep_t *native_ifspec;
    /*
    ** Assume success...
    */
    *status = NSI_S_OK;
    /*
    ** If if_spec is null or has nil UUID, then set native_ifspec to NULL
    */
```

Example 7-1: Wrapper Routine (continued)

```
if (if_spec == (NSI)INTERFACE_ID_T *) NULL)                              ❶
    native_ifspec = (homesupn_rpc_if_rep_t *) NULL;
else
    {
    if (uuid_is_nil(&(if_spec->interface_id.uuid),&st))
        native_ifspec = (homespun_rpc_if_rep_t *) NULL;
    else
        {
        /*
        ** Allocate and fill native interface handle               ❷
        */
        native_ifspec = (homespun_rpc_if_rep_t *)
                    rpc_ss_allocate (sizeof(homespun_rpc_if_rep_t));
        handcraft_an_ifspec (native_ifspec, if_spec );
        }
    }
/*
** Convert unicode entry name to ascii
*/
unicode_to_ascii (entry_name);                                          ❸
/*
** Unexport bindings
*/
rpc_ns_binding_unexport ( entry_name_syntax,                            ❹
                          entry_name,
                          native_ifspec,
                          object_uuid_vec,
                          &st
                        );
if (st != error_status_ok)                                             ❺
    *status = translate_error( st );
return;
}
```

❶ The procedure first checks the incoming interface spec. If it is zero or has a UUID that is zero, then it passes zero on to the native *rpc_ns_binding_unexport* call.

❷ If it isn't zero, then we create a native representation of an interface handle.

❸ Convert the entry name from a UNICODE representation to ASCII.

❹ Call *rpc_ns_binding_unexport* to remove the exported bindings from CDS.

❺ Check status, convert if necessary, and return.

Implementing wrapper routines as remote procedures is also useful in the cases where you do have control over all of the code in an application. Using wrappers provides a new API for new distributed applications that want to use it, as well as retaining the old API for monolithic applications that stick with the traditional use of the API.

You may have good reasons for keeping some applications monolithic, even though they use the API that you are trying to provide remotely. Perhaps you have a multitude of smaller monolithic programs that aren't worth converting because they call only one or two functions in the API set. Or possibly you have users who have written monolithic programs that simply don't want to change them. If you avoid modifying the existing API by using wrappers, then your monolithic applications don't have to change, and you only need to change the remodeled applications to use the new remote API.

Referring back to Example 7-1, note that you can still write applications on the DCE host that calls *rpc_ns_binding_unexport* directly, and remote Windows NT clients can call the wrapper procedure *nsi_binding_unexport*.

Another approach to remodeling an application over which you have complete control is to define the APIs themselves as remote procedures. If you're able to do the remodeling this way, then it can result in a much cleaner implementation. For one thing, you don't end up supporting two separate APIs as you do in the case where you have to write wrapper routines.

After you've decided what to put in the server and how to put it there, the next step is to think about your client implementation. Is a simple console or command-line interface suitable? You're free to put a more user-friendly graphical interface on the client, and you may not have had that option in the past.

Once you've finished the client side and have your application working, you can stand back and survey your work. Maybe you like the result well enough that you're happy leaving it just as it is. On the other hand, perhaps a more substantial reconstruction is called for. Even if your conclusion is that the application is still in need of a major rewrite, a number of benefits may already be yours:

- You now have some experience with using the application as a set of remote procedures. Whether further work on the interface is incremental or substantial, this is information you didn't have when you started.

- You should have a better idea about what kind of client interface makes sense. You may have increased the applications's usability by providing a windowed interface.

- You're making more efficient use of your computing resources.

A

API Differences

This appendix lists some of the differences between DCE and Microsoft RPC. We've masked most of these differences by defining API correspondences in the *dceport.h* header file (see Appendix E).

Runtime Library

Microsoft RPC Version 1.0 supports most of the RPC APIs provided by OSF DCE. Table A-1 shows the correspondence between the DCE and Microsoft RPC APIs. Functions might not be equally supported in both environments. For instance, the Microsoft API *RpcServerUseProtseq* includes an additional parameter that is not available in the DCE RPC API. "N/A" indicates an unsupported API.

Table A-1: DCE and Microsoft RPC Function Correspondence

DCE Function Name	*Microsoft RPC Function Name*
dce_error_inq_text	N/A
N/A	RpcAbnormalTermination[1]
rpc_binding_copy	RpcBindingCopy
rpc_binding_free	RpcBindingFree
rpc_binding_from_string_binding	RpcBindingFromStringBinding
N/A	RpcEndExcept[1]
N/A	RpcEndFinally[1]
N/A	RpcExcept[1]
N/A	RpcExceptionCode[1]
N/A	RpcFinally[1]
rpc_binding_inq_auth_client	RpcBindingInqAuthClient
rpc_binding_inq_auth_info	RpcBindingInqAuthInfo
rpc_binding_inq_object	RpcBindingInqObject

Table A-1: DCE and Microsoft RPC Function Correspondence (continued)

DCE Function Name	Microsoft RPC Function Name
rpc_binding_reset	RpcBindingReset
rpc_binding_server_from_client	N/A
rpc_binding_set_auth_info	RpcBindingSetAuthInfo
rpc_binding_set_object	RpcBindingSetObject
rpc_binding_to_string_binding	RpcBindingToStringBinding
rpc_binding_vector_free	RpcBindingVectorFree
rpc_ep_register	RpcEpRegister
rpc_ep_register_no_replace	RpcEpRegisterNoReplace
rpc_ep_resolve_binding	RpcEpResolveBinding
rpc_ep_unregister	RpcEpUnregister
rpc_if_id_vector_free	RpcIfIdVectorFree
rpc_if_inq_id	RpcIfInqId
rpc_if_register_auth_info	N/A
N/A	RpcImpersonateClient
N/A	RpcMgmtEnableIdleCleanup
rpc_mgmt_ep_elt_inq_begin	N/A
rpc_mgmt_ep_elt_inq_done	N/A
rpc_mgmt_ep_elt_inq_next	N/A
rpc_mgmt_ep_unregister	N/A
rpc_mgmt_inq_com_timeout	RpcMgmtInqComTimeout
rpc_mgmt_inq_dflt_authn_level	N/A
rpc_mgmt_inq_dflt_protect_level	N/A
rpc_mgmt_inq_if_ids	N/A
rpc_mgmt_inq_server_princ_name	N/A
rpc_mgmt_inq_stats	RpcMgmtInqStats
rpc_mgmt_is_server_listening	RpcMgmtIsServerListening
rpc_mgmt_set_authorization_fn	N/A
rpc_mgmt_set_cancel_timeout	N/A
rpc_mgmt_set_com_timeout	RpcMgmtSetComTimeout
rpc_mgmt_set_server_stack_size	RpcMgmtSetServerStackSize
rpc_mgmt_stats_vector_free	RpcMgmtStatsVectorFree
rpc_mgmt_stop_server_listening	RpcMgmtStopServerListening
N/A	RpcMgmtWaitServerListen
rpc_network_inq_protseqs	RpcNetworkInqProtseqs
rpc_network_is_protseq_valid	RpcNetworkIsProtseqValid
rpc_ns_binding_export	RpcNsBindingExport
rpc_ns_binding_import_begin	RpcNsBindingImportBegin
rpc_ns_binding_import_done	RpcNsBindingImportDone
rpc_ns_binding_import_next	RpcNsBindingImportNext
rpc_ns_binding_inq_entry_name	RpcNsBindingInqEntryName
rpc_ns_binding_lookup_begin	RpcNsBindingLookupBegin
rpc_ns_binding_lookup_done	RpcNsBindingLookupDone
rpc_ns_binding_lookup_next	RpcNsBindingLookupNext

Table A-1: DCE and Microsoft RPC Function Correspondence (continued)

DCE Function Name	Microsoft RPC Function Name
rpc_ns_binding_select	RpcNsBindingSelect
rpc_ns_binding_unexport	RpcNsBindingUnexport
rpc_ns_entry_expand_name	RpcNsEntryExpandName
rpc_ns_entry_object_inq_begin	RpcNsEntryObjectInqBegin
rpc_ns_entry_object_inq_done	RpcNsEntryObjectInqDone
rpc_ns_entry_object_inq_next	RpcNsEntryObjectInqNext
rpc_ns_group_delete	RpcNsGroupDelete[2]
rpc_ns_group_mbr_add	RpcNsGroupMbrAdd
rpc_ns_group_mbr_inq_begin	RpcNsGroupMbrInqBegin
rpc_ns_group_mbr_inq_done	RpcNsGroupMbrInqDone
rpc_ns_group_mbr_inq_next	RpcNsGroupMbrInqNext
rpc_ns_group_mbr_remove	RpcNsGroupMbrRemove
rpc_ns_mgmt_binding_unexport	RpcNsMgmtBindingUnexport
rpc_ns_mgmt_entry_create	RpcNsMgmtEntryCreate
rpc_ns_mgmt_entry_delete	RpcNsMgmtEntryDelete
rpc_ns_mgmt_entry_inq_if_ids	RpcNsMgmtEntryInqIfIds
rpc_ns_mgmt_handle_set_exp_age	RpcNsMgmtHandleSetExpAge
rpc_ns_mgmt_inq_exp_age	RpcNsMgmtInqExpAge
rpc_ns_mgmt_set_exp_age	RpcNsMgmtSetExpAge
rpc_ns_profile_delete	RpcNsProfileDelete
rpc_ns_profile_elt_add	RpcNsProfileEltAdd
rpc_ns_profile_elt_inq_begin	RpcNsProfileEltInqBegin
rpc_ns_profile_elt_inq_done	RpcNsProfileEltInqDone
rpc_ns_profile_elt_inq_next	RpcNsProfileEltInqNext
rpc_ns_profile_elt_remove	RpcNsProfileEltRemove
rpc_object_inq_type	RpcObjectInqType
rpc_object_set_inq_fn	RpcObjectSetInqFn
rpc_object_set_type	RpcObjectSetType
rpc_protseq_vector_free	RpcProtseqVectorFree
N/A	RpcRaiseException[1]
N/A	RpcRevertToSelf
rpc_server_inq_bindings	RpcServerInqBindings
rpc_server_inq_if	RpcServerInqIf
rpc_server_listen	RpcServerListen
rpc_server_register_auth_info	RpcServerRegisterAuthInfo(no DLL)
rpc_server_register_if	RpcServerRegisterIf
rpc_server_unregister_if	RpcServerUnregisterIf
rpc_server_use_all_protseqs	RpcServerUseAllProtseqs
rpc_server_use_all_protseqs_if	RpcServerUseAllProtseqsIf
rpc_server_use_protseq	RpcServerUseProtseq
rpc_server_use_protseq_ep	RpcServerUseProtseqEp
rpc_server_use_protseq_if	RpcServerUseProtseqIf
rpc_ss_allocate	N/A

Table A-1: DCE and Microsoft RPC Function Correspondence (continued)

DCE Function Name	Microsoft RPC Function Name
rpc_ss_destroy_client_context	RpcSsDestroyClientContext
rpc_ss_disable_allocate	N/A
rpc_ss_enable_allocate	N/A
rpc_ss_free	N/A
rpc_ss_get_thread_handle	N/A
rpc_ss_register_auth_info	N/A
rpc_ss_set_client_alloc_free	N/A
rpc_ss_set_thread_handle	N/A
rpc_ss_swap_client_alloc_free	N/A
rpc_string_binding_compose	RpcStringBindingCompose
rpc_string_binding_parse	RpcStringBindingParse
rpc_string_free	RpcStringFree
N/A	RpcTryExcept[1]
N/A	RpcTryFinally[1]
N/A	RpcWinSetYieldInfo
uuid_compare	N/A
uuid_create	UuidCreate
uuid_create_nil	N/A
uuid_equal	N/A
uuid_from_string	UuidFromString
uuid_hash	N/A
uuid_is_nil	N/A
uuid_to_string	UuidToString
N/A	YieldFunctionName

[1] Microsoft exception handling macros
[2] Supported for use with CDS only

RPC Status Information

DCE RPC routines generally include status information as a parameter, as in the following code:

```
void rpc_binding_copy(
    rpc_binding_handle_t source_binding,
    rpc_binding_handle_t *destination_binding,
    unsigned32 *status);
```

Microsoft RPC generally provides status as a function return value, as shown below:

```
RPC_STATUS RPC_ENTRY RpcBindingCopy(
    RPC_BINDING_HANDLE SourceBinding,
    RPC_BINDING_HANDLE * DestinationBinding);
```

Base Data Types

The interface definition languages DCE IDL and Microsoft MIDL use similar base data types. Table A-2 compares the data types supported by the two languages and explains some of the differences. As you can see, many rows in the table have no explanation. These data types are used consistently between environments so there's no need for a workaround of any kind here.

Table A-2: Interface Definition Language Differences

IDL Type	MIDL Type	Explanation
Data Types		
`boolean`	`boolean`	
`byte`	`byte`	
`void`	`void`	
`void *`	`void *`	
`handle_t` or `rpc_ binding_handle`	`handle_t` or `RPC_HANDLE`	The IDL `handle_t` and `rpc_ binding_handle` data types are equivalent. The MIDL `handle_t` and `RPC_HANDLE` data types are equivalent. The IDL and MIDL `handle_t` type exists only for compatibility with earlier RPC versions.
`error_status_t`	`error_status_t`	DCE systems convert `error_ status_t` arguments to the host-specific error_status format. Microsoft Windows and Microsoft Windows NT systems convert `error_sta- tus_t` arguments from the values defined in *winerror.h* to those in *rpcsts.h*.
Integers		
`small`	`small`	
`short`	`short`	
`long`	`long`	
`hyper`		Not implemented in MIDL V1.0
`unsigned small`	`unsigned small`	
`unsigned short`	`unsigned short`	
`unsigned long`	`unsigned long`	
`unsigned hyper`		Not implemented in MIDL V1.0
	`wchar_t`	Not supported by IDL

Table A-2: Interface Definition Language Differences (continued)

IDL Type	MIDL Type	Explanation
Floating Point		
float double	float double	
International Characters		
ISO_LATIN_1 ISO_UCS ISO_MULTI_LINGUAL		Although MIDL doesn't support these international character sets, you can use the MIDL wchar_t data type to support UNICODE character data.

The Use of Pipes for Data Transfer

DCE supports the use of pipes to transfer bulk data while Microsoft RPC does not. (This is the IDL pipe data type, and has nothing to do with named pipes.)

Pointer Support

Microsoft RPC supports the use of reference pointers and unique pointers. DCE implementations based on OSF DCE versions prior to Version 1.0.3 might not support the use of unique pointers. Microsoft RPC partially supports full pointers, treating them like unique pointers.

Explicit Binding

In DCE, you can ask the stub compiler to automatically generate a binding handle as an argument to a remote procedure call. This is done by including the [explicit_handle] attribute in an ACF file. In Microsoft RPC, you have to write the binding handle into the argument list of the interface definition file in order to use explicit binding.

Error Handling

Microsoft MIDL does not provide the [comm_status] and [fault_status] ACF attributes. However, it does provide the capabilities offered by these attributes. You must declare a variable of the type *error_status_t* as a parameter in your remote procedure. See Chapter 3.

Name Service Support

Microsoft RPC uses the Microsoft Locator name service. DCE uses the DCE Directory Service. Cross environment applications that use a name service must use the DCE Directory Service. DCE provides a name service proxy agent called *nsid* which is a gateway to the DCE Directory Service for Microsoft RPC systems.

Distributed Application Security

Microsoft RPC Version 1.0 builds security into the named pipes transport which is part of the file system. DCE uses a distributed form of security referred to as the DCE Security Service. These two forms of security do not work together.

Interface Specification Naming

The DCE IDL compiler creates interface specification names like *search_v1_0_s_ifspec*. The Microsoft RPC MIDL compiler creates interface specification names like *search_ServerIfHandle*.

Exception Handling

DCE uses exception macros like TRY and CATCH to handle exceptions. Microsoft RPC uses Microsoft C keywords like *try* and *except*.

Memory Management

Microsoft RPC requires user-supplied procedures *MIDL_user_allocate* and *MIDL_user_free* to manage memory in both clients and servers. DCE relies on special stub support routines *rpc_ss_allocate* and *rpc_ss_free* to manage server memory.

Managing the RPC Endpoint Map

DCE has a control program *rpccp* that allows you to view and manage server endpoint maps. Microsoft RPC has no such control program. Microsoft RPC does not document a means to print server endpoint information on the screen.

Protocol Support

Although Microsoft RPC and DCE can run over several network protocols, the only protocol they share in common is TCP/IP.

Threads

DCE threads conforms to the POSIX 1003.4a standard. Microsoft Windows NT provides its own threads library, which is not POSIX compatible.

Error Codes

When your distributed application encounters an error, DCE and Microsoft RPC runtime libraries can return an error message describing the error. The DCE and Microsoft RPC error messages differ in minor ways:

- DCE uses lowercase rather than uppercase characters.
- Microsoft RPC supports fewer error codes than DCE.
- Microsoft RPC renames DCE UUID-related error codes.

While many DCE error codes and Microsoft error codes apply only to their native environment, some error codes are similar and can apply to either environment. The API mapping file *dceport.h* defines correspondence between similar DCE and Microsoft RPC error codes. The following two tables show the error code mapping imposed by *dceport.h*. Table A-3 is alphabetically sorted by DCE error code. Table A-4 is sorted by Microsoft RPC error code.

At the time this book went to press, Microsoft had not yet shipped Windows NT as a final product. As a result, there may be some differences between the error messages that we list here and those that are part of the Windows NT product.

Table A-3: DCE to Microsoft RPC Error Code Mappings

DCE Error Codes	Microsoft RPC Error Codes
ept_s_cant_perform_op	EPT_S_CANT_PERFORM_OP
ept_s_invalid_entry	EPT_S_INVALID_ENTRY
ept_s_not_registered	EPT_S_NOT_REGISTERED
error_status_ok	RPC_S_OK
rpc_s_already_listening	RPC_S_ALREADY_LISTENING
rpc_s_already_registered	RPC_S_ALREADY_REGISTERED
rpc_s_binding_has_no_auth	RPC_S_BINDING_HAS_NO_AUTH
rpc_s_call_failed	RPC_S_CALL_FAILED
rpc_s_cant_bind_socket	RPC_S_CANNOT_BIND
rpc_s_cant_create_socket	RPC_S_CANT_CREATE_ENDPOINT
rpc_s_comm_failure	RPC_S_SERVER_UNAVAILABLE
rpc_s_connect_no_resources	RPC_S_OUT_OF_RESOURCES
rpc_s_cthread_create_failed	RPC_S_OUT_OF_THREADS
rpc_s_endpoint_not_found	RPC_S_NO_ENDPOINT_FOUND
rpc_s_entry_already_exists	RPC_S_ENTRY_ALREADY_EXISTS
rpc_s_entry_not_found	RPC_S_ENTRY_NOT_FOUND

Table A-3: DCE to Microsoft RPC Error Code Mappings (continued)

DCE Error Codes	Microsoft RPC Error Codes
rpc_s_fault_addr_error	RPC_S_ADDRESS_ERROR
rpc_s_fault_fp_div_by_zero	RPC_S_FP_DIV_ZERO
rpc_s_fault_fp_overflow	RPC_S_FP_OVERFLOW
rpc_s_fault_fp_underflow	RPC_S_FP_UNDERFLOW
rpc_s_fault_int_div_by_zero	RPC_S_ZERO_DIVIDE
rpc_s_fault_invalid_bound	RPC_S_INVALID_BOUND
rpc_s_fault_invalid_tag	RPC_S_INVALID_TAG
rpc_s_fault_remote_no_memory	RPC_S_SERVER_OUT_OF_MEMORY
rpc_s_incomplete_name	RPC_S_INCOMPLETE_NAME
rpc_s_interface_not_found	RPC_S_INTERFACE_NOT_FOUND
rpc_s_internal_error	RPC_S_INTERNAL_ERROR
rpc_s_inval_net_addr	RPC_S_INVALID_NET_ADDR
rpc_s_invalid_arg	RPC_S_INVALID_ARG
rpc_s_invalid_binding	RPC_S_INVALID_BINDING
rpc_s_invalid_endpoint_format	RPC_S_INVALID_ENDPOINT_FORMAT
rpc_s_invalid_naf_id	RPC_S_INVALID_NAF_IF
rpc_s_invalid_name_syntax	RPC_S_INVALID_NAME_SYNTAX
rpc_s_invalid_rpc_protseq	RPC_S_INVALID_RPC_PROTSEQ
rpc_s_invalid_string_binding	RPC_S_INVALID_STRING_BINDING
rpc_s_invalid_timeout	RPC_S_INVALID_TIMEOUT
rpc_s_invalid_vers_option	RPC_S_INVALID_VERS_OPTION
rpc_s_max_calls_too_small	RPC_S_MAX_CALLS_TOO_SMALL
rpc_s_name_service_unavailable	RPC_S_NAME_SERVICE_UNAVAILABLE
rpc_s_no_bindings	RPC_S_NO_BINDINGS
rpc_s_no_entry_name	RPC_S_NO_ENTRY_NAME
rpc_s_no_interfaces_exported	RPC_S_NO_INTERFACES_EXPORTED
rpc_s_no_memory	RPC_S_OUT_OF_MEMORY
rpc_s_no_more_bindings	RPC_S_NO_MORE_BINDINGS
rpc_s_no_more_members	RPC_S_NO_MORE_MEMBERS
rpc_s_no_protseqs	RPC_S_NO_PROTSEQS
rpc_s_no_protseqs_registered	RPC_S_NO_PROTSEQS_REGISTERED
rpc_s_not_rpc_tower	RPC_S_CANNOT_SUPPORT
rpc_s_not_supported	RPC_S_CANNOT_SUPPORT
rpc_s_nothing_to_unexport	RPC_S_NOTHING_TO_UNEXPORT
rpc_s_object_not_found	RPC_S_OBJECT_NOT_FOUND
rpc_s_ok	RPC_S_OK
rpc_s_protocol_error	RPC_S_PROTOCOL_ERROR
rpc_s_protseq_not_supported	RPC_S_PROTSEQ_NOT_SUPPORTED
rpc_s_server_too_busy	RPC_S_SERVER_TOO_BUSY
rpc_s_string_too_long	RPC_S_STRING_TOO_LONG
rpc_s_type_already_registered	RPC_S_TYPE_ALREADY_REGISTERED
rpc_s_unknown_authn_service	RPC_S_UNKNOWN_AUTHN_SERVICE
rpc_s_unknown_if	RPC_S_UNKNOWN_IF

Table A-3: DCE to Microsoft RPC Error Code Mappings (continued)

DCE Error Codes	Microsoft RPC Error Codes
rpc_s_unknown_mgr_type	RPC_S_UNKNOWN_MGR_TYPE
rpc_s_unsupported_name_syntax	RPC_S_UNSUPPORTED_NAME_SYNTAX
rpc_s_unsupported_type	RPC_S_UNSUPPORTED_TYPE
rpc_s_wrong_kind_of_binding	RPC_S_WRONG_KIND_OF_BINDING
rpc_x_comm_failure	RPC_S_SERVER_UNAVAILABLE
rpc_x_connect_no_resources	RPC_S_OUT_OF_RESOURCES
rpc_x_entry_not_found	RPC_S_ENTRY_NOT_FOUND
rpc_x_incomplete_name	RPC_S_INCOMPLETE_NAME
rpc_x_invalid_arg	RPC_S_INVALID_ARG
rpc_x_invalid_binding	RPC_S_INVALID_BINDING
rpc_x_invalid_bound	RPC_X_INVALID_BOUND
rpc_x_invalid_endpoint_format	RPC_S_INVALID_ENDPOINT_FORMAT
rpc_x_invalid_naf_id	RPC_S_INVALID_NAF_IF
rpc_x_invalid_name_syntax	RPC_S_INVALID_NAME_SYNTAX
rpc_x_invalid_rpc_protseq	RPC_S_INVALID_RPC_PROTSEQ
rpc_x_invalid_tag	RPC_X_INVALID_TAG
rpc_x_invalid_timeout	RPC_S_INVALID_TIMEOUT
rpc_x_no_memory	RPC_X_NO_MEMORY
rpc_x_object_not_found	RPC_S_OBJECT_NOT_FOUND
rpc_x_protocol_error	RPC_S_PROTOCOL_ERROR
rpc_x_protseq_not_supported	RPC_S_PROTSEQ_NOT_SUPPORTED
rpc_x_server_too_busy	RPC_S_SERVER_TOO_BUSY
rpc_x_ss_char_trans_open_fail	RPC_X_SS_CHAR_TRANS_OPEN_FAIL
rpc_x_ss_char_trans_short_file	RPC_X_SS_CHAR_TRANS_SHORT_FILE
rpc_x_ss_context_damaged	RPC_X_SS_CONTEXT_DAMAGED
rpc_x_ss_context_mismatch	RPC_X_SS_CONTEXT_MISMATCH
rpc_x_ss_in_null_context	RPC_X_SS_IN_NULL_CONTEXT
rpc_x_string_too_long	RPC_S_STRING_TOO_LONG
rpc_x_unknown_if	RPC_S_UNKNOWN_IF
rpc_x_unknown_mgr_type	RPC_S_UNKNOWN_MGR_TYPE
rpc_x_unsupported_name_syntax	RPC_S_UNSUPPORTED_NAME_SYNTAX
rpc_x_unsupported_type	RPC_S_UNSUPPORTED_TYPE
rpc_x_wrong_kind_of_binding	RPC_S_WRONG_KIND_OF_BINDING
uuid_s_internal_error	RPC_S_INTERNAL_ERROR
uuid_s_invalid_string_uuid	RPC_S_INVALID_STRING_UUID
uuid_s_no_address	RPC_S_UUID_NO_ADDRESS
uuid_x_internal_error	RPC_S_INTERNAL_ERROR

Some Microsoft RPC error codes correspond to both a DCE error code (rpc_s*) and a DCE exception (rpc_x*). For instance, Microsoft's RPC_S_SERVER_UNAVAILABLE maps to both rpc_s_comm_failure and rpc_x_comm_failure. This is because Microsoft makes no distinction between an exception and a status; the Microsoft RPC runtime library returns a status, and the stub looks at the return value. If you have a [comm_status] or a [fault_status] variable, the stub will return the status in it, otherwise the stub will raise the exception.

Table A-4: Microsoft RPC to DCE Error Code Mappings

Microsoft RPC Error Codes	*DCE Error Codes*
EPT_S_CANT_PERFORM_OP	ept_s_cant_perform_op
EPT_S_INVALID_ENTRY	ept_s_invalid_entry
EPT_S_NOT_REGISTERED	ept_s_not_registered
RPC_S_ADDRESS_ERROR	rpc_s_fault_addr_error
RPC_S_ALREADY_LISTENING	rpc_s_already_listening
RPC_S_ALREADY_REGISTERED	rpc_s_already_registered
RPC_S_BINDING_HAS_NO_AUTH	rpc_s_binding_has_no_auth
RPC_S_CALL_FAILED	rpc_s_call_failed
RPC_S_CANNOT_BIND	rpc_s_cant_bind_socket
RPC_S_CANNOT_SUPPORT	rpc_s_not_rpc_tower
RPC_S_CANNOT_SUPPORT	rpc_s_not_supported
RPC_S_CANT_CREATE_ENDPOINT	rpc_s_cant_create_socket
RPC_S_ENTRY_ALREADY_EXISTS	rpc_s_entry_already_exists
RPC_S_ENTRY_NOT_FOUND	rpc_s_entry_not_found
RPC_S_ENTRY_NOT_FOUND	rpc_x_entry_not_found
RPC_S_FP_DIV_ZERO	rpc_s_fault_fp_div_by_zero
RPC_S_FP_OVERFLOW	rpc_s_fault_fp_overflow
RPC_S_FP_UNDERFLOW	rpc_s_fault_fp_underflow
RPC_S_INCOMPLETE_NAME	rpc_s_incomplete_name
RPC_S_INCOMPLETE_NAME	rpc_x_incomplete_name
RPC_S_INTERFACE_NOT_FOUND	rpc_s_interface_not_found
RPC_S_INTERNAL_ERROR	rpc_s_internal_error
RPC_S_INTERNAL_ERROR	uuid_s_internal_error
RPC_S_INTERNAL_ERROR	uuid_x_internal_error
RPC_S_INVALID_ARG	rpc_s_invalid_arg
RPC_S_INVALID_ARG	rpc_x_invalid_arg
RPC_S_INVALID_BINDING	rpc_s_invalid_binding
RPC_S_INVALID_BINDING	rpc_x_invalid_binding
RPC_S_INVALID_BOUND	rpc_s_fault_invalid_bound
RPC_S_INVALID_ENDPOINT_FORMAT	rpc_s_invalid_endpoint_format
RPC_S_INVALID_ENDPOINT_FORMAT	rpc_x_invalid_endpoint_format
RPC_S_INVALID_NAF_IF	rpc_s_invalid_naf_id
RPC_S_INVALID_NAF_IF	rpc_x_invalid_naf_id
RPC_S_INVALID_NAME_SYNTAX	rpc_s_invalid_name_syntax
RPC_S_INVALID_NAME_SYNTAX	rpc_x_invalid_name_syntax
RPC_S_INVALID_NET_ADDR	rpc_s_inval_net_addr
RPC_S_INVALID_RPC_PROTSEQ	rpc_s_invalid_rpc_protseq
RPC_S_INVALID_RPC_PROTSEQ	rpc_x_invalid_rpc_protseq

Table A-4: Microsoft RPC to DCE Error Code Mappings (continued)

Microsoft RPC Error Codes	DCE Error Codes
RPC_S_INVALID_STRING_BINDING	rpc_s_invalid_string_binding
RPC_S_INVALID_STRING_UUID	uuid_s_invalid_string_uuid
RPC_S_INVALID_TAG	rpc_s_fault_invalid_tag
RPC_S_INVALID_TIMEOUT	rpc_s_invalid_timeout
RPC_S_INVALID_TIMEOUT	rpc_x_invalid_timeout
RPC_S_INVALID_VERS_OPTION	rpc_s_invalid_vers_option
RPC_S_MAX_CALLS_TOO_SMALL	rpc_s_max_calls_too_small
RPC_S_NAME_SERVICE_UNAVAILABLE	rpc_s_name_service_unavailable
RPC_S_NOTHING_TO_UNEXPORT	rpc_s_nothing_to_unexport
RPC_S_NO_BINDINGS	rpc_s_no_bindings
RPC_S_NO_ENDPOINT_FOUND	rpc_s_endpoint_not_found
RPC_S_NO_ENTRY_NAME	rpc_s_no_entry_name
RPC_S_NO_INTERFACES_EXPORTED	rpc_s_no_interfaces_exported
RPC_S_NO_MORE_BINDINGS	rpc_s_no_more_bindings
RPC_S_NO_MORE_MEMBERS	rpc_s_no_more_members
RPC_S_NO_PROTSEQS	rpc_s_no_protseqs
RPC_S_NO_PROTSEQS_REGISTERED	rpc_s_no_protseqs_registered
RPC_S_OBJECT_NOT_FOUND	rpc_s_object_not_found
RPC_S_OBJECT_NOT_FOUND	rpc_x_object_not_found
RPC_S_OK	error_status_ok
RPC_S_OK	rpc_s_ok
RPC_S_OUT_OF_MEMORY	rpc_s_no_memory
RPC_S_OUT_OF_RESOURCES	rpc_s_connect_no_resources
RPC_S_OUT_OF_RESOURCES	rpc_x_connect_no_resources
RPC_S_OUT_OF_THREADS	rpc_s_cthread_create_failed
RPC_S_PROTOCOL_ERROR	rpc_s_protocol_error
RPC_S_PROTOCOL_ERROR	rpc_x_protocol_error
RPC_S_PROTSEQ_NOT_SUPPORTED	rpc_s_protseq_not_supported
RPC_S_PROTSEQ_NOT_SUPPORTED	rpc_x_protseq_not_supported
RPC_S_SERVER_OUT_OF_MEMORY	rpc_s_fault_remote_no_memory
RPC_S_SERVER_TOO_BUSY	rpc_s_server_too_busy
RPC_S_SERVER_TOO_BUSY	rpc_x_server_too_busy
RPC_S_SERVER_UNAVAILABLE	rpc_s_comm_failure
RPC_S_SERVER_UNAVAILABLE	rpc_x_comm_failure
RPC_S_STRING_TOO_LONG	rpc_s_string_too_long
RPC_S_STRING_TOO_LONG	rpc_x_string_too_long
RPC_S_TYPE_ALREADY_REGISTERED	rpc_s_type_already_registered
RPC_S_UNKNOWN_AUTHN_SERVICE	rpc_s_unknown_authn_service
RPC_S_UNKNOWN_IF	rpc_s_unknown_if
RPC_S_UNKNOWN_IF	rpc_x_unknown_if
RPC_S_UNKNOWN_MGR_TYPE	rpc_s_unknown_mgr_type
RPC_S_UNKNOWN_MGR_TYPE	rpc_x_unknown_mgr_type
RPC_S_UNSUPPORTED_NAME_SYNTAX	rpc_s_unsupported_name_syntax

Table A-4: Microsoft RPC to DCE Error Code Mappings (continued)

Microsoft RPC Error Codes	DCE Error Codes
RPC_S_UNSUPPORTED_NAME_SYNTAX	rpc_x_unsupported_name_syntax
RPC_S_UNSUPPORTED_TYPE	rpc_s_unsupported_type
RPC_S_UNSUPPORTED_TYPE	rpc_x_unsupported_type
RPC_S_UUID_NO_ADDRESS	uuid_s_no_address
RPC_S_WRONG_KIND_OF_BINDING	rpc_s_wrong_kind_of_binding
RPC_S_WRONG_KIND_OF_BINDING	rpc_x_wrong_kind_of_binding
RPC_S_ZERO_DIVIDE	rpc_s_fault_int_div_by_zero
RPC_X_INVALID_BOUND	rpc_x_invalid_bound
RPC_X_INVALID_TAG	rpc_x_invalid_tag
RPC_X_NO_MEMORY	rpc_x_no_memory
RPC_X_SS_CHAR_TRANS_OPEN_FAIL	rpc_x_ss_char_trans_open_fail
RPC_X_SS_CHAR_TRANS_SHORT_FILE	rpc_x_ss_char_trans_short_file
RPC_X_SS_CONTEXT_DAMAGED	rpc_x_ss_context_damaged
RPC_X_SS_CONTEXT_MISMATCH	rpc_x_ss_context_mismatch
RPC_X_SS_IN_NULL_CONTEXT	rpc_x_ss_in_null_context

B

The Simple Phonebook Application

This appendix describes the source code for the phonebook application example. The simple version of phonebook takes a server name passed on the command line. It does not use a name service to find a server.

Simple Phonebook Source File Descriptions

This section describes the phonebook source files you can use to build an executable PC client and DCE server. The server runs on OSF/1, ULTRIX, Microsoft Windows NT, and OpenVMS. The client runs on these platforms and on DOS and Microsoft Windows with a character-based interface. We also provide a client with a Microsoft Windows interface.

We are not describing intermediate files like objects and stub files because they are created and handled automatically by the build tools. The DCE portability header file included by these sources is shown in Appendix E.

phnbk.idl
    Example B-1 is an interface definition file that contains procedure declarations and defines data types so that clients and servers can interpret each other's data. This file is compiled with the attribute configuration file to produce stub files and header files.

phnbk.acf
    Example B-2 is an attribute configuration file that tells the phonebook client and server to use implicit bindings. This file is compiled with the interface definition file to produce stub files and header files.

client.c
    Example B-3 is a client application program that provides a user interface for the phonebook server and invokes remote procedure calls.

server.c

Example B-4 is a server initialization file that prepares the phonebook server to handle incoming remote procedure calls. During server startup, the file invokes RPC routines to register the interface and to set the server so it listens for incoming calls.

manager.c

Example B-5 is a file containing the remote procedure. This procedure responds to client requests to browse or search for information contained in the *phnbk.txt* data file.

phnbk.txt

Example B-6 is an ASCII text file that contains the database of names used by the phonebook server. We created it using a text editor. You can add your own lines to this file. Make sure lines are under 100 characters in length.

wclient.c

Example B-7 is the Windows phonebook client source file that provides a Windows interface for the phonebook server.

wphnbk.h

Example B-8 is a header file that defines constants used in *wphnbk.c* and in the resource file *wphnbk.rc*.

wphnbk.def

Example B-9 is a Windows module definition file. It defines the name of the application, the type of image to be produced, and other attributes of the application.

wphnbk.rc

Example B-10 is a Windows resource file. It describes the size and appearance of the Windows dialog box and controls (such as buttons, edit boxes) used by the application.

makefile.unx

Example B-11 is a description file (makefile) used by the ULTRIX *make* program to build (compile and link) executable client and server programs for ULTRIX.

makefile.osf

Example B-12 is a description file used by the OSF/1 *make* program to build executable client and server programs for OSF/1.

makefile.nt

Example B-13 is a description file used by the Microsoft Windows NT *nmake* program to build an executable client and server program for Microsoft Windows NT.

makefile.dos

Example B-14 is a description file used by the DOS *nmake* program to build an executable DOS client program.

makefile.win

Example B-15 is a description file used by the Microsoft Windows *nmake* program to build an executable client program with a Windows interface.

makefile.com

Example B-16 is a description file used by OpenVMS systems to build executable client and server programs for OpenVMS.

Simple Phonebook Source File Listings

Example B-1: The Simple Phonebook IDL File

```
/*
**   Interface Definition File for Simple phnbk Client
*/
[
 uuid(F2FE85A0-0C28-1068-A726-AA0004007EFF),
 version(1.0),
 pointer_default(ref)]
interface phnbk
{
/*
** Constant for maximum line size
*/
const long LINESIZE = 100;
/*
** Flag for hitting end of phonebook file
*/
const short END = -1;
/*
** Flag for normal completion of operation
*/
const short NORMAL = 0;
/*
** Define all possible operations on phonebook file
*/
typedef enum
            {
             FIRSTMATCH,
             NEXTMATCH,
             BROWSE,
             RESET,
             BROWSE_RESET
            } operations;
```

Example B-1: The Simple Phonebook IDL File (continued)

```
/*
** Perform some operation on the phonebook
*/
short
lookup
      (
      [in]           operations operation,
      [in,string]    char        search_string[LINESIZE],
      [out,string]   char        return_string[LINESIZE]
      );
}
```

Example B-2: The Simple Phonebook Attribute Configuration File

```
[
implicit_handle (handle_t xhandle)
]
interface phnbk
{}
```

Example B-3: The Simple Phonebook Client Program File

```
/*
**
**
** MODULE: client.c
**
**
** PROGRAM: Portable PHNBK Application (OpenVMS,DOS,NT,OSF/1,ULTRIX)
**
**
** ABSTRACT: PHNBK is a sample RPC application intended to illustrate
**           the basics of RPC interoperation between DCE platforms
**           and Microsoft platforms.
**
**
*/
#include <stdio.h>
#include <string.h>
#include <stdlib.h>
#ifndef VMS
#include <malloc.h>
#endif
#include "phnbk.h"
#if defined(MSDOS) || defined(WIN32)
#include "dceport.h"
#endif
#ifdef WIN32
```

Example B-3: The Simple Phonebook Client Program File (continued)

```
#define MAIN_DECL _CRTAPI1
#else
#define MAIN_DECL
#endif
int
MAIN_DECL main
                (
                ac,
                av
                )
int    ac;
char *av[];
{
    int             i;
    int             lookup_status;      /* lookup return status */
    error_status_t  status;             /* rpc status */
    idl_char        input[LINESIZE];    /* 'find' search string */
    idl_char        output[LINESIZE];   /* string returned from database*/
    idl_char        oldmatch[LINESIZE]; /* previous 'find' string */
    char            command;            /* lookup command */
    unsigned char   server[80];         /* string binding for server */

    /*
    ** Initialize some strings
    */
    oldmatch[0] = '\0';
    server[0]   = '\0';

    if (ac < 2)
        {
        /*
        ** With this version of phonbook, the user must specify the
        **    server's binding as a string on the command line.  If the
        **    user hasn't done that, then tell them about the error and
        **    exit the program so they can try again.
        **
        */
        printf("\nPlease specify a server name on the command line:\n");
        printf("\n\tphnbk myhost\n\n");

        exit (EXIT_FAILURE);
        }
    else
        {
        /*
        ** The user has specified a string binding
        */
        strcat ((char *)server,"ncacn_ip_tcp:");
        strcat ((char *)server,av[1]);
        }
```

Example B-3: The Simple Phonebook Client Program File (continued)

```
/*
** Display the server in use
*/
printf("\n\t(Selected server binding: %s)\n\n",server);
/*
** Convert the character string binding into an RPC handle
*/
rpc_binding_from_string_binding
            (
             server,
             &xhandle,
             &status
            );
if (status)
    {
    printf("Invalid string binding\n");
    exit (EXIT_FAILURE);
    }
/*
** Usage -- present user with a list of valid commands
*/
printf("Valid commands are:\n");
printf("(b)rowse        - List next entry\n");
printf("(r)eset         - Reset to beginning of file\n");
printf("(f)ind <string> - Find a substring\n");
printf("(f)ind          - Find next occurrence of <string>\n");
printf("(q)uit          - Exit program\n\n");

/*
** Keep looking for further commands until the user issues the
**      (q)uit command...
*/
while(1)
    {
    /*
    ** Initialize input and output strings
    */
    input[0]  = '\0';
    output[0] = '\0';
    /*
    ** Wait for user input
    */
    command = getchar();
    /*
    ** Select on user input
    */
    switch(command)
        {
```

Example B-3: The Simple Phonebook Client Program File (continued)

```
/*
** Command "f" means find the given search
**    string, or find the next occurrence
**    of the previously supplied search string
*/
case 'f' :

    i = 0;
    /*
    ** skip spaces
    */
    while ((command = getchar()) == ' ');

    /*
    ** Retrieve search string (if there is one)
    */
    input[i++] = command;

    if (command != '\n')
        {
        /*
        ** There is a search string so retrieve it
        */
        while ((input[i++] = getchar()) != '\n');
        input[--i] = '\0';
        strcpy ( (char *)oldmatch, (char *)input );
        /*
        ** Try to find a match for the search string
        **    in the phonebook file
        */
        lookup_status = lookup
                            (
                            FIRSTMATCH,
                            input,
                            output
                            );
        /*
        ** Print the search results: either a
        **    match was found or it wasn't...
        */
        if (lookup_status == END)
            printf("No matches found\n");
        else
            printf("Entry is: %s\n",output);
        }
    /*
    ** No search string: search for next occurrence
    **    of the search string given previously
    */
```

Example B-3: The Simple Phonebook Client Program File (continued)

```
                else
                    {
                    input[0] = '\0';
                    /*
                    ** restore search string
                    */
                    strcpy ((char *)input, (char *)oldmatch);
                    /*
                    ** search for match
                    */
                    lookup_status = lookup
                                            (
                                            NEXTMATCH,
                                            input,
                                            output
                                            );
                    /*
                    ** Print search results
                    */
                    if (lookup_status == END)
                        printf("No further matches found\n");
                    else
                        printf("Entry is: %s\n",output);
                    }

            break;
        /*
        ** Command "b" means just return the next entry
        **     in the phonebook file.
        */
        case 'b' :

            /*
            ** Display next entry from wherever we happen to be
            **     positioned in the phonebook
            */
            lookup_status = lookup
                                    (
                                    BROWSE,
                                    input,
                                    output
                                    );
            /*
            ** Echo entry or rewind database if we're at the end
            **     of the phonebook
            */
            if (lookup_status != END)
                printf("Entry is: %s\n", output);
            else
                printf("Resetting...\n");
            break;
```

Example B-3: The Simple Phonebook Client Program File (continued)

```
            /*
            ** Command "r" means reset file position to
            **     the beginning of the phonebook file
            */
            case 'r' :

                input[0] = '\0';
                /*
                ** Reset phonebook position to beginning
                */
                lookup_status = lookup
                                    (
                                        RESET,
                                        input,
                                        output
                                    );
                printf("Resetting...\n");
                break;

            /*
            ** Command "q" means exit the program
            */
            case 'q' :

                /*
                ** Free binding handle
                */
                rpc_binding_free
                            (
                                &xhandle,
                                &status
                            );
                /*
                ** Exit program
                */
                printf("Exiting...\n");
                exit(EXIT_SUCCESS);
            default :
                break;
            /*
            ** End of "switch" block
            */
            }

    /*
    ** End of "while" block
    */
    }

}
#if defined(MSDOS) || defined(WIN32)
```

Example B-3: The Simple Phonebook Client Program File (continued)

```
/***********************************************************************/
/***                 MIDL_user_allocate / MIDL_user_free          ***/
/***********************************************************************/
void * __RPC_API
MIDL_user_allocate
            (
             size
            )
size_t size;
{
    unsigned char * ptr;
    ptr = malloc( size );
    return ( (void *)ptr );

}
void __RPC_API
MIDL_user_free
            (
             object
            )
void * object;
{
    free (object);
}
#endif
```

Example B-4: The Simple Phonebook Server Initialization File

```
/*
**
**
** MODULE: server.c
**
**
** PROGRAM: Portable PHNBK Application (OpenVMS,DOS,NT,OSF/1,ULTRIX)
**
**
** ABSTRACT: PHNBK is a sample RPC application intended to illustrate
**           the basics of RPC interoperation between DCE platforms
**           and Microsoft platforms.
**
**
**
**
*/
#include <stdio.h>
#include <string.h>
#include <stdlib.h>
#ifndef VMS
#include <malloc.h>
```

Example B-4: The Simple Phonebook Server Initialization File (continued)

```
#endif
#include "phnbk.h"
#ifdef WIN32
#include "dceport.h"
#define MAIN_DECL _CRTAPI1
#define IFSPEC phnbk_ServerIfHandle
#else
#define MAIN_DECL
#define IFSPEC phnbk_v1_0_s_ifspec
#include <dce/rpcexc.h>
#endif
#define SERVER_ENTRY1 "/.:/subsys/DEC/examples/phnbk_srv_"
#define SERVER_ENTRY2 "/.:/phnbk_srv_"
FILE * filehandle;        /*File handle used for phonebook file*/
short previous_operation; /*Keeps track of previous phonebook operation*/
int
MAIN_DECL main
            (
             ac,
             av
            )
int    ac;
char *av[];
{
    unsigned int            i;
    error_status_t          status;
    unsigned_char_t         *string_binding;
    rpc_binding_vector_p_t  bvec;
    /*
    **
    ** Specify TCP/IP as a protocol sequences
    */
    rpc_server_use_protseq
            (
             (unsigned_char_t *) "ncacn_ip_tcp",
             5,
             &status
            );
    if (status != error_status_ok)
        {
        printf("No available protocol sequences\n");
        exit(EXIT_FAILURE);
        }
    /*
    ** register the server interface
    */
    rpc_server_register_if
            (
             IFSPEC,
             NULL,
             NULL,
```

Example B-4: The Simple Phonebook Server Initialization File (continued)

```
                &status
                );
if (status != error_status_ok)
    {
    printf("Can't register interface \n");
    exit(EXIT_FAILURE);
    }
/*
** find out what binding information is actually available
*/
rpc_server_inq_bindings
            (
            &bvec,
            &status
            );
if (status != error_status_ok)
    {
    printf("Can't inquire bindings \n");
    exit(EXIT_FAILURE);
    }
/*
** register with endpoint mapper
*/
rpc_ep_register
            (
            IFSPEC,
            bvec,
            NULL,
            (unsigned_char_t *)"phnbk endpoint",
            &status
            );
if (status != error_status_ok)
    {
    printf("Can't register endpoint\n");
    exit(EXIT_FAILURE);
    }
/*
** Get the string bindings and print them
*/
for (i = 0; i < bvec->count; i++)
    {
    /*
    ** For each binding, convert it to a
    **    string representation
    */
    rpc_binding_to_string_binding
                (
                bvec->binding_h[i],
                &string_binding,
                &status
                );
```

Example B-4: The Simple Phonebook Server Initialization File (continued)

```
        if (status != error_status_ok)
            {
            printf("Can't get string binding \n");
            exit(EXIT_FAILURE);
            }
        printf("%s\n", string_binding);
        }
    /*
    ** Open the phonebook file
    */
    filehandle = fopen("phnbk.txt","r");
    /*
    ** Server is all ready to start listening for client
    **      requests...
    */
    rpc_server_listen
                (
                (long)2,
                &status
                );
    if (status != error_status_ok)
        printf("Error: rpc_server_listen() returned \n");
    return (EXIT_FAILURE);
}
#ifdef WIN32
/**************************************************************************/
/***                 MIDL_user_allocate / MIDL_user_free            ***/
/**************************************************************************/
void * __RPC_API
MIDL_user_allocate
            (
            size
            )
size_t size;
{
    unsigned char * ptr;
    ptr = malloc( size );
    return ( (void *)ptr );

}
void __RPC_API
MIDL_user_free
            (
            object
            )
void * object;
{
    free (object);
}
#endif
```

Example B-5: The Simple Phonebook Remote Procedures

```
/*
**
**
** MODULE: manager.c
**
**
** PROGRAM: Portable PHNBK Application (OpenVMS,DOS,NT,OSF/1,ULTRIX)
**
**
** ABSTRACT: PHNBK is a sample RPC application intended to illustrate
**           the basics of RPC interoperation between DCE platforms
**           and Microsoft platforms.
**
**
**
**
*/
#include <stdio.h>
#include <string.h>
#include <stdlib.h>
#ifndef VMS
#include <malloc.h>
#endif
#include "phnbk.h"
#ifdef WIN32
#include "dceport.h"
#endif
extern FILE *filehandle;          /* Phonebook file filehandle */
extern short previous_operation; /* Keeps track of previous operation */
/*
**
** FUNCTION:  getfileline
**
** PURPOSE:
**      Retrieve Lines from input file
**
*/
int
getfileline
            (
             line,
             phone
            )
idl_char * line;
FILE * phone;
{
    /*
    ** Each call of this routine returns a line of the
    **    phonebook file.  On EOF, it returns -1.
    */
    char ch;
```

Example B-5: The Simple Phonebook Remote Procedures (continued)

```
    while ((ch = fgetc(phone)) != '\n' && ch != EOF)
        {
        /*
        ** Tabs are unpredictable, so substitute
        **     three spaces if you run across a tab...
        */
        if (ch == '\t')
            {
            *line++ = ' ';
            *line++ = ' ';
            *line++ = ' ';
            }
        else
            *line++ = ch;


        }
    *line++ = '\0';
    if (ch == EOF)
        return (END);
    else
        return (NORMAL);
}
/*
**
** FUNCTION:  lookup
**
** PURPOSE:
**     Lookup up entries in database
**
*/
short
lookup
        (
        op,
        stringin,
        stringout
        )
operations  op;
idl_char stringin[LINESIZE];
idl_char stringout[LINESIZE];
{
    idl_char buf[LINESIZE];
    /*
    ** Switch on requested operation
    */
    switch (op)
        {
        case  RESET:
            /*
            **  Reset context
            */
```

Example B-5: The Simple Phonebook Remote Procedures (continued)

```
            printf("Phonbook:\tRESET\n");
            rewind(filehandle);
            previous_operation = FIRSTMATCH;
            return(NORMAL);
            break;
    case  FIRSTMATCH:
        /*
        **  Look for first match of a string, starting at the
        **      beginning of the file...
        */
        printf("Phonbook:\tFIRSTMATCH\n");
        rewind(filehandle);
        break;
    case  NEXTMATCH:
        /*
        **  Nothing special here, fall out and continue search
        */
        printf("Phonbook:\tNEXTMATCH\n");
        break;
    case  BROWSE:
        /*
        **  A BROWSE operation just returns the next entry...
        **
        **  If the last operation was a BROWSE that got an EOF,
        **      then rewind and start cycling through again.
        */
        printf("Phonbook:\tBROWSE\n");
        if (previous_operation == BROWSE_RESET)
            rewind (filehandle);

        if ((getfileline(buf,filehandle)) != -1)
            {
            /*
            **  If not EOF, then just return next entry.
            */
            strcpy ((char *)stringout,(char *)buf);
            printf("Phonbook: \tFound %s\n", buf);
            previous_operation = BROWSE;
            return(NORMAL);
            }
        else
            {
            /*
            **  This allows the client to flag "no more entries"
            **  before cycling through the file again on
            **  another BROWSE request.
            */
            previous_operation = BROWSE_RESET;
```

Example B-5: The Simple Phonebook Remote Procedures (continued)

```
                    return(END);
                    }
        }
    /*
    ** Keep track of previous operation in p_context
    */
    previous_operation = op;
    /*
    **  Either return the line of the file that contains a string
    **  match, or return -1...
    */
    while ((getfileline(buf,filehandle)) != -1)
        {
        if ((strstr((char *)buf, (char *)stringin)) != (char *) NULL)
            {
            printf("Phonbook: \tFound %s\n", buf);
            strcpy ((char *)stringout,(char *)buf);
            return(NORMAL);
            }
        }
    return(END);
}
```

Example B-6: The Simple Phonebook Server Database File phnbk.txt

```
Mickey Mouse 555-2345
Donald Duck 555-2342
Pluto 555-4564
James T. Kirk 555-2342
Fred Flintstone   555-2342
Spider Man 555-2345
Bat Man 555-2342
George Jetson 555-2342
Peter Pan 555-4312
John Doe 555-8888
Charlie Brown 555-2374
```

Example B-7: The Windows Phonebook Client

```
/*
**
**
** MODULE: wclient.c
**
**
** PROGRAM: Windows WPHNBK Application
**
**
```

Example B-7: The Windows Phonebook Client (continued)

```
** ABSTRACT: WPHNBK is a sample RPC application intended to illustrate
**          the basics of RPC interoperation between DCE platforms
**          and Microsoft Windows platforms.
**
**
**
**
*/
#include <windows.h>
#include <stdlib.h>
#include <string.h>
#include <ctype.h>
#include "phnbk.h"
#include "wphnbk.h"
#include "dceport.h"
int            lookup_status;    /* lookup return status           */
error_status_t status;           /* rpc status                     */
idl_char       input[LINESIZE];  /* 'find' search string           */
idl_char       output[LINESIZE]; /* string returned from database  */
idl_char       oldmatch[LINESIZE];/* previous 'find' string        */
unsigned char  server[80];       /* string binding for server      */
short          operation;        /* operation requested            */
short          no_handle;        /* handle not initialized flag    */
unsigned char  hostname[32];     /* phnbk server host name         */
long FAR PASCAL WndProc (HWND, WORD, WORD, LONG) ;
int
PASCAL WinMain
            (
            HANDLE hInstance,
            HANDLE hPrevInstance,
            LPSTR lpszCmdLine,
            int nCmdShow
            )
{
    char szAppName [] = "WPHNBK" ;
    HWND        hwnd ;
    MSG         msg;
    WNDCLASS    wndclass ;
    /*
    ** Initialize strings
    */
    input[0]    = '\0';
    output[0]   = '\0';
    oldmatch[0] = '\0';
    server[0]   = '\0';
    hostname[0] = '\0';
    no_handle = TRUE;
    /*
    ** Standard Windows stuff...
    */
```

Example B-7: The Windows Phonebook Client (continued)

```
        if (!hPrevInstance)
            {
            wndclass.style          = CS_HREDRAW | CS_VREDRAW;
            wndclass.lpfnWndProc    = WndProc ;
            wndclass.cbClsExtra     = 0 ;
            wndclass.cbWndExtra     = DLGWINDOWEXTRA ;
            wndclass.hInstance      = hInstance ;
            wndclass.hIcon          = LoadIcon(NULL,IDI_APPLICATION);
            wndclass.hCursor        = LoadCursor (NULL, IDC_ARROW) ;
            wndclass.hbrBackground  = COLOR_WINDOW + 1 ;
            wndclass.lpszMenuName   = NULL ;
            wndclass.lpszClassName  = szAppName ;
            RegisterClass (&wndclass) ;
            }
        hwnd = CreateDialog (hInstance, szAppName, 0, NULL) ;
        ShowWindow (hwnd, nCmdShow) ;
        SetFocus ( GetDlgItem (hwnd, HOSTNAMEBOX ) );
        /*
        ** Start accepting messages
        */
        while ( GetMessage (&msg, NULL, 0, 0) )
            {
            TranslateMessage (&msg) ;
            DispatchMessage (&msg) ;
            }
        return msg.wParam ;
}
short
InitHandle
            (
            HWND hwnd
            )
{
    /*
    ** Read server host name
    */
    GetDlgItemText (hwnd, HOSTNAMEBOX, hostname, 16 );

    /*
    ** Warn user if they haven't specified a host name
    */
    if (hostname[0] == '\0')
        {
        MessageBox
                (
                hwnd,
                "Please enter server host name",
                "ERROR",
                MB_OK
                );
```

Example B-7: The Windows Phonebook Client (continued)

```
            SetFocus ( GetDlgItem (hwnd, HOSTNAMEBOX) );
            return (-1);
            }
    /*
    ** Build server string binding
    */
    strcat (server, "ncacn_ip_tcp:");
    strcat (server, hostname);
    /*
    ** Convert the character string binding into an RPC handle
    */
    rpc_binding_from_string_binding
                (
                  server,
                  &xhandle,
                  &status
                );
    if (status)
        {
        MessageBox
                (
                  hwnd,
                  "Invalid string binding",
                  "ERROR",
                  MB_OK
                );
        exit (EXIT_FAILURE);
        }

    no_handle = FALSE;
    return (0);
}
void
ShowResult
            (
              HWND hwnd
            )
{
    /*
    ** Display lookup results, based on the context of
    **    the requested operation
    */
    if (operation == BROWSE)
        {
        /*
        ** BROWSE -- return next entry
        */
        if (lookup_status == NORMAL)
            /*
            ** Everything ok, display next entry
            */
```

Example B-7: The Windows Phonebook Client (continued)

```
                SetDlgItemText (hwnd,RESULTSBOX,output);
        else
            {
            /*
            ** Othwise, we hit end of file...
            */
            SetDlgItemText (hwnd,RESULTSBOX,"");
            SetDlgItemText (hwnd,INFOBOX,"No more entries");
            }
        }
    else
        {
        /*
        ** Operation was a Find or Find Next...tailor message
        **     syntax to reflect the operation.
        */
        if (lookup_status == NORMAL)
            {
            /*
            ** Print results
            */
            SetDlgItemText (hwnd,RESULTSBOX,output);

            /*
            ** Determine if this was first match, or subsequent match
            */
            if (operation == FIRSTMATCH)
                SetDlgItemText (hwnd,INFOBOX,"Match found");
            else
                SetDlgItemText (hwnd,INFOBOX,"Another match found");
            }
        else
            /*
            ** Hit end of file during search
            */
            if (operation == FIRSTMATCH)
                SetDlgItemText (hwnd,INFOBOX,"Match not found");
            else
                SetDlgItemText (hwnd,INFOBOX,"No other matches found");
        }
    return;
    }
long
FAR PASCAL WndProc
                (
                HWND hwnd,
                WORD message,
                WORD wParam,
                LONG lParam
                )
```

Example B-7: The Windows Phonebook Client (continued)

```
{
/*
** We switch cursors to the hourglass during
**     a lookup RPC.  This is for saving the
**     regular pointer.
*/
HCURSOR OldCursor;
/*
** First thing, save the match string from last time around
*/
strcpy (oldmatch, input);
/*
** Switch on the incoming message type (standard Windows
**     programming)
*/
switch (message)
    {
    /*
    ** Got a button pushed
    */
    case WM_COMMAND:
        switch (wParam)
            {
            /*
            ** Either a Find or a Find Next
            */
            case FINDBUTTON:
                if (no_handle)
                    if (InitHandle(hwnd)) break;
                /*
                ** Clear current text
                */
                SetDlgItemText(hwnd,RESULTSBOX,"");
                SetDlgItemText(hwnd,INFOBOX,"");
                /*
                ** Read the search string
                */
                GetDlgItemText(hwnd,SEARCHBOX,input,32);
                /*
                ** Make sure user entered a search string
                */
                if (input[0] == NULL)
                    {
                    MessageBox
                            (
                            hwnd,
                            "Missing Search String!",
                            "ERROR",
                            MB_OK
                            );
```

Example B-7: The Windows Phonebook Client (continued)

```
                            /*
                            ** Set focus back to SEARCHBOX so user can
                            **     enter search string
                            */
                            SetFocus ( GetDlgItem (hwnd, SEARCHBOX) );
                            }
                    else
                        {
                        /*
                        ** Search string is present. Save existing
                        **     pointer and display hourglass
                        */
                        OldCursor = SetCursor (LoadCursor(NULL,IDC_WAIT));
                        ShowCursor (TRUE);
                        /*
                        ** Determine desired operation
                        */
                        if (strcmp(oldmatch,input))
                            operation = FIRSTMATCH;
                        else
                            operation = NEXTMATCH;
                        /*
                        ** Perform the requested operation
                        */
                        lookup_status = lookup
                                            (
                                            operation,
                                            input,
                                            output
                                            );
                        /*
                        ** Restore pointer cursor
                        */
                        ShowCursor (FALSE);
                        SetCursor ( OldCursor );

                        /*
                        ** Display lookup results
                        */
                        ShowResult(hwnd);
                        }

            break;
    /*
    ** BROWSE -- return next entry
    */
    case BROWSEBUTTON:
        if (no_handle)
            if(InitHandle(hwnd)) break;
        /*
        ** Clear existing text and display status
```

Example B-7: The Windows Phonebook Client (continued)

```
                              */
                              SetDlgItemText(hwnd,RESULTSBOX,"");
                              SetDlgItemText(hwnd,SEARCHBOX,"");
                              SetDlgItemText(hwnd,INFOBOX,"Browsing...");
                              /*
                              ** Switch to hourglass cursor
                              */
                              OldCursor = SetCursor (LoadCursor(NULL,IDC_WAIT));
                              ShowCursor (TRUE);

                              operation = BROWSE;
                              /*
                              ** Perform the requested operation
                              */
                              lookup_status = lookup
                                                     (
                                                      operation,
                                                      input,
                                                      output
                                                     );
                              /*
                              ** Restore pointer cursor
                              */
                              ShowCursor (FALSE);
                              SetCursor ( OldCursor );

                              /*
                              ** Display operation results
                              */
                              ShowResult(hwnd);

                              break;
                /*
                ** User has requested a RESET.  This clears all
                **     text and rewinds the phonebook file
                */
                case RESETBUTTON:
                    if (no_handle)
                        if (InitHandle(hwnd)) break;
                    /*
                    ** Clear all text
                    */
                    SetDlgItemText(hwnd,RESULTSBOX,"");
                    SetDlgItemText(hwnd,INFOBOX,"");
                    SetDlgItemText(hwnd,SEARCHBOX,"");
                    input[0] = '\0';
                    operation = RESET;
                    /*
                    ** Perform the requested operation
                    */
```

Example B-7: The Windows Phonebook Client (continued)

```
                lookup_status = lookup
                                    (
                                    operation,
                                    input,
                                    output
                                    ) ;
            break;
        }
    return 0 ;
/*
** User has closed the application
*/
case WM_DESTROY:
    if (!no_handle)
        {
        /*
        ** Free binding handle, post quit message and leave
        */
        rpc_binding_free
                    (
                    &xhandle,
                    &status
                    ) ;
        }
    PostQuitMessage (0) ;
    return 0 ;
/*
** Ignore other messages
*/
default:
    return DefWindowProc (hwnd, message, wParam, lParam) ;
    }
}
```

Example B-8: The Windows Phonebook Header File wphnbk.h

```
#define SEARCHBOX 102
#define RESULTSBOX 104
#define INFOBOX 106
#define FINDBUTTON 113
#define BROWSEBUTTON 112
#define RESETBUTTON 110
#define HOSTNAMEBOX 109
```

Example B-9: The Windows Phonebook Definition File: wphnbk.def

```
;-----------------------------------
; WPHNBK.DEF module definition file
;-----------------------------------
NAME            WPHNBK
DESCRIPTION     'Windows RPC Phonebook'
EXETYPE         WINDOWS
STUB            'WINSTUB.EXE'
CODE            PRELOAD FIXED DISCARDABLE
DATA            PRELOAD FIXED MULTIPLE
HEAPSIZE        8192
STACKSIZE       8192
EXPORTS         WndProc
```

Example B-10: The Windows Phonebook Resource File

```
#include <windows.h>
#include "wphnbk.h"
WPHNBK DIALOG  15, 33, 315, 102
CAPTION "Windows RPC Phonebook"
STYLE WS_OVERLAPPED | WS_BORDER | WS_CAPTION | WS_SYSMENU | WS_MINIMIZEBOX
CLASS "WPHNBK"
BEGIN
  CONTROL "Search String:", 100, "static", SS_LEFT | WS_CHILD, 13, 18,
          47, 10
  CONTROL "Input", 101, "button", BS_GROUPBOX | WS_TABSTOP | WS_CHILD,
          5, 3, 173, 32
  CONTROL "", 102, "edit", ES_LEFT | WS_BORDER | WS_TABSTOP | WS_CHILD,
          63, 17, 108, 12
  CONTROL "Search Results:", 103, "static", SS_LEFT | WS_CHILD, 6, 50,
          58, 7
  CONTROL "", 104, "edit", ES_LEFT | WS_BORDER | WS_TABSTOP | WS_CHILD,
          64, 48, 239, 12
  CONTROL "Status:", 105, "static", SS_LEFT | WS_CHILD, 6, 80, 26, 8
  CONTROL "", 106, "edit", ES_LEFT | WS_BORDER | WS_TABSTOP | WS_CHILD,
          30, 78, 133, 12
  CONTROL "Output", 108, "button", BS_GROUPBOX | WS_TABSTOP | WS_CHILD,
          4, 36, 305, 31
  CONTROL "Information", 111, "button", BS_GROUPBOX | WS_TABSTOP |
          WS_CHILD, 4, 68, 305, 31
  CONTROL "Find / Find Next", 113, "button", BS_PUSHBUTTON | WS_TABSTOP
          | WS_CHILD, 192, 6, 112, 14
  CONTROL "Reset", 110, "button", BS_PUSHBUTTON | WS_TABSTOP | WS_CHILD,
          192, 22, 50, 14
  CONTROL "Browse", 112, "button", BS_PUSHBUTTON | WS_TABSTOP | WS_CHILD,
          258, 22, 46, 14
  CONTROL "", HOSTNAMEBOX, "edit", ES_LEFT | WS_BORDER | WS_TABSTOP |
          WS_CHILD, 228, 78, 76, 12
  CONTROL "Server Host Name:",107, "static", SS_LEFT | WS_CHILD, 166, 80,
          62, 8
END
```

Example B-11: The Simple Phonebook Makefile for ULTRIX

```
#
#
# Build PHNBK client and server for ULTRIX
#
#
ALPHA_LIBFLAGS  = -ldce -lpthreads -lmach -lc_r
LIBS            = -ldce -lcma -ldnet -li
CFLAGS          = -I. -c
all: phnbk phnbkd
#
# Link simple client
#
phnbk: client.o phnbk_cstub.o
        $(CC) -o phnbk client.o phnbk_cstub.o $(LIBS)
#
# Link server
#
phnbkd: server.o manager.o phnbk_sstub.o
        $(CC) -o phnbkd server.o manager.o phnbk_sstub.o $(LIBS)
#
# Compile client source code
#
client.o: client.c phnbk.h
        $(CC) $(CFLAGS) client.c
#
# Compile server source code
#
server.o: server.c phnbk.h
        $(CC) $(CFLAGS) server.c
manager.o: manager.c phnbk.h
        $(CC) $(CFLAGS) manager.c
#
# Generate stubs and header file from interface definition
#
phnbk.h: phnbk.idl phnbk.acf
        idl phnbk.idl
#
# Clean up for fresh build
#
clean:
        rm -f *.o
        rm -f phnbk.h
        rm -f *ub.c
#
# Clean up all byproducts of build
#
clobber: clean
        rm -f phnbk
        rm -f phnbkd
```

Example B-12: The Simple Phonebook Makefile for OSF/1

```
#
#
# Build PHNBK client and server for DEC OSF/1
#
#
ALPHA_LIBFLAGS  = -ldce -lpthreads -lmach -lc_r
LIBS            = -ldce -lpthreads -lmach -lc_r -ldnet
CFLAGS          = -I. -std1 -c
all: phnbk phnbkd
#
# Link client
#
phnbk: client.o phnbk_cstub.o
    $(CC) -o phnbk client.o phnbk_cstub.o $(LIBS)
#
# Link server
#
phnbkd: server.o manager.o phnbk_sstub.o
    $(CC) -o phnbkd server.o manager.o phnbk_sstub.o $(LIBS)
#
# Compile client source code
#
client.o: client.c phnbk.h
    $(CC) $(CFLAGS) client.c
#
# Compile server source code
#
server.o: server.c phnbk.h
    $(CC) $(CFLAGS) server.c
manager.o: manager.c phnbk.h
    $(CC) $(CFLAGS) manager.c
#
# Generate stubs and header file from interface definition
#
phnbk.h: phnbk.idl phnbk.acf
    idl phnbk.idl
#
# Clean up for fresh build
#
clean:
    rm -f *.o
    rm -f phnbk.h
    rm -f *ub.c
#
# Clean up all byproducts of build
#
clobber: clean
    rm -f phnbk
    rm -f phnbkd
```

Example B-13: The Simple Phonebook Makefile for NT

```
#
#
# Build PHNBK client and server for Windows NT
#
#
!INCLUDE <ntwin32.mak>
includes =  -I.
all : phnbk.exe phnbkd.exe
#
# Link simple client
#
phnbk.exe: client.obj phnbk_c.obj phnbk_x.obj
    $(link) $(linkdebug) $(conflags) -out:phnbk.exe \
      client.obj phnbk_c.obj phnbk_x.obj \
      rpcrt4.lib rpcns4.lib rpcndr.lib $(conlibs)
#
# Link server
#
phnbkd.exe: server.obj manager.obj phnbk_s.obj phnbk_y.obj
    $(link) $(linkdebug) $(conflags) -out:phnbkd.exe \
      server.obj manager.obj phnbk_s.obj phnbk_y.obj \
      rpcrt4.lib rpcns4.lib rpcndr.lib $(conlibs)
#
# Compile simple client source code
#
client.obj: client.c phnbk.h
   $(cc) $(cflags) $(cvars) $(scall) $(includes) client.c
#
# Compile server source code
#
server.obj: server.c phnbk.h
   $(cc) $(cflags) $(cvars) $(scall) $(includes) server.c
manager.obj: manager.c phnbk.h
   $(cc) $(cflags) $(cvars) $(scall) $(includes) manager.c
#
# Compile client stubs
#
phnbk_c.obj : phnbk_c.c
    $(cc) $(cflags) $(cvars) $(scall) $(includes) phnbk_c.c
phnbk_x.obj : phnbk_x.c
    $(cc) $(cflags) $(cvars) $(scall) $(includes) phnbk_x.c
#
# Compile server stubs
#
phnbk_s.obj : phnbk_s.c
    $(cc) $(cflags) $(cvars) $(scall) $(includes) phnbk_s.c
phnbk_y.obj : phnbk_y.c
    $(cc) $(cflags) $(cvars) $(scall) $(includes) phnbk_y.c
#
# Generate stubs and header file from interface definition
#
phnbk.h : phnbk.idl phnbk.acf
```

Example B-13: The Simple Phonebook Makefile for NT (continued)

```
    midl phnbk.idl
#
# Clean up for fresh build
#
clean :
    del phnbk_*.*
    del *.obj
    del phnbk.h
#
# Clean up all byproducts of build
#
clobber : clean
    del phnbk.exe
    del phnbkd.exe
```

Example B-14: The Simple Phonebook Makefile for DOS

```
[.phnbk]MAKEFILE.DOS
#
#
# Build PHNBK client for DOS
#
#
DEV   = c:\c700
LIBS  =   $(DEV)\lib\llibce $(DEV)\lib\rpc $(DEV)\lib\rpcndr
CFLAGS = -AL -c -w -nologo -Zp -Zi -Oatelr -I$(DEV)\include\dos
all: phnbk.exe
#
# Link simple client
#
phnbk.exe: client.obj phnbk_c.obj phnbk_x.obj
    link /co /nologo client.obj phnbk_c.obj phnbk_x.obj,\
    phnbk.exe,,/nod $(LIBS);
#
# Compile simple client source code
#
client.obj: client.c phnbk.h
    $(CC) $(CFLAGS) $*.c
#
# Compile client stubs
#
phnbk_c.obj : phnbk_c.c
    $(CC) $(CFLAGS) $*.c
phnbk_x.obj : phnbk_x.c
    $(CC) $(CFLAGS) $*.c
#
# Generate stubs and header file from interface definition
#
phnbk.h : phnbk.idl phnbk.acf
    midl phnbk.idl
```

Example B-14: The Simple Phonebook Makefile for DOS (continued)

```
#
# Clean up for fresh build
#
clean:
    del phnbk_*.*
    del *.obj
    del phnbk.h
#
# Clean up all byproducts of build
#
clobber: clean
    del phnbk.exe
```

Example B-15: The Simple Phonebook Makefile for Windows

```
[.phnbk]MAKEFILE.WIN
#
# Build WPHNBK client for Windows
#
DEV    = c:\c700
LIBS   = $(DEV)\lib\libw $(DEV)\lib\llibcew \
         $(DEV)\lib\rpcw $(DEV)\lib\rpcndrw
CFLAGS = -AL -c -w -nologo -Gsw -Zp -Zi -Otelr -I$(DEV)\include\win
all: wphnbk.exe
#
# Link simple client
#
wphnbk.exe: wphnbk.lnk wphnbk.res
    link /co /nologo @wphnbk.lnk
    rc wphnbk.res
#
# Make .LNK file
#
wphnbk.lnk: wclient.obj phnbk_c.obj phnbk_x.obj
    echo @<<wphnbk.lnk
        wclient.obj phnbk_c.obj phnbk_x.obj
        wphnbk.exe

        ,
        /noe/nod $(LIBS)
        wphnbk.def
<<KEEP
#
# Compile simple client source code
#
wclient.obj : wclient.c phnbk.h
    $(CC) $(CFLAGS) $*.c
#
# Compile client stubs
#
```

Example B-15: The Simple Phonebook Makefile for Windows (continued)

```
phnbk_c.obj : phnbk_c.c
    $(CC) $(CFLAGS) $*.c
phnbk_x.obj : phnbk_x.c
    $(CC) $(CFLAGS) $*.c
#
# Generate stubs and header file from interface definition
#
phnbk.h : phnbk.idl phnbk.acf
    midl phnbk.idl
#
# Generate resource file
#
wphnbk.res: wphnbk.rc wphnbk.ico
    rc -I $(DEV)\include -r wphnbk.rc
#
# Clean up for fresh build
#
clean:
    del *.obj
    del wphnbk.lnk
    del wphnbk.res
    del phnbk_*.*
    del phnbk.h
#
# Clean up all byproducts of build
#
clobber: clean
    del wphnbk.exe
```

Example B-16: The Simple Phonebook Makefile for OpenVMS

```
$!
$! This is file MAKEFILE.COM to build the PHNBK
$! example application on an OpenVMS system.
$!
$!
$! Enable the universal IDL command interface
$  idl            := $sys$system:dce$idl.exe
$
$! Compile the interface definition
$! -keep all is used to keep the IDL output for training purposes
$ idl PHNBK.IDL -keep all -trace all -trace log_manager
$
$! Compile the client application files
$ cc CLIENT.C
$
$! Link the client application
$ link /exe=phnbk.exe client, phnbk_cstub, sys$input:/options
        sys$share:dce$lib_shr/share
        sys$share:vaxc2decc.exe/share
```

Example B-16: The Simple Phonebook Makefile for OpenVMS (continued)

```
$ write sys$output "PHNBK.EXE done."
$
$! Compile the server application files
$ cc server.c, manager.c
$
$! Link the server application
$ link/exe=phnbkd.exe server, manager, phnbk_sstub, sys$input:/options
        sys$share:dce$lib_shr/share
        sys$share:vaxc2decc.exe/share
$ write sys$output "PHNBKD.EXE done."
```

C

The Complete Phonebook Application

This appendix describes the source code for the complete phonebook application example. The complete version of phonebook uses CDS to find servers. It also uses context handles to enable the server to handle requests from multiple clients.

Complete Phonebook Source File Descriptions

Here, we describe the phonebook source files you can use to build an executable client and server. The server runs on OSF/1, ULTRIX, Microsoft Windows NT, and OpenVMS. The client runs on these platforms and on DOS and Microsoft Windows with a character-based interface. We also provide a client with a Microsoft Windows interface.

We are not describing intermediate files like objects and stub files because they are created and handled automatically by the build tools. The DCE portability header file included by these sources is shown in Appendix E.

phnbk2.idl
>   Example C-1 is an interface definition file that contains procedure declarations and defines data types so that clients and servers can interpret each other's data. This file is compiled with the attribute configuration file to produce stub files and header files.

phnbk2.acf
>   Example C-2 is an attribute configuration file that tells the phonebook client and server to use implicit bindings. This file is compiled with the interface definition file to produce stub files and header files.

client.c

> Example C-3 is a client application program that provides a user interface for the phonebook server and invokes remote procedure calls. This client uses the CDS name service to get server binding information.

server.c

> Example C-4 is a server initialization file that prepares the phonebook server to handle incoming remote procedure calls. During server startup, the file invokes RPC routines to register the interface and to set the server so it listens for incoming calls.

manager.c

> Example C-5 is a file containing the remote procedures. These procedures respond to client requests to browse or search for information contained in the *phnbk.txt* data file.

phnbk.txt

> Example C-6 is an ASCII text file that contains the database of names used by the phonbook server. We created it using a text editor. You can add your own lines to this file. Make sure lines are under 100 characters in length.

wclient.c

> Example C-7 is the Windows phnbk2 client source file that provides a Windows interface for the phnbk2 server.

wphnbk2.h

> Example C-8 is a header file you write that defines constants used in *wphnbk2.c* and in the resource file *wphnbk2.rc*.

wphnbk2.def

> Example C-9 is a Windows module definition file. This file defines the name of the applications, the type of image to be produced, and other attributes of the application.

wphnbk2.rc

> Example C-10 is a Windows resource file. It describes the size and appearance of the Windows dialog box and controls (such as buttons, edit boxes) used by the application.

makefile.unx

> Example C-10 is a description file (makefile) used by the ULTRIX *make* program to build (compile and link) executable client and server programs for ULTRIX.

makefile.osf

> Example C-11 is a description file used by the OSF/1 *make* program to build executable client and server programs for OSF/1.

makefile.nt

> Example C-12 is a description file used by the Microsoft Windows NT *nmake* program to build an executable client and server program for Microsoft Windows NT.

makefile.dos

> Example C-13 is a description file used by the DOS *nmake* program to build an executable DOS client program.

makefile.win

> Example C-14 is a description file used by the Microsoft Windows *nmake* program to build an executable client program with a Windows interface.

makefile.com

> Example C-15 is a description file used by VMS systems to build executable client and server programs for VMS.

Complete Phonebook Source File Listings

Example C-1: The Complete Phonebook IDL File

```
/*
**   Interface Definition File for Implicit phnbk Client
*/
[
 uuid(65C6918A-667E-11CC-BAF0-08002B24389A),
 version(1.0),
 pointer_default(ref)]
interface phnbk2
{
/*
** Constant for maximum line size
*/
const long LINESIZE = 100;
/*
** Flag for hitting end of phonebook file
*/
const short END = -1;
/*
** Flag for normal completion of operation
*/
const short NORMAL = 0;
/*
** Define all possible operations on phonebook file
*/
typedef enum
            {
              FIRSTMATCH,
              NEXTMATCH,
              BROWSE,
```

Example C-1: The Complete Phonebook IDL File (continued)

```
                RESET,
                BROWSE_RESET
                } operations;
/*
** Context handle definition
*/
typedef [context_handle] void * phonebook_handle;
/*
** Establish context handle
*/
void
open_phonebook_file
            (
             [out] phonebook_handle *ph
            );
/*
** Clean up context handle
*/
void
close_phonebook_file
            (
             [in,out] phonebook_handle *ph
            );
/*
** Perform some operation on the phonebook
*/
short
lookup
        (
          [in]          phonebook_handle ph,
          [in]          operations       operation,
          [in,string]   char             search_string[LINESIZE],
          [out,string]  char             return_string[LINESIZE]
        );
}
```

Example C-2: The Complete Phonebook Attribute Configuration File

```
[
implicit_handle (handle_t xhandle)
]
interface phnbk
{}
```

Example C-3: The Complete Phonebook Client Program File

```
/*
**
**
** MODULE: client.c
**
**
** PROGRAM: Portable PHNBK2 Application (OpenVMS,DOS,NT,OSF/1,ULTRIX)
**
**
** ABSTRACT: PHNBK2 is a sample RPC application intended to illustrate
**           the basics of RPC interoperation between DCE platforms
**           and Microsoft platforms.  PHNBK2 extends the capabilities
**           of PHNBK by using context handles, and the CDS nameservice.
**
**
**
**
*/
#include <stdio.h>
#include <string.h>
#include <stdlib.h>
#ifndef VMS
#include <malloc.h>
#endif
#include "phnbk2.h"
#if defined(MSDOS) || defined(WIN32)
#include "dceport.h"
#define IFSPEC phnbk2_ClientIfHandle
#else
#include <pthread_exc.h>
#define IFSPEC phnbk2_v1_0_c_ifspec
#endif
#ifdef WIN32
#define MAIN_DECL _CRTAPI1
#else
#define MAIN_DECL
#endif
#define SERVER_ENTRY_NAME  "/.:/phnbk2_srv_"
#define SERVER_ENTRY_NAME2 "/.:/subsys/DEC/examples/phnbk2_srv_"
/*
** Internal function prototype
*/
static int find_servers();
int
MAIN_DECL main
              (
               ac,
               av
              )
int   ac;
```

Example C-3: The Complete Phonebook Client Program File (continued)

```
char *av[];
{
    int              i;
    int              lookup_status;      /* lookup return status */
    error_status_t   status;             /* rpc status */
    idl_char         input[LINESIZE];    /* 'find' search string */
    idl_char         output[LINESIZE];   /* string returned */
    idl_char         oldmatch[LINESIZE]; /* previous 'find' string */
    char             command;            /* lookup command */
    unsigned char    server[80];         /* string binding for server */
    phonebook_handle ph;                 /* phonebook context handle */

    /*
    ** Initialize some strings
    */
    oldmatch[0] = '\0';
    server[0]   = '\0';
    /*
    ** Call the find_servers procedure to locate a suitable
    **     phonebook server using the nameservice...
    */
    if (find_servers(server))
        {
        printf("\nServer lookup failed:\n\n\t %s\n",server);
        exit (EXIT_FAILURE);
        }
    /*
    ** Display the server in use
    */
    printf("\n\t(Selected server binding: %s)\n\n", server);
    /*
    ** Convert the character string binding into an RPC handle
    */
    rpc_binding_from_string_binding
              (
               server,
               &xhandle,
               &status
              );
    if (status)
        {
        printf("Invalid string binding\n");
        exit (EXIT_FAILURE);
        }
    /*
    ** Initialize the phonebook context handle to NULL
    */
    ph = NULL;
    /*
    ** Establish the phonebook context handle
    */
```

Example C-3: The Complete Phonebook Client Program File (continued)

```
open_phonebook_file
            (
            &ph
            );
/*
** Usage -- present user with a list of valid commands
*/
printf("Valid commands are:\n");
printf("(b)rowse        - List next entry\n");
printf("(r)eset         - Reset to beginning of file\n");
printf("(f)ind <string> - Find a substring\n");
printf("(f)ind          - Find next occurrence of <string>\n");
printf("(q)uit          - Exit program\n\n");

/*
** Keep looking for further commands until the user issues the
**    (q)uit command...
*/
while(1)
    {
    /*
    ** Initialize input and output strings
    */
    input[0]  = '\0';
    output[0] = '\0';
    /*
    ** Wait for user input
    */
    command = getchar();
    /*
    ** Select on user input
    */
    switch(command)
        {
        /*
        ** Command "f" means find the given search
        **    string, or find the next occurrence
        **    of the previously supplied search string
        */
        case 'f' :

            i = 0;
            /*
            ** skip spaces
            */
            while ((command = getchar()) == ' ');

            /*
            ** Retrieve search string (if there is one)
            */
            input[i++] = command;
```

Example C-3: The Complete Phonebook Client Program File (continued)

```
if (command != '\n')
    {
    /*
    ** There is a search string so retrieve it
    */
    while ((input[i++] = getchar()) != '\n');
    input[--i] = '\0';
    strcpy ( (char *)oldmatch, (char *)input );
    /*
    ** Try to find a match for the search string
    **     in the phonebook file
    */
    lookup_status = lookup
                            (
                            ph,
                            FIRSTMATCH,
                            input,
                            output
                            );
    /*
    ** Print the search results: either a
    **     match was found or it wasn't...
    */
    if (lookup_status == END)
        printf("No matches found\n");
    else
        printf("Entry is: %s\n",output);
    }
/*
** No search string: search for next occurrence
**     of the search string given previously
*/
else
    {
    input[0] = '\0';
    /*
    ** restore search string
    */
    strcpy ((char *)input, (char *)oldmatch);
    /*
    ** search for match
    */
    lookup_status = lookup
                            (
                            ph,
                            NEXTMATCH,
                            input,
                            output
                            );
```

Example C-3: The Complete Phonebook Client Program File (continued)

```
                    /*
                    ** Print search results
                    */
                    if (lookup_status == END)
                        printf("No further matches found\n");
                    else
                        printf("Entry is: %s\n",output);
                    }

            break;
        /*
        ** Command "b" means just return the next entry
        **     in the phonebook file.
        */
        case 'b' :

            /*
            ** Display next entry from wherever we happen to be
            **     positioned in the phonebook
            */
            lookup_status = lookup
                                    (
                                    ph,
                                    BROWSE,
                                    input,
                                    output
                                    );
            /*
            ** Echo entry or rewind database if we're at the end
            **     of the phonebook
            */
            if (lookup_status != END)
                printf("Entry is: %s\n", output);
            else
                printf("Resetting...\n");
            break;
        /*
        ** Command "r" means reset file position to
        **     the beginning of the phonebook file
        */
        case 'r' :

            input[0] = '\0';
            /*
            ** Reset phonebook position to beginning
            */
            lookup_status = lookup
                                    (
                                    ph,
                                    RESET,
                                    input,
```

Example C-3: The Complete Phonebook Client Program File (continued)

```
                                output
                                ) ;
               printf("Resetting...\n");
               break;

           /*
           ** Command "q" means exit the program
           */
           case 'q' :

               /*
               ** Clean up phonebook context
               */
               close_phonebook_file
                       (
                        &ph
                       ) ;
               /*
               ** Free binding handle
               */
               rpc_binding_free
                       (
                        &xhandle,
                        &status
                       ) ;
               /*
               ** Exit program
               */
               printf("Exiting...\n");
               exit(EXIT_SUCCESS);
           default :
               break;
           /*
           ** End of "switch" block
           */
           }

       /*
       ** End of "while" block
       */
       }

}
#if defined(MSDOS) || defined(WIN32)
/*********************************************************************/
/***            MIDL_user_allocate / MIDL_user_free            ***/
/*********************************************************************/
void * __RPC_API
```

Example C-3: The Complete Phonebook Client Program File (continued)

```
MIDL_user_allocate
            (
             size
            )
size_t size;
{
    unsigned char * ptr;
    ptr = malloc( size );
    return ( (void *)ptr );

}
void __RPC_API
MIDL_user_free
            (
             object
            )
void * object;
{
    free (object);
}
#endif
/*
** ROUTINE NAME: find_servers
**
** SCOPE:        PUBLIC
**
** DESCRIPTION
**
**      The purpose of this routine is to retrieve a phnbk2
**      server from the default CDS server and return it as
**      a parameter.
**
** INPUTS:
**
**      none
**
** OUTPUTS:
**
**      server   character string
**
** FUNCTION VALUE
**
**      0 success
**      1 failure
**
*/
static int
find_servers
            (
             server
            )
```

Example C-3: The Complete Phonebook Client Program File (continued)

```
unsigned char server[80];
{
    unsigned char    *string_binding;
    unsigned char    *protseq;
    handle_t          handle;
    long              entry_name_syntax=3;
    rpc_ns_handle_t   import_context;
    int               found=0;
    error_status_t    status;
    error_status_t    status2;
 TRY
    /*
    ** Get ready to import bindings that match the
    **     given entry name
    */
    rpc_ns_binding_import_begin
                (
                 rpc_c_ns_syntax_default,
                 (unsigned char *)SERVER_ENTRY_NAME,
                 IFSPEC,
                 NULL,
                 &import_context,
                 &status
                );
    if (status)
        {
        strcpy((char *)server, "rpc_ns_binding_import_begin failure");
        return (1);
        }
    /*
    ** search for TCP binding
    */
    while (!found)
        {
        /*
        ** Get next binding
        */
        rpc_ns_binding_import_next
                    (
                     import_context,
                     &handle,
                     &status
                    );
        if (status)
            {
            strcpy((char *)server, "server not found");
            return (1);
            }
        /*
        ** Convert binding to string binding
        */
```

Example C-3: The Complete Phonebook Client Program File (continued)

```
rpc_binding_to_string_binding
            (
            handle,
            &string_binding,
            &status
            );
if (status)
    {
    strcpy((char *)server, "rpc_binding_to_string_binding failure");
    return (1);
    }
else
    {
    /*
    ** Parse the binding into its individual components...
    **      actually all we care about here is the protocol
    **      sequence...
    */
    rpc_string_binding_parse
                (
                string_binding,
                NULL,
                &protseq,
                NULL,
                NULL,
                NULL,
                &status
                );


    if (status)
        {
        strcpy((char *)server, "rpc_string_binding_parse failure");
        return(1);
        }
    else
        {
        /*
        ** Check for a TCP/IP protocol sequence
        */
        if (!(strcmp((char *)protseq, "ncacn_ip_tcp")))
            /*
            ** Got one!
            */
            {
            strcpy((char *)server, (char *)string_binding);
            /*
            ** Free the string binding
            */
```

Example C-3: The Complete Phonebook Client Program File (continued)

```
                        rpc_string_free
                                (
                                &string_binding,
                                &status2
                                );
                        found = 1;
                        /*
                        ** finish the search
                        */
                        rpc_ns_binding_import_done(&import_context, &status);
                        }
                else
                        rpc_string_free
                                (
                                &string_binding,
                                &status2
                                );
                }
            }
    /*
    ** End of while block
    */
    }
 CATCH_ALL
#if defined (WIN32) || defined (MSDOS)
    /*
    ** If MSDOS or Windows NT, print the specific error code
    **     and exit
    */
    unsigned long Exception;
    Exception = RpcExceptionCode();
    printf("\n\tException # %d in find_servers...exiting\n",Exception);
#else
    /*
    ** Else, with a "native" DCE platform, let the operating system
    **     take care of printing the exception
    */
    RERAISE;
#endif
    exit (EXIT_FAILURE);
 ENDTRY
    /*
    ** Only way to return successfully
    */
    return (0);
}
```

Example C-4: The Complete Phonebook Server Initialization File

```
/*
**
**
** MODULE: server.c
**
**
** PROGRAM: Portable PHNBK2 Application (OpenVMS,DOS,NT,OSF/1,ULTRIX)
**
**
** ABSTRACT: PHNBK2 is a sample RPC application intended to illustrate
**           the basics of RPC interoperation between DCE platforms
**           and Microsoft platforms.  PHNBK2 extends the capabilities
**           of PHNBK by using context handles and the CDS nameservice.
**
**
**
**
*/
#include <stdio.h>
#include <string.h>
#include <stdlib.h>
#ifndef VMS
#include <malloc.h>
#endif
#ifdef WIN32
#include <process.h>
#define IFSPEC phnbk2_ServerIfHandle
#else
#include <dce/rpcexc.h>
#define IFSPEC phnbk2_v1_0_s_ifspec
#endif
#include "phnbk2.h"
#ifdef WIN32
#include "dceport.h"
#define MAIN_DECL _CRTAPI1
#else
#define MAIN_DECL
#endif
#define SERVER_ENTRY_NAME   "/.:/phnbk2_srv_"
#define SERVER_ENTRY_NAME2 "/.:/subsys/DEC/examples/phnbk2_srv_"
int
MAIN_DECL main
               (
                ac,
                av
                )
int    ac;
char *av[];
{
    unsigned int              i;
    error_status_t            status;
    unsigned_char_t           *string_binding;
```

Example C-4: The Complete Phonebook Server Initialization File (continued)

```
rpc_binding_vector_p_t        bvec;
/*
**
** Specify TCP/IP as a protocol sequences
*/
rpc_server_use_protseq
            (
             (unsigned_char_t *)"ncacn_ip_tcp",
             5,
             &status
            );
if (status != error_status_ok)
    {
    printf("No available protocol sequences\n");
    exit(EXIT_FAILURE);
    }
/*
** register the server interface
*/
rpc_server_register_if
            (
             IFSPEC,
             NULL,
             NULL,
             &status
            );
if (status != error_status_ok)
    {
    printf("Can't register interface \n");
    exit(EXIT_FAILURE);
    }
/*
** find out what binding information is actually available
*/
rpc_server_inq_bindings
            (
             &bvec,
             &status
            );
if (status != error_status_ok)
    {
    printf("Can't inquire bindings \n");
    exit(EXIT_FAILURE);
    }
/*
** register endpoint with the name server
*/
rpc_ns_binding_export
            (
             rpc_c_ns_syntax_default,
             (unsigned_char_t *) SERVER_ENTRY_NAME,
```

Example C-4: The Complete Phonebook Server Initialization File (continued)

```
                IFSPEC,
                bvec,
                NULL,
                &status
                );
if (status != error_status_ok)
    {
    printf("Can't register entry with name service\n");
    exit(EXIT_FAILURE);
    }
/*
** register with endpoint mapper
*/
rpc_ep_register
                (
                IFSPEC,
                bvec,
                NULL,
                (unsigned_char_t *)"phonebook endpoint",
                &status
                );
if (status != error_status_ok)
    {
    printf("Can't register endpoint\n");
    exit(EXIT_FAILURE);
    }
/*
** Get the string bindings and print them
*/
for (i = 0; i < bvec->count; i++)
    {
    /*
    ** For each binding, convert it to a
    **     string representation
    */
    rpc_binding_to_string_binding
                    (
                    bvec->binding_h[i],
                    &string_binding,
                    &status
                    );
    if (status != error_status_ok)
        {
        printf("Can't get string binding \n");
        exit(EXIT_FAILURE);
        }
    printf("%s\n", string_binding);
    }
/*
** Server is all ready to start listening for client
**     requests...
```

Example C-4: The Complete Phonebook Server Initialization File (continued)

```
    */
    rpc_server_listen
            (
             (long)2,
             &status
            );
    if (status != error_status_ok)
        printf("Error: rpc_server_listen() returned \n");
    return (EXIT_FAILURE);
}
#ifdef WIN32
/*************************************************************************/
/***                MIDL_user_allocate / MIDL_user_free            ***/
/*************************************************************************/
void * __RPC_API
MIDL_user_allocate
            (
             size
            )
size_t size;
{
    unsigned char * ptr;
    ptr = malloc( size );
    return ( (void *)ptr );

}
void __RPC_API
MIDL_user_free
            (
             object
            )
void * object;
{
    free (object);
}
#endif
```

Example C-5: The Complete Phonebook Remote Procedures

```
/*
**
**
** MODULE: manager.c
**
**
** PROGRAM: Portable PHNBK2 Application (OpenVMS,DOS,NT,OSF/1,ULTRIX)
**
**
** ABSTRACT: PHNBK2 is a sample RPC application intended to illustrate
**           the basics of RPC interoperation between DCE platforms
```

Example C-5: The Complete Phonebook Remote Procedures (continued)

```
**              and Microsoft platforms.  PHNBK2 extends the capabilities
**              of PHNBK by using context handles, and the CDS nameservice.
**
**
**
*/
#include <stdio.h>
#include <string.h>
#include <stdlib.h>
#include "phnbk2.h"
#ifndef VMS
#include <malloc.h>
#endif
#ifdef WIN32
#include "dceport.h"
#endif
typedef struct _p_context
    {
    /*
    ** Phonebook handle
    */
    FILE * filehandle;
    /*
    ** Previous phonebook operation
    */
    short previous_operation;
    } p_context;
/*
**
** FUNCTION:  getfileline
**
** PURPOSE:
**      Retrieve Lines from input file
**
*/
int
getfileline
            (
             line,
             phone
            )
idl_char * line;
FILE * phone;
{
    /*
    ** Each call of this routine returns a line of the
    **      phonebook file.  On EOF, it returns -1.
    */
    char ch;
    while ((ch = fgetc(phone)) != '\n' && ch != EOF)
        {
```

Example C-5: The Complete Phonebook Remote Procedures (continued)

```
        /*
        ** Tabs are unpredictable, so substitute
        **    three spaces if you run across a tab...
        */
        if (ch == '\t')
            {
            *line++ = ' ';
            *line++ = ' ';
            *line++ = ' ';
            }
        else
            *line++ = ch;

        }
    *line++ = '\0';
    if (ch == EOF)
        return (END);
    else
        return (NORMAL);
}
/*
**
** FUNCTION:  open_phonebook_file
**
** PURPOSE:
**     Open phonebook file and establish a context handle that
**     reflects the client's phonebook "state"
**
*/
void
open_phonebook_file
            (
             ph
            )
phonebook_handle *ph;
{
    /*
    ** This structure is defined in phnbk2.idl, and contains both
    **   a filehandle and a short that keeps track of the previous
    **   phonebook operation.
    */
    p_context *pc_p;
    /*
    ** Allocate the required amount of memory for a p_context
    **     structure
    */
    pc_p = (p_context *) malloc ( sizeof (p_context) );
    /*
    ** Allocate a file handle for this client's operations
    */
    pc_p->filehandle = fopen ("phnbk.txt","r");
```

Example C-5: The Complete Phonebook Remote Procedures (continued)

```
    /*
    ** Initialize the p_context...
    **
    ** The previous operation is 0 (no previous operation yet)
    */
    pc_p->previous_operation = 0;
    /*
    ** Return the context handle
    */
    *ph = (phonebook_handle) pc_p;

    return ;
}


/*
**
** FUNCTION:  phonebook_handle_rundown
**
** PURPOSE:
**      This routine releases resources associated with the
**      context handle if the connection goes away.
**
*/
void
phonebook_handle_rundown
            (
             ph
            )
phonebook_handle ph;
{
    p_context *pc_p;
    pc_p = (p_context *)ph;
    /*
    ** Close the file associated with the filehandle
    */
    fclose (pc_p->filehandle);
    /*
    ** ...and free the memory associated with this p_context struct
    */
    free(pc_p);
    return;
}
/*
**
** FUNCTION:  close_phonebook_file
**
** PURPOSE:
**      This routine does an orderly close of the phonebook file handle
**      and frees resources associated with the context handle.
**
*/
```

Example C-5: The Complete Phonebook Remote Procedures (continued)

```
void
close_phonebook_file
          (
           ph
          )
phonebook_handle *ph;
{
    /*
    ** Effect a context handle cleanup by calling on the
    **     rundown routine -- it already does what we want
    **     to do
    */
    phonebook_handle_rundown
              (
               *ph
              ) ;
    /*
    ** Reset the context handle to NULL
    */
    *ph = NULL;
    return;
}
/*
**
** FUNCTION:  lookup
**
** PURPOSE:
**      Lookup up entries in database
**
*/
short
lookup
      (
       phone,
       op,
       stringin,
       stringout
      )
phonebook_handle phone;
operations       op;
idl_char stringin[LINESIZE];
idl_char stringout[LINESIZE];
{
    idl_char buf[LINESIZE];
    p_context *pc_p;
    /*
    ** Remember that our context handle is a pointer to a
    **     p_context structure
    */
    pc_p = (p_context *)phone;
```

Example C-5: The Complete Phonebook Remote Procedures (continued)

```
/*
** Switch on requested operation
*/
switch (op)
    {
    case  RESET:
        /*
        **  Reset context
        */
        printf("Phonbook:\tRESET\n");
        rewind(pc_p->filehandle);
        pc_p->previous_operation = FIRSTMATCH;
        return(NORMAL);
        break;
    case  FIRSTMATCH:
        /*
        **  Look for first match of a string, starting at the
        **     beginning of the file...
        */
        printf("Phonbook:\tFIRSTMATCH\n");
        rewind(pc_p->filehandle);
        break;
    case  NEXTMATCH:
        /*
        **  Nothing special here, fall out and continue search
        */
        printf("Phonbook:\tNEXTMATCH\n");
        break;
    case  BROWSE:
        /*
        **  A BROWSE operation just returns the next entry...
        **
        **  If the last operation was a BROWSE that got an EOF,
        **     then rewind and start cycling through again.
        */
        printf("Phonbook:\tBROWSE\n");
        if (pc_p->previous_operation == BROWSE_RESET)
            rewind (pc_p->filehandle);

        if ((getfileline(buf,pc_p->filehandle)) != -1)
            {
            /*
            **  If not EOF, then just return next entry.
            */
            strcpy ((char *)stringout,(char *)buf);
            printf("Phonbook: \tFound %s\n", buf);
            pc_p->previous_operation = BROWSE;
            return(NORMAL);
            }
```

Example C-5: The Complete Phonebook Remote Procedures (continued)

```
            else
                {
                /*
                **   This allows the client to flag "no more entries"
                **   before cycling through the file again on
                **   another BROWSE request.
                */
                pc_p->previous_operation = BROWSE_RESET;

                return(END);
                }
        }
    /*
    ** Keep track of previous operation in p_context
    */
    pc_p->previous_operation = op;
    /*
    **   Either return the line of the file that contains a string
    **   match, or return -1...
    */
    while ((getfileline(buf,pc_p->filehandle)) != -1)
        {
        if ((strstr((char *)buf, (char *)stringin)) != (char *) NULL)
            {
            printf("Phonbook: \tFound %s\n", buf);
            strcpy ((char *)stringout,(char *)buf);
            return(NORMAL);
            }
        }
    return(END);
}
```

Example C-6: The Complete Phonebook Server Database File phnbk.txt

```
Micky Mouse 555-2345
Donald Duck 555-2342
Pluto 555-4564
James T. Kirk 555-2342
Fred Flintstone   555-2342
Spider Man 555-2345
Bat Man      555-2342
George Jettson 555-2342
Peter Pan 555-4312
John Doe 555-8888
Charlie Brown 555-2374
```

Example C-7: The Complete Windows Phonebook Client

```
/*
**
**
** MODULE: wclient.c
**
**
** PROGRAM: Windows WPHNBK2 Application
**
**
** ABSTRACT: WPHNBK2 is a sample RPC application intended to illustrate
**           the basics of RPC interoperation between DCE platforms
**           and Microsoft Windows platforms.  WPHNBK2 extends the
**           capabilities of WPHNBK by using context handles, and the
**           CDS nameservice.
**
**
**
**
*/
#include <windows.h>
#include <stdlib.h>
#include <string.h>
#include <ctype.h>
#include "phnbk2.h"
#include "wphnbk2.h"
#include "dceport.h"
#define IFSPEC phnbk2_ClientIfHandle
#define SERVER_ENTRY_NAME "/.:/phnbk2_srv_"
#define SERVER_ENTRY_NAME2  "/.:/subsys/DEC/examples/phnbk2_srv_"
int             lookup_status;      /* lookup return status         */
error_status_t status;              /* rpc status                   */
idl_char        input[LINESIZE];    /* 'find' search string         */
idl_char        output[LINESIZE];   /* string returned from database */
idl_char        oldmatch[LINESIZE]; /* previous 'find' string       */
unsigned char   server[80];         /* string binding for server    */
operations      operation;          /* operation requested          */
short           no_handle;          /* handle not initialized flag  */
phonebook_handle ph;                /* phnbk context handle         */
long FAR PASCAL WndProc (HWND, WORD, WORD, LONG) ;


int
PASCAL WinMain
                (
                HANDLE hInstance,
                HANDLE hPrevInstance,
                LPSTR lpszCmdLine,
                int nCmdShow
                )
{
    char szAppName [] = "WPHNBK2" ;
    HWND        hwnd ;
    MSG         msg;
```

Example C-7: The Complete Windows Phonebook Client (continued)

```
        WNDCLASS    wndclass ;
        /*
        ** Initialize strings
        */
        input[0]    = '\0';
        output[0]   = '\0';
        oldmatch[0] = '\0';
        server[0]   = '\0';
        no_handle = TRUE;
        /*
        ** Standard Windows stuff...
        */
        if (!hPrevInstance)
            {
            wndclass.style          = CS_HREDRAW | CS_VREDRAW;
            wndclass.lpfnWndProc     = WndProc ;
            wndclass.cbClsExtra      = 0 ;
            wndclass.cbWndExtra      = DLGWINDOWEXTRA ;
            wndclass.hInstance       = hInstance ;
            wndclass.hIcon           = LoadIcon(NULL,IDL_APPLICATION);
            wndclass.hCursor         = LoadCursor (NULL, IDC_ARROW) ;
            wndclass.hbrBackground   = COLOR_WINDOW + 1 ;
            wndclass.lpszMenuName    = NULL ;
            wndclass.lpszClassName   = szAppName ;
            RegisterClass (&wndclass) ;
            }
    hwnd = CreateDialog (hInstance, szAppName, 0, NULL) ;
    ShowWindow (hwnd, nCmdShow) ;
    SetFocus ( GetDlgItem (hwnd, SEARCHBOX ) );
    /*
    ** Start accepting messages
    */
    while ( GetMessage (&msg, NULL, 0, 0) )
        {
        TranslateMessage (&msg) ;
        DispatchMessage (&msg) ;
        }
    return msg.wParam ;
}
void
ErrorBox
        (
        HWND hwnd,
        unsigned char *error_string
        )
{
    /*
    ** This is just a convenience procedure for
    **      generating message boxes when errors
    **      are encountered.
    */
```

Example C-7: The Complete Windows Phonebook Client (continued)

```
    MessageBox
                (
                hwnd,
                error_string,
                "ERROR",
                MB_OK
                );
}
short
InitHandle
            (
             HWND hwnd
            )
{
    /*
    ** This procedure goes to the CDS nameservice to locate
    **      a PHNBK2 server, initializes the binding handle,
    **      and establishes the context handle.
    */
    unsigned char    *string_binding;
    unsigned char    *protseq;
    handle_t          import_handle;
    long              entry_name_syntax=3;
    rpc_ns_handle_t   import_context;
    int               found=0;
    error_status_t    status;
    error_status_t    status2;

  TRY
    /*
    ** Get ready to import bindings that match the
    **      given entry name
    */
    rpc_ns_binding_import_begin
                (
                 rpc_c_ns_syntax_default,
                 SERVER_ENTRY_NAME,
                 IFSPEC,
                 NULL,
                 &import_context,
                 &status
                );
    if (status)
        {
        ErrorBox(hwnd,"import_begin failure");
        exit (EXIT_FAILURE);
        }
    /*
    ** search for TCP binding
    */
```

Example C-7: The Complete Windows Phonebook Client (continued)

```
while (!found)
    {
    /*
    ** Get next binding
    */
    rpc_ns_binding_import_next
            (
                import_context,
                &import_handle,
                &status
            );
    if (status)
        {
        ErrorBox(hwnd,"server not found");
        exit (EXIT_FAILURE);
        }
    /*
    ** Convert binding to string binding
    */
    rpc_binding_to_string_binding
            (
                import_handle,
                &string_binding,
                &status
            );
    if (status)
        {
        ErrorBox(hwnd,"binding_to_string_binding failure");
        exit (EXIT_FAILURE);
        }
    else
        {
        /*
        ** Parse the binding into its individual components...
        **      actually all we care about here is the protocol
        **      sequence...
        */
        rpc_string_binding_parse
                (
                    string_binding,
                    NULL,
                    &protseq,
                    NULL,
                    NULL,
                    NULL,
                    &status
                );
```

Example C-7: The Complete Windows Phonebook Client (continued)

```
                  if (status)
                      {
                      ErrorBox(hwnd,"string_binding_parse failure");
                      exit (EXIT_FAILURE);
                      }
                  else
                      {
                      /*
                      ** Check for a TCP/IP protocol sequence
                      */
                      if (!(strcmp((char *)protseq, "ncacn_ip_tcp")))
                          /*
                          ** Got one!
                          */
                          {
                          strcpy(server, (char *)string_binding);
                          /*
                          ** Free the string binding
                          */
                          rpc_string_free
                                      (
                                       &string_binding,
                                       &status2
                                      );
                          found = 1;
                          /*
                          ** finish the search
                          */
                          rpc_ns_binding_import_done(&import_context, &status);
                          }
                      else
                          rpc_string_free
                                      (
                                       &string_binding,
                                       &status2
                                      );
                      }
              }
    /*
    ** End of while block
    */
    }
    rpc_binding_from_string_binding
                (
                 server,
                 &xhandle,
                 &status
                );
    if (status)
        {
        ErrorBox(hwnd,"invalid string binding");
```

Example C-7: The Complete Windows Phonebook Client (continued)

```
                exit (EXIT_FAILURE);
                }
        /*
        ** Initialize context handle to NULL
        */
        ph = NULL;
        /*
        ** Establish the phonebook context handle
        */
        open_phonebook_file
                        (
                        &ph
                        );
    CATCH_ALL
        /*
        ** Catch all exceptions from above code
        */
        unsigned long exception;
        unsigned char error_code[6];
        exception = RpcExceptionCode();
        ltoa (exception,error_code,10);

        ErrorBox (hwnd,strcat("Exception: ",error_code));
        exit (EXIT_FAILURE);
    ENDTRY
        /*
        ** Only way to return successfully
        */

        no_handle = FALSE;
        return (0);
}
void
ShowResult
                (
                HWND hwnd
                )
{
        /*
        ** Display lookup results, based on the context of
        **     the requested operation
        */
        if (operation == BROWSE)
                {
                /*
                ** BROWSE -- return next entry
                */
                if (lookup_status == NORMAL)
                        /*
                        ** Everything ok, display next entry
                        */
```

Example C-7: The Complete Windows Phonebook Client (continued)

```
                SetDlgItemText (hwnd,RESULTSBOX,output);
        else
            {
            /*
            ** Othwise, we hit end of file...
            */
            SetDlgItemText (hwnd,RESULTSBOX,"");
            SetDlgItemText (hwnd,INFOBOX,"No more entries");
            }
        }
    else
        {
        /*
        ** Operation was a Find or Find Next...tailor message
        **    syntax to reflect the operation.
        */
        if (lookup_status == NORMAL)
            {
            /*
            ** Print results
            */
            SetDlgItemText (hwnd,RESULTSBOX,output);

            /*
            ** Determine if this was first match, or subsequent match
            */
            if (operation == FIRSTMATCH)
                SetDlgItemText (hwnd,INFOBOX,"Match found");
            else
                SetDlgItemText (hwnd,INFOBOX,"Another match found");
            }
        else
            /*
            ** Hit end of file during search
            */
            if (operation == FIRSTMATCH)
                SetDlgItemText (hwnd,INFOBOX,"Match not found");
            else
                SetDlgItemText (hwnd,INFOBOX,"No other matches found");
        }
    return;
    }
long
FAR PASCAL WndProc
                    (
                    HWND hwnd,
                    WORD message,
                    WORD wParam,
                    LONG lParam
                    )
```

Example C-7: The Complete Windows Phonebook Client (continued)

```
{
/*
** We switch cursors to the hourglass during
**     a lookup RPC.  This is for saving the
**     regular pointer.
*/
HCURSOR OldCursor;
/*
** First thing, save the match string from last time around
*/
strcpy (oldmatch, input);
/*
** Switch on the incoming message type (standard Windows
**     programming)
*/
switch (message)
    {
    /*
    ** Got a button pushed
    */
    case WM_COMMAND:
        switch (wParam)
            {
            /*
            ** Either a Find or a Find Next
            */
            case FINDBUTTON:
                /*
                ** Make sure our handle is initialized
                */
                if (no_handle)
                    if (InitHandle(hwnd)) break;
                /*
                ** Clear current text
                */
                SetDlgItemText(hwnd,RESULTSBOX,"");
                SetDlgItemText(hwnd,INFOBOX,"");
                /*
                ** Read the search string
                */
                GetDlgItemText(hwnd,SEARCHBOX,input,32);
                /*
                ** Make sure user entered a search string
                */
                if (input[0] == NULL)
                    {
                    ErrorBox (
                            hwnd,
                             "Missing Search String!"
                            );
```

Example C-7: The Complete Windows Phonebook Client (continued)

```
                        /*
                        ** Set focus back to SEARCHBOX so user can
                        **    enter search string
                        */
                        SetFocus ( GetDlgItem (hwnd, SEARCHBOX) );
                        }
            else
                {
                /*
                ** Search string is present. Save existing
                **    pointer and display hourglass
                */
                OldCursor = SetCursor (LoadCursor(NULL,IDC_WAIT));
                ShowCursor (TRUE);
                /*
                ** Determine desired operation
                */
                if (strcmp(oldmatch,input))
                    operation = FIRSTMATCH;
                else
                    operation = NEXTMATCH;
                /*
                ** Perform the requested operation
                */
                lookup_status = lookup
                                    (
                                    ph,
                                    operation,
                                    input,
                                    output
                                    );
                /*
                ** Restore pointer cursor
                */
                ShowCursor (FALSE);
                SetCursor ( OldCursor );

                /*
                ** Display lookup results
                */
                ShowResult(hwnd);
                }

        break;
    /*
    ** BROWSE -- return next entry
    */
    case BROWSEBUTTON:
        /*
        ** Make sure handle is initialized
        */
```

Example C-7: The Complete Windows Phonebook Client (continued)

```
        if (no_handle)
            if(InitHandle(hwnd)) break;
        /*
        ** Clear existing text and display status
        */
        SetDlgItemText(hwnd,RESULTSBOX,"");
        SetDlgItemText(hwnd,SEARCHBOX,"");
        SetDlgItemText(hwnd,INFOBOX,"Browsing...");
        /*
        ** Switch to hourglass cursor
        */
        OldCursor = SetCursor (LoadCursor(NULL,IDC_WAIT));
        ShowCursor (TRUE);

        operation = BROWSE;
        /*
        ** Perform the requested operation
        */
        lookup_status = lookup
                            (
                            ph,
                            operation,
                            input,
                            output
                            );
        /*
        ** Restore pointer cursor
        */
        ShowCursor (FALSE);
        SetCursor ( OldCursor );

        /*
        ** Display operation results
        */
        ShowResult(hwnd);

        break;
    /*
    ** User has requested a RESET.  This clears all
    **     text and rewinds the phonebook file
    */
    case RESETBUTTON:
        /*
        ** Make sure handle is initialized
        */
        if (no_handle)
            if (InitHandle(hwnd)) break;
        /*
        ** Clear all text
        */
        SetDlgItemText(hwnd,RESULTSBOX,"");
```

Example C-7: The Complete Windows Phonebook Client (continued)

```
                    SetDlgItemText(hwnd,INFOBOX,"");
                    SetDlgItemText(hwnd,SEARCHBOX,"");
                    input[0] = '\0';
                    operation = RESET;
                    /*
                    ** Perform the requested operation
                    */
                    lookup_status = lookup
                                        (
                                        ph,
                                        operation,
                                        input,
                                        output
                                        );
                break;
            }
        return 0 ;
    /*
    ** User has closed the application
    */
    case WM_DESTROY:
        if (!no_handle)
            {
            /*
            ** Free resources associated with context handle
            */
            close_phonebook_file
                        (
                        &ph
                        );
            /*
            ** Free binding handle, post quit message and leave
            */
            rpc_binding_free
                        (
                        &xhandle,
                        &status
                        );
            }
        PostQuitMessage (0) ;
        return 0 ;
    /*
    ** Ignore other messages
    */
    default:
        return DefWindowProc (hwnd, message, wParam, lParam) ;
    }
}
```

Example C-8: The Complete Windows Phonebook Header File wphnbk2.h

```
#define SEARCHBOX 102
#define RESULTSBOX 104
#define INFOBOX 106
#define FINDBUTTON 113
#define BROWSEBUTTON 112
#define RESETBUTTON 110
```

Example C-9: The Complete Windows Phonebook Definition File

```
;------------------------------------
; WPHNBK2.DEF module definition file
;------------------------------------
NAME            WPHNBK2
DESCRIPTION     'Windows RPC Phonebook 2'
EXETYPE         WINDOWS
STUB            'WINSTUB.EXE'
CODE            PRELOAD FIXED DISCARDABLE
DATA            PRELOAD FIXED MULTIPLE
HEAPSIZE        8192
STACKSIZE       8192
EXPORTS         WndProc
```

Example C-10: The Complete Windows Phonebook Resource File

```
#include <windows.h>
#include "wphnbk2.h"
WPHNBK2 DIALOG  15, 33, 315, 102
CAPTION "Windows RPC Phonebook 2"
STYLE WS_OVERLAPPED | WS_BORDER | WS_CAPTION | WS_SYSMENU | WS_MINIMIZEBOX
CLASS "WPHNBK2"
BEGIN
    CONTROL "Search String:", 100, "static", SS_LEFT | WS_CHILD, 13, 18,
            47, 10
    CONTROL "Input", 101, "button", BS_GROUPBOX | WS_TABSTOP | WS_CHILD,
            5, 3, 173, 32
    CONTROL "", 102, "edit", ES_LEFT | WS_BORDER | WS_TABSTOP | WS_CHILD,
            63, 17, 108, 12
    CONTROL "Search Results:", 103, "static", SS_LEFT | WS_CHILD, 6, 50,
            58, 7
    CONTROL "", 104, "edit", ES_LEFT | WS_BORDER | WS_TABSTOP | WS_CHILD,
            64, 48, 239, 12
    CONTROL "Status:", 105, "static", SS_LEFT | WS_CHILD, 6, 80, 26, 8
    CONTROL "", 106, "edit", ES_LEFT | WS_BORDER | WS_TABSTOP | WS_CHILD,
            30, 78, 133, 12
    CONTROL "Output", 108, "button", BS_GROUPBOX | WS_TABSTOP | WS_CHILD,
            4, 36, 305, 31
    CONTROL "Information", 111, "button", BS_GROUPBOX | WS_TABSTOP |
            WS_CHILD, 4, 68, 305, 31
```

Example C-10: The Complete Windows Phonebook Resource File (continued)

```
        CONTROL "Find / Find Next", 113, "button", BS_PUSHBUTTON | WS_TABSTOP
                | WS_CHILD, 192, 6, 112, 14
        CONTROL "Reset", 110, "button", BS_PUSHBUTTON | WS_TABSTOP | WS_CHILD,
                192, 22, 50, 14
        CONTROL "Browse", 112, "button", BS_PUSHBUTTON | WS_TABSTOP | WS_CHILD,
                258, 22, 46, 14
END
#
#
# Build PHNBK2 client and server for ULTRIX
#
#
ALPHA_LIBFLAGS  = -ldce -lpthreads -lmach -lc_r
LIBS            = -ldce -lcma -ldnet -li
CFLAGS          = -I. -c
all: phnbk2 phnbk2d
#
# Link client
#
phnbk2: client.o phnbk2_cstub.o
        $(CC) -o phnbk2 client.o phnbk2_cstub.o $(LIBS)
#
# Link server
#
phnbk2d: server.o manager.o phnbk2_sstub.o
        $(CC) -o phnbk2d server.o manager.o phnbk2_sstub.o $(LIBS)
#
# Compile client source code
#
client.o: client.c phnbk2.h
        $(CC) $(CFLAGS) client.c
#
# Compile server source code
#
server.o: server.c phnbk2.h
        $(CC) $(CFLAGS) server.c
manager.o: manager.c phnbk2.h
        $(CC) $(CFLAGS) manager.c
#
# Generate stubs and header file from interface definition
#
phnbk2.h: phnbk2.idl phnbk2.acf
        idl phnbk2.idl
#
# Clean up for fresh build
#
clean:
        rm -f *.o
        rm -f phnbk2.h
        rm -f *ub.c
```

Example C-10: The Complete Windows Phonebook Resource File (continued)

```
#
# Clean up all byproducts of build
#
clobber: clean
        rm -f phnbk2
        rm -f phnbk2d
```

Example C-11: The Complete Phonebook Makefile for OSF/1

```
#
#
# Build PHNBK2 client and server for OSF/1
#
#
ALPHA_LIBFLAGS  = -ldce -lpthreads -lmach -lc_r
LIBS            = -ldce -lpthreads -lmach -lc_r -ldnet
CFLAGS          = -I. -std1 -c
all: phnbk2 phnbk2d
#
# Link client
#
phnbk2: client.o phnbk2_cstub.o
        $(CC) -o phnbk2 client.o phnbk2_cstub.o $(LIBS)
#
# Link server
#
phnbk2d: server.o manager.o phnbk2_sstub.o
        $(CC) -o phnbk2d server.o manager.o phnbk2_sstub.o $(LIBS)
#
# Compile client source code
#
client.o: client.c phnbk2.h
        $(CC) $(CFLAGS) client.c
#
# Compile server source code
#
server.o: server.c phnbk2.h
        $(CC) $(CFLAGS) server.c
manager.o: manager.c phnbk2.h
        $(CC) $(CFLAGS) manager.c
#
# Generate stubs and header file from interface definition
#
phnbk2.h: phnbk2.idl phnbk2.acf
        idl phnbk2.idl
#
# Clean up for fresh build
#
clean:
        rm -f *.o
```

Example C-11: The Complete Phonebook Makefile for OSF/1 (continued)

```
        rm -f phnbk2.h
        rm -f *ub.c
#
# Clean up all byproducts of build
#
clobber: clean
        rm -f phnbk2
        rm -f phnbk2d
```

Example C-12: The Complete Phonebook Makefile for NT

```
#
#
# Build PHNBK2 client and server for Windows NT
#
#
!INCLUDE <ntwin32.mak>
includes =  -I.
all : phnbk2.exe phnbk2d.exe
#
# Link client
#
phnbk2.exe: client.obj phnbk2_c.obj phnbk2_x.obj
    $(link) $(linkdebug) $(conflags) -out:phnbk2.exe \
      client.obj phnbk2_c.obj phnbk2_x.obj \
      rpcrt4.lib rpcns4.lib rpcndr.lib $(conlibs)
#
# Link server
#
phnbk2d.exe: server.obj manager.obj phnbk2_s.obj phnbk2_y.obj
    $(link) $(linkdebug) $(conflags) -out:phnbk2d.exe \
      server.obj manager.obj phnbk2_s.obj phnbk2_y.obj \
      rpcrt4.lib rpcns4.lib rpcndr.lib $(conlibs)
#
# Compile client source code
#
client.obj: client.c phnbk2.h
   $(cc) $(cflags) $(cvars) $(scall) $(includes) client.c
#
# Compile server source code
#
server.obj: server.c phnbk2.h
   $(cc) $(cflags) $(cvars) $(scall) $(includes) server.c
manager.obj: manager.c phnbk2.h
   $(cc) $(cflags) $(cvars) $(scall) $(includes) manager.c
#
# Compile client stubs
#
phnbk2_c.obj : phnbk2_c.c
    $(cc) $(cflags) $(cvars) $(scall) $(includes) phnbk2_c.c
```

Example C-12: The Complete Phonebook Makefile for NT (continued)

```
phnbk2_x.obj : phnbk2_x.c
    $(cc) $(cflags) $(cvars) $(scall) $(includes) phnbk2_x.c
#
# Compile server stubs
#
phnbk2_s.obj : phnbk2_s.c
    $(cc) $(cflags) $(cvars) $(scall) $(includes) phnbk2_s.c
phnbk2_y.obj : phnbk2_y.c
    $(cc) $(cflags) $(cvars) $(scall) $(includes) phnbk2_y.c
#
# Generate stubs and header file from interface definition
#
phnbk2.h : phnbk2.idl phnbk2.acf
    midl phnbk2.idl
#
# Clean up for fresh build
#
clean :
    del phnbk2_*.*
    del *.obj
    del phnbk2.h
#
# Clean up all byproducts of build
#
clobber : clean
    del phnbk2.exe
    del phnbk2d.exe
```

Example C-13: The Complete Phonebook Makefile for DOS

```
#
#
# Build PHNBK2 client for DOS
#
#
DEV    = c:\c700
LIBS   = $(DEV)\lib\llibce $(DEV)\lib\rpc $(DEV)\lib\rpcndr
CFLAGS = -AL -c -w -nologo -Zp -Zi -Oatelr -I$(DEV)\include\dos
all: phnbk2.exe
#
# Link client
#
phnbk2.exe: client.obj phnbk2_c.obj phnbk2_x.obj
    link /co /nologo client.obj phnbk2_c.obj phnbk2_x.obj,\
    phnbk2.exe,,/nod $(LIBS);
#
# Compile client source code
#
client.obj: client.c phnbk2.h
    $(CC) $(CFLAGS) $*.c
```

Example C-13: The Complete Phonebook Makefile for DOS (continued)

```
#
# Compile client stubs
#
phnbk2_c.obj : phnbk2_c.c
    $(CC) $(CFLAGS) $*.c
phnbk2_x.obj : phnbk2_x.c
    $(CC) $(CFLAGS) $*.c
#
# Generate stubs and header file from interface definition
#
phnbk2_c.c phnbk2.h phnbk2_x.c : phnbk2.idl phnbk2.acf
    midl phnbk2.idl
#
# Clean up for fresh build
#
clean:
    del phnbk2_*.*
    del *.obj
    del phnbk2.h
#
# Clean up all byproducts of build
#
clobber: clean
    del phnbk2.exe
```

Example C-14: The Complete Phonebook Makefile for Windows

```
#
# Build WPHNBK2 client for Windows
#
DEV    = c:\c700
LIBS   = $(DEV)\lib\libw $(DEV)\lib\llibcew $(DEV)\lib\rpcw \
         $(DEV)\lib\rpcndrw $(DEV)\lib\oldnames
CFLAGS = -AL -c -w -nologo -Gsw -Zp -Zi -Otelr -I$(DEV)\include\win
all: wphnbk2.exe
#
# Link simple client
#
wphnbk2.exe: wphnbk2.lnk wphnbk2.res
    link /co /nologo @wphnbk2.lnk
    rc wphnbk2.res
#
# Make .LNK file
#
wphnbk2.lnk: wclient.obj phnbk2_c.obj phnbk2_x.obj
    echo @<<wphnbk2.lnk
        wclient.obj phnbk2_c.obj phnbk2_x.obj
```

Example C-14: The Complete Phonebook Makefile for Windows (continued)

```
        wphnbk2.exe
        ,
        /noe/nod $(LIBS)
        wphnbk2.def
#
# Compile simple client source code
#
wclient.obj : wclient.c phnbk2.h
    $(CC) $(CFLAGS) $*.c
#
# Compile client stubs
#
phnbk2_c.obj : phnbk2_c.c
    $(CC) $(CFLAGS) $*.c
phnbk2_x.obj : phnbk2_x.c
    $(CC) $(CFLAGS) $*.c
#
# Generate stubs and header file from interface definition
#
phnbk2.h : phnbk2.idl phnbk2.acf
    midl phnbk2.idl
#
# Generate resource file
#
wphnbk2.res: wphnbk2.rc wphnbk2.ico
    rc -I $(DEV)\include -r wphnbk2.rc
#
# Clean up for fresh build
#
clean:
    del *.obj
    del wphnbk2.lnk
    del wphnbk2.res
    del phnbk2_*.*
    del phnbk2.h
#
# Clean up all byproducts of build
#
clobber: clean
    del wphnbk2.exe
```

Example C-15: The Complete Phonebook Makefile for OpenVMS

```
$!
$! This is file MAKEFILE.COM to build the PHNBK2
$! example application on an OpenVMS system.
$!
$! Enable the universal IDL command interface
$ idl            := $sys$system:dce$idl.exe
$
```

Example C-15: The Complete Phonebook Makefile for OpenVMS (continued)

```
$! Compile the interface definition
$! -keep all is used to keep the IDL output for training purposes
$ idl PHNBK2.IDL -keep all -trace all -trace log_manager
$
$! Compile the client application files
$ cc CLIENT.C
$
$! Link the client application
$ link /exe=phnbk2.exe client, phnbk2_cstub, sys$input:/options
        sys$share:dce$lib_shr/share
        sys$share:vaxc2decc.exe/share
$ write sys$output "PHNBK2.EXE done."
$
$! Compile the server application files
$ cc server.c, manager.c
$
$! Link the server application
$ link/exe=phnbk2d.exe server,manager,phnbk2_sstub,sys$input:/options
        sys$share:dce$lib_shr/share
        sys$share:vaxc2decc.exe/share
$ write sys$output "PHNBKD2.EXE done."
```

D

Remote Search Application

This appendix describes the *searchit* application that allows client users to search a file on a server system for a string. This example application uses customized binding handles to enable clients to pass a remote filename and search string along with the binding information to the server. We also show the use of [comm_status] and [fault_status] ACF attributes for error handling purposes.

search.idl

Example D-1 is an interface definition file that contains procedure declarations and defines data types so that clients and servers can interpret each other's data. This file is compiled with the attribute configuration file to produce stub files and header files.

search.acf

Example D-2 is an attribute configuration file that declares the [comm_status] and [fault_status] ACF attributes for use with the remote procedure. This enables Microsoft RPC clients to catch exceptions and return them as status variables through error_status_t declared in the remote procedure.

client.c

Example D-3 is a client application program that takes a hostname, filename, and search string as arguments on the client command line.

server.c

Example D-4 is a server initialization file that prepares the searchit server to handle incoming remote procedure calls. During server startup, the file invokes RPC routines to register the interface and to set the server so it listens for incoming calls.

manager.c

Example D-5 is a file containing the remote procedure. This procedure responds to client requests to search for a string in a file specified by the client.

makefile.unx

Example D-6 is a description file (makefile) used by the ULTRIX *make* program to build (compile and link) executable client and server programs for ULTRIX.

makefile.osf

Example D-7 is a description file used by the OSF/1 *make* program to build executable client and server programs for OSF/1.

makefile.nt

Example D-8 is a description file used by the Microsoft Windows NT *nmake* program to build an executable client and server program for Microsoft Windows NT.

makefile.dos

Example D-9 is a description file used by the DOS *nmake* program to build an executable DOS client program.

makefile.com

Example D-10 is a description file used by OpenVMS systems to build executable client and server programs for OpenVMS.

Example D-1: Remote Search Interface Definition File: search.idl

```
/*
** Interface Definition File for Search program
*/
[
 uuid(2450F730-5170-101A-9A93-08002B2BC829),
 version(1.0),
 pointer_default(ref)]
interface search
{
/*
** Constant for maximum line size
*/
const long LINESIZE = 100;
/*
** Constant for file name length
*/
const long FILENAME_SIZE = 100;
/*
** Constant for host name size
*/
const long BINDING_SIZE = 32;
```

Example D-1: Remote Search Interface Definition File: search.idl (continued)

```
/*
** Status for search file error
*/
const short FILE_ERROR = -1;
/*
** Status for no match found
*/
const short NO_MATCH = 0;
/*
** Customized binding handle definition -- it
**      contains the file name and the string
**      binding to use.
*/
typedef [handle] struct
                        {
                         unsigned char binding[BINDING_SIZE];
                         unsigned char filename[FILENAME_SIZE];
                        } search_spec;
/*
** Search for a string match on the file specified
**      in the customized binding handle above.
*/
short
searchit
        (
        [in]            search_spec    custom_handle,
        [in,string]     char           search_string[LINESIZE],
        [out,string]    char           return_string[LINESIZE],
        [out]           error_status_t *error
        );
}
```

Example D-2: Remote Search Attribute Configuration File: search.acf

```
interface search
{
searchit([comm_status,fault_status] error);
}
```

Example D-3: Remote Search Client Program File: client.c

```
/*
**
**
** MODULE: client.c
**
**
** PROGRAM: Portable SEARCH Application (OpenVMS,DOS,NT,OSF/1,ULTRIX)
```

Example D-3: Remote Search Client Program File: client.c (continued)

```
**
**
** ABSTRACT: SEARCH is a sample RPC application intended to illustrate
**           the basics of RPC interoperation between DCE platforms
**           and Microsoft platforms.
**
**
**
**
*/
#include <stdio.h>
#include <string.h>
#include <stdlib.h>
#include "search.h"
#ifndef VMS
#include <malloc.h>
#endif
#if defined(MSDOS) || defined(WIN32)
#include "dceport.h"
#else
#define __RPC_API
#endif
#ifdef WIN32
#define MAIN_DECL _CRTAPI1
#else
#define MAIN_DECL
#endif
int
MAIN_DECL main
                (
                ac,
                av
                )
int    ac;
char *av[];
{
    short            search_status;   /* status from search          */
    error_status_t   rpc_status;      /* comm/fault status code      */
    idl_char         result[LINESIZE]; /* string that matched         */
    idl_char         match[LINESIZE];  /* string to look for          */
    search_spec      custom_handle;   /* search customized handle */

    /*
    ** Initialize some strings
    */
    match[0]  = '\0';
    custom_handle.binding[0]  = '\0';
    custom_handle.filename[0] = '\0';
    /*
    ** There should be 4 parameters to searchit:
    **
```

Example D-3: Remote Search Client Program File: client.c (continued)

```
**      searchit <hostname> <filename> <matchstring>
**
** where
**
**      <hostname> is the hostname where the file to be searched
**                 exists.
**
**      <filename> is the name of the file to be searched.
**
**      <matchstring> is the string to search <filename> for.
**
*/
if (ac != 4)
 {
 /*
 ** Not the right number of parameters
 */
 printf("\t\nUsage: searchit <hostname> <filename> <matchstring>\n\n");
 exit(EXIT_FAILURE);
 }
/*
** Set up the string binding, the filename, and the
**      match string from the command line.
*/
strcpy ((char *)custom_handle.binding,  "ncacn_ip_tcp:");
strcat ((char *)custom_handle.binding,  av[1]);
strcpy ((char *)custom_handle.filename, av[2]);
strcpy ((char *)match, av[3]);
/*
** Search the given file on the given host for the
**      given string...
*/
search_status = searchit
                        (
                         custom_handle,
                         match,
                         result,
                         &rpc_status
                        );
/*
** Most importantly...did we get an RPC error?
*/
if (rpc_status)
    {
    printf("RPC error: %d\n",rpc_status);
    exit(EXIT_FAILURE);
    }


/*
** Check the return status
*/
```

Example D-3: Remote Search Client Program File: client.c (continued)

```
    switch (search_status)
        {
        /*
        ** If FILE_ERROR is returned, then we either couldn't find
        **     the requested file, or we couldn't open it.
        */
        case FILE_ERROR:
            {
            printf("Couldn't find or open requested file\n");
            exit(EXIT_FAILURE);
            }
        /*
        ** If NO_MATCH is returned, then we didn't find the string
        **     in the file
        */
        case NO_MATCH:
            {
            printf("Couldn't find %s in %s \n",av[3],av[2]);
            exit(EXIT_SUCCESS);
            }
        /*
        ** Otherwise, the returned value is the line number where
        **     we found the match
        */
        default:
            {
            printf("Found a match on line number %d:\n\n\t %s\n",
                    search_status,result);
            break;
            }
        }

    return (EXIT_SUCCESS);

}
#if defined(MSDOS) || defined(WIN32)
/************************************************************************/
/***               MIDL_user_allocate / MIDL_user_free             ***/
/************************************************************************/
void * __RPC_API
MIDL_user_allocate
            (
            size
            )
size_t size;
{
    unsigned char * ptr;
    ptr = malloc( size );
    return ( (void *)ptr );

}
```

Example D-3: Remote Search Client Program File: client.c (continued)

```
void __RPC_API
MIDL_user_free
            (
              object
            )
void * object;
{
    free (object);
}
#endif
/*
** FUNCTION: search_spec_bind
**
** PURPOSE: search_spec_bind is called from the client
**           stub to establish a customized binding
**           handle for this remote procedure call.
**
*/
handle_t __RPC_API
search_spec_bind
            (
              custom_handle
            )
search_spec custom_handle;
{
    rpc_binding_handle_t xhandle;
    error_status_t       status;
    /*
    ** Display the server in use
    */
    printf("\n\t(Selecting server binding: %s)\n\n",
          custom_handle.binding);
    /*
    ** Convert the character string binding into an RPC handle
    */
    rpc_binding_from_string_binding
                (
                  custom_handle.binding,
                  &xhandle,
                  &status
                );
    if (status)
        {
        printf("Invalid string binding\n");
        exit (EXIT_FAILURE);
        }

    return ( xhandle );
}
```

Example D-3: Remote Search Client Program File: client.c (continued)

```
/*
**
** FUNCTION: search_spec_unbind
**
** PURPOSE: search_spec_unbind is called by the client stub
**           to free the customized binding handle used
**           by this remote procedure call.
**
*/
void __RPC_API
search_spec_unbind
          (
            custom_handle,
            xhandle
          )
search_spec custom_handle;
handle_t  xhandle;
{
    error_status_t status;
    /*
    ** Free the binding handle
    */
    rpc_binding_free
              (
              &xhandle,
              &status
              );
    return;
}
```

Example D-4: Remote Search Server Initialization File: server.c

```
/*
**
**
** MODULE: server.c
**
**
** PROGRAM: Portable SEARCH Application (OpenVMS,DOS,NT,OSF/1,ULTRIX)
**
**
** ABSTRACT: SEARCH is a sample RPC application intended to illustrate
**           the basics of RPC interoperation between DCE platforms
**           and Microsoft platforms.
**
**
**
*/
#include <stdio.h>
#include <string.h>
```

Example D-4: Remote Search Server Initialization File: server.c (continued)

```
#include <stdlib.h>
#ifndef VMS
#include <malloc.h>
#endif
#include "search.h"
#ifdef WIN32
#include "dceport.h"
#define MAIN_DECL _CRTAPI1
#define IFSPEC search_ServerIfHandle
#else
#define MAIN_DECL
#define IFSPEC search_v1_0_s_ifspec
#endif
int
MAIN_DECL main
            (
             ac,
             av
            )
int    ac;
char *av[];
{
    unsigned int              i;
    error_status_t            status;
    unsigned_char_t           *string_binding;
    rpc_binding_vector_p_t     bvec;
    /*
    **
    ** Specify TCP/IP as a protocol sequences
    */
    rpc_server_use_protseq
            (
             (unsigned_char_t *)"ncacn_ip_tcp",
             5,
             &status
            );
    if (status != error_status_ok)
        {
        printf("No available protocol sequences\n");
        exit(EXIT_FAILURE);
        }
    /*
    ** Register the server interface
    */
    rpc_server_register_if
            (
             IFSPEC,
             NULL,
             NULL,
             &status
            );
```

Example D-4: Remote Search Server Initialization File: server.c (continued)

```
if (status != error_status_ok)
    {
    printf("Can't register interface \n");
    exit(EXIT_FAILURE);
    }
/*
** Find out what binding information is actually available
*/
rpc_server_inq_bindings
            (
             &bvec,
             &status
            );
if (status != error_status_ok)
    {
    printf("Can't inquire bindings \n");
    exit(EXIT_FAILURE);
    }
/*
** Register with endpoint mapper
*/
rpc_ep_register
            (
             IFSPEC,
             bvec,
             NULL,
             (unsigned_char_t *)"SEARCH endpoint",
             &status
            );
if (status != error_status_ok)
    {
    printf("Can't register endpoint\n");
    exit(EXIT_FAILURE);
    }
/*
** Get the string bindings and print them
*/
for (i = 0; i < bvec->count; i++)
    {
    /*
    ** For each binding, convert it to a
    **     string representation
    */
    rpc_binding_to_string_binding
                (
                 bvec->binding_h[i],
                 &string_binding,
                 &status
                );
```

Example D-4: Remote Search Server Initialization File: server.c (continued)

```
        if (status != error_status_ok)
            {
            printf("Can't get string binding \n");
            exit(EXIT_FAILURE);
            }
        printf("%s\n", string_binding);
        }
    /*
    ** Server is all ready to start listening for client
    **      requests...
    */
    rpc_server_listen
                (
                 (long)2,
                 &status
                );
    if (status != error_status_ok)
        printf("Error: rpc_server_listen() returned \n");
    return (EXIT_FAILURE);
}
#ifdef WIN32
/***********************************************************************/
/***                MIDL_user_allocate / MIDL_user_free        ***/
/***********************************************************************/
void * __RPC_API
MIDL_user_allocate
            (
             size
            )
size_t size;
{
    unsigned char * ptr;
    ptr = malloc( size );
    return ( (void *)ptr );

}
void __RPC_API
MIDL_user_free
            (
             object
            )
void * object;
{
    free (object);
}
#endif
```

Example D-5: Remote Search Remote Procedures: manager.c

```
/*
**
**
** MODULE: manager.c
**
**
** PROGRAM: Portable SEARCH Application (OpenVMS,DOS,NT,OSF/1,ULTRIX)
**
**
** ABSTRACT: SEARCH is a sample RPC application intended to illustrate
**          the basics of RPC interoperation between DCE platforms
**          and Microsoft platforms.
**
**
*/
#include <stdio.h>
#include <string.h>
#include <stdlib.h>
#ifndef VMS
#include <malloc.h>
#endif
#include "search.h"
#ifdef WIN32
#include "dceport.h"
#endif
/*
**
** FUNCTION:  getfileline
**
** PURPOSE:
**      Retrieve lines from input file
**
*/
int
getfileline
            (
              line,
              file_handle
            )
idl_char *line;
FILE     *file_handle;
{
    /*
    ** Each call of this routine returns a line of the
    **     file referred to by the file handle.  On EOF, it
    **     returns -1.
    */
    char ch;
    while ((ch = fgetc(file_handle)) != '\n' && ch != EOF)
        {
```

Example D-5: Remote Search Remote Procedures: manager.c (continued)

```
        /*
        ** Tabs are unpredictable, so substitute
        **    three spaces if you run across a tab...
        */
        if (ch == '\t')
            {
            *line++ = ' ';
            *line++ = ' ';
            *line++ = ' ';
            }
        else
            *line++ = ch;


        }
    *line++ = '\0';
    if (ch == EOF)
        return (-1);
    else
        return (0);
}
/*
**
** FUNCTION:  searchit
**
** PURPOSE:   Find a string in a file
**
*/
short
searchit
        (
         custom_handle,
         stringin,
         stringout,
         rpc_status
        )
search_spec        custom_handle;
idl_char            stringin[LINESIZE];
idl_char            stringout[LINESIZE];
error_status_t    *rpc_status;
{
    idl_char buf[LINESIZE];
    FILE *file_handle;
    short line_number = 0;
    *rpc_status = error_status_ok;

    /*
    ** Return FILE_ERROR if we can't find the file or can't open it
    */
    if ((file_handle = fopen ((char *)custom_handle.filename,"r")) == NULL)
        return (FILE_ERROR);
```

Example D-5: Remote Search Remote Procedures: manager.c (continued)

```
    /*
    **  Either return the line of the file that contains a string
    **  match, or return NO_MATCH
    */
    while ((getfileline(buf,file_handle)) != -1)
        {
        /*
        ** Keep track of line number
        */
        line_number++;
        /*
        ** Does this line of the file contain the string?
        */
        if ((strstr((char *)buf, (char *)stringin)) != (char *) NULL)
            {
            /*
            ** Yes!  Return the matching line and the line number
            **     after closing the file.
            */
            strcpy ((char *)stringout,(char *)buf);
            fclose(file_handle);
            return(line_number);
            }
        }
    /*
    ** Couldn't find it.  Close the file and return.
    */
    fclose(file_handle);
    return(NO_MATCH);
}
```

Example D-6: Remote Search Makefile for ULTRIX: makefile.unx

```
#
#
# Build SEARCH client and server ULTRIX
#
#
ALPHA_LIBFLAGS    = -ldce -lpthreads -lmach -lc_r
LIBS              = -ldce -lcma -ldnet -li
CFLAGS            = -I. -c
all: searchit searchd
#
# Link client
#
searchit: client.o search_cstub.o
      $(CC) -o searchit client.o search_cstub.o $(LIBS)
```

Example D-6: Remote Search Makefile for ULTRIX: makefile.unx (continued)

```
#
# Link server
#
searchd: server.o manager.o search_sstub.o
        $(CC) -o searchd server.o manager.o search_sstub.o $(LIBS)
#
# Compile client source code
#
client.o: client.c search.h
        $(CC) $(CFLAGS) client.c
#
# Compile server source code
#
server.o: server.c search.h
        $(CC) $(CFLAGS) server.c
manager.o: manager.c search.h
        $(CC) $(CFLAGS) manager.c
#
# Generate stubs and header file from interface definition
#
search.h: search.idl search.acf
        idl search.idl
#
# Clean up for fresh build
#
clean:
        rm -f *.o
        rm -f search.h
        rm -f *ub.c
#
# Clean up all byproducts of build
#
clobber: clean
        rm -f searchit
        rm -f searchd
```

Example D-7: Remote Search Makefile for OSF/1: makefile.osf

```
#
#
# Build SEARCH client and server for DEC OSF/1
#
#
ALPHA_LIBFLAGS = -ldce -lpthreads -lmach -lc_r
LIBS           = -ldce -lpthreads -lmach -lc_r -ldnet
CFLAGS         = -I. -std1 -c
all: searchit searchd
#
# Link client
#
```

Example D-7: Remote Search Makefile for OSF/1: makefile.osf (continued)

```
searchit: client.o search_cstub.o
     $(CC) -o searchit client.o search_cstub.o $(LIBS)
#
# Link server
#
searchd: server.o manager.o search_sstub.o
     $(CC) -o searchd server.o manager.o search_sstub.o $(LIBS)
#
# Compile client source code
#
client.o: client.c search.h
     $(CC) $(CFLAGS) client.c
#
# Compile server source code
#
server.o: server.c search.h
     $(CC) $(CFLAGS) server.c
manager.o: manager.c search.h
     $(CC) $(CFLAGS) manager.c
#
# Generate stubs and header file from interface definition
#
search.h: search.idl search.acf
     idl search.idl
#
# Clean up for fresh build
#
clean:
     rm -f *.o
     rm -f search.h
     rm -f *ub.c
#
# Clean up all byproducts of build
#
clobber: clean
     rm -f searchit
     rm -f searchd
```

Example D-8: Remote Search Makefile for Windows NT: makefile.nt

```
#
#
# Build SEARCH client and server for Windows NT
#
#
!INCLUDE <ntwin32.mak>
includes =  -I.
all : searchit.exe searchd.exe
```

Example D-8: Remote Search Makefile for Windows NT: makefile.nt (continued)

```
#
# Link client
#
searchit.exe: client.obj search_c.obj search_x.obj
    $(link) $(linkdebug) $(conflags) -out:searchit.exe \
        client.obj search_c.obj search_x.obj \
        rpcrt4.lib rpcns4.lib rpcndr.lib $(conlibs)
#
# Link server
#
searchd.exe: server.obj manager.obj search_s.obj search_y.obj
    $(link) $(linkdebug) $(conflags) -out:searchd.exe \
        server.obj manager.obj search_s.obj search_y.obj \
        rpcrt4.lib rpcns4.lib rpcndr.lib $(conlibs)
#
# Compile client source code
#
client.obj: client.c search.h
    $(cc) $(cflags) $(cvars) $(scall) $(includes) client.c
#
# Compile server source code
#
server.obj: server.c search.h
    $(cc) $(cflags) $(cvars) $(scall) $(includes) server.c
manager.obj: manager.c search.h
    $(cc) $(cflags) $(cvars) $(scall) $(includes) manager.c
#
# Compile client stubs
#
search_c.obj : search_c.c
    $(cc) $(cflags) $(cvars) $(scall) $(includes) search_c.c
search_x.obj : search_x.c
    $(cc) $(cflags) $(cvars) $(scall) $(includes) search_x.c
#
# Compile server stubs
#
search_s.obj : search_s.c
    $(cc) $(cflags) $(cvars) $(scall) $(includes) search_s.c
search_y.obj : search_y.c
    $(cc) $(cflags) $(cvars) $(scall) $(includes) search_y.c
#
# Generate stubs and header file from interface definition
#
search.h : search.idl search.acf
    midl search.idl
#
# Clean up for fresh build
#
```

Example D-8: Remote Search Makefile for Windows NT: makefile.nt (continued)

```
clean :
    del search_*.*
    del *.obj
    del search.h
#
# Clean up all byproducts of build
#
clobber : clean
    del searchit.exe
    del searchd.exe
```

Example D-9: Remote Search Makefile for DOS: makefile.dos

```
#
#
# Build SEARCHIT client for DOS
#
#
DEV    = c:\c700
LIBS   =  $(DEV)\lib\llibce $(DEV)\lib\rpc $(DEV)\lib\rpcndr
CFLAGS = -AL -c -w -nologo -Zp -Zi -Oatelr -I$(DEV)\include\dos
all: searchit.exe
#
# Link client
#
searchit.exe: client.obj search_c.obj search_x.obj
    link /co /nologo client.obj search_c.obj search_x.obj,\
    searchit.exe,,/nod $(LIBS);
#
# Compile client source code
#
client.obj: client.c search.h
    $(CC) $(CFLAGS) $*.c
#
# Compile client stubs
#
search_c.obj : search_c.c
    $(CC) $(CFLAGS) $*.c
search_x.obj : search_x.c
    $(CC) $(CFLAGS) $*.c
#
# Generate stubs and header file from interface definition
#
search.h : search.idl search.acf
    midl search.idl
#
# Clean up for fresh build
#
clean:
    del search_*.*
```

Example D-9: Remote Search Makefile for DOS: makefile.dos (continued)

```
        del *.obj
        del search.h
        del searchit.map
#
# Clean up all byproducts of build
#
clobber: clean
        del searchit.exe
```

Example D-10: Remote Search Makefile for OpenVMS: makefile.com

```
$!
$! This is file SEARCH.COM to build the
$! SEARCH example application on OpenVMS.
$!
$! Enable the universal IDL command interface
$   idl            := $sys$system:dce$idl.exe
$
$! Compile the interface definition
$! -keep all is used to keep the IDL output for training purposes
$ idl search.idl -keep all -trace all -trace log_manager
$
$! Compile the client application files
$ cc client.c
$
$! Link the client application
$ link /exe=searchit.exe client, search_cstub, sys$input:/options
        sys$share:dce$lib_shr/share
        sys$share:vaxc2decc.exe/share
$ write sys$output "searchit.exe done."
$
$! Compile the server application files
$ cc server.c, manager.c
$
$! Link the server application
$ link/exe=searchd.exe server, manager, search_sstub, sys$input:/options
        sys$share:dce$lib_shr/share
        sys$share:vaxc2decc.exe/share
$ write sys$output "searchd.exe done."
```

E

DCEPORT.H API Map

This appendix contains the header file that enables programmers to use DCE coding conventions in Microsoft RPC clients and servers. This file is included with the phonebook and calendar application example programs when they're compiled on Microsoft RPC systems.

Example E-1: The DCEPORT.H RPC API Mapping File

```
/*
** File:     DCEPORT.H
**
** Purpose: A list of macros to aid in porting of DCE RPC applications
**          to the Microsoft RPC environment.
**
** Date      6-22-93
**
** Version:  0.7
**
*/
#ifndef DCEPORT_H
#define DCEPORT_H
/*
** Define various idl types
*/
#define idl_char          unsigned char
#define idl_boolean       unsigned char
#define idl_byte          unsigned char
#define idl_usmall_int    unsigned char
#define idl_small_int     char
#define idl_short_int     signed short
#define idl_ushort_int    unsigned short
#define idl_long_int      long
#define idl_ulong_int     unsigned long
#define unsigned32        unsigned long
#define idl_true          1
```

Example E-1: The DCEPORT.H RPC API Mapping File (continued)

```
#define idl_false        0
typedef unsigned char    *unsigned_char_p_t;
typedef unsigned char    unsigned_char_t;
typedef void * idl_void_p_t;
#ifndef _ERROR_STATUS_T_DEFINED
typedef unsigned long error_status_t;
#define _ERROR_STATUS_T_DEFINED
#endif
/*
** Undefine and redefine some vectors in a DCE-portable
**    way
*/
#undef rpc_binding_vector_t
#undef rpc_binding_vector_p_t
typedef struct
{
    unsigned long          count;
    handle_t               binding_h[1];
} rpc_binding_vector_t, *rpc_binding_vector_p_t;
#define rpc_endpoint_vector_elt_t   RPC_PROTSEQ_ENDPOINT
#define rpc_endpoint_vector_elt_p_t PRPC_PROTSEQ_ENDPOINT
#define rpc_endpoint_vector_t       RPC_IF_ID_VECTOR
#undef uuid_vector_t
#undef uuid_vector_p_t
typedef uuid_t *uuid_p_t;
typedef struct
{
    unsigned long          count;
    uuid_p_t               uuid[1];
} uuid_vector_t, *uuid_vector_p_t;
#define rpc_if_id_vector_t RPC_IF_ID_VECTOR
#define rpc_if_id_t         RPC_IF_ID
#define rpc_ns_handle_t RPC_NS_HANDLE
#define rpc_if_handle_t RPC_IF_HANDLE
/*
** Define various default constants
*/
#define rpc_c_ns_syntax_default RPC_C_NS_SYNTAX_DEFAULT
#define rpc_c_protseq_max_reqs_default RPC_C_PROTSEQ_MAX_REQS_DEFAULT
#define rpc_c_protseq_max_calls_default RPC_C_PROTSEQ_MAX_REQS_DEFAULT
#define rpc_c_listen_max_calls_default RPC_C_LISTEN_MAX_CALLS_DEFAULT
/*
** Define version matching options
*/
#define rpc_c_vers_all          1
#define rpc_c_vers_compatible 2
#define rpc_c_vers_exact        3
#define rpc_c_vers_major_only 4
#define rpc_c_vers_upto         5
```

Example E-1: The DCEPORT.H RPC API Mapping File (continued)

```
/*
** Define profile element options
*/
#define rpc_c_profile_default_elt    1
#define rpc_c_profile_all_elts       2
#define rpc_c_profile_match_by_if    3
#define rpc_c_profile_match_by_mbr   4
#define rpc_c_profile_match_by_both  5
/*
** Define DCE API equivalents
*/
#define rpc_binding_copy(source,dest,status) \
        *status = RpcBindingCopy(source,dest)
#define rpc_binding_free(binding,status) \
        *status = RpcBindingFree(binding)
#define rpc_binding_from_string_binding(string_binding,binding,status)\
        *status = RpcBindingFromStringBinding(string_binding,binding)
#define rpc_binding_inq_auth_client(binding,privs,princ_name,\
        protect_level,authn_svc,authz_svc,status) \
        *status = RpcBindingInqAuthClient(binding,privs,princ_name,\
        protect_level,authn_svc,authz_svc)
#define rpc_binding_inq_auth_info(binding,princ_name,protect_level,\
        authn_svc,auth_identity,authz_svc,status) \
        *status = RpcBindingInqAuthInfo(binding,princ_name, \
        protect_level,authn_svc,auth_identity,authz_svc)
#define rpc_binding_inq_object(binding,object_uuid,status) \
        *status = RpcBindingInqObject(binding,object_uuid)
#define rpc_binding_reset(binding,status) \
        *status = RpcBindingReset(binding)
#define rpc_binding_server_from_client(client,server,status) \
        *status = RpcBindingServerFromClient(client,server)
#define rpc_binding_set_auth_info(binding,princ_name,protect_level,\
        authn_svc,auth_identity,authz_svc,status) \
        *status = RpcBindingSetAuthInfo(binding,princ_name,\
        protect_level,authn_svc,auth_identity,authz_svc)
#define rpc_binding_set_object(binding,object_uuid,status) \
        *status = RpcBindingSetObject(binding,object_uuid)
#define rpc_binding_to_string_binding(binding,string_binding,status) \
        *status = RpcBindingToStringBinding(binding,string_binding)
#define rpc_binding_vector_free(binding_vector,status) \
        *status = RpcBindingVectorFree((RPC_BINDING_VECTOR **)\
        binding_vector)
#define rpc_ep_register(if_spec,binding_vec,object_uuid_vec,\
        annotation,status) \
        *status = RpcEpRegister(if_spec,\
        (RPC_BINDING_VECTOR *)binding_vec,object_uuid_vec,\
        annotation)
#define rpc_ep_register_no_replace(if_spec,binding_vec,\
        object_uuid_vec,annotation,status) \
        *status = RpcEpRegisterNoReplace(if_spec,\
```

Example E-1: The DCEPORT.H RPC API Mapping File (continued)

```
                (RPC_BINDING_VECTOR *)binding_vec,\
                object_uuid_vec,annotation)
#define rpc_ep_resolve_binding(binding_h,if_spec,status) \
                *status = RpcEpResolveBinding(binding_h,if_spec)
#define rpc_ep_unregister(if_spec,binding_vec,object_uuid_vec,status) \
                *status = RpcEpUnregister(if_spec,\
                (RPC_BINDING_VECTOR *)binding_vec,object_uuid_vec)
#define rpc_if_id_vector_free(if_id_vector,status) \
                *status = RpcIfIdVectorFree(if_id_vector)
#define rpc_if_inq_id(if_spec,if_id,status) \
                *status = RpcIfInqId(if_spec,if_id)
#define rpc_if_register_auth_info(if_spec,princ_name,protect_level,\
                authn_svc,auth_identity,authz_svc,status) \
                *status = RpcIfRegisterAuthInfo(if_spec,princ_name,\
                protect_level,authn_svc,auth_identity,authz_svc)
#define rpc_mgmt_ep_elt_inq_begin(ep_binding,inquiry_type,if_id,\
                vers_option,object_uuid,inquiry_context,status) \
                *status = RpcMgmtEpEltInqBegin(ep_binding,inquiry_type,\
                if_id,vers_option,object_uuid,inquiry_context)
#define rpc_mgmt_ep_elt_inq_done(inquiry_context,status) \
                *status = RpcMgmtEpEltInqDone(inquiry_context)
#define rpc_mgmt_ep_elt_inq_next(inquiry_context,if_id,binding,\
                object_uuid,annotation,status) \
                *status = RpcMgmtEpEltInqNext(inquiry_context,if_id,binding,\
                object_uuid,annotation)
#define rpc_mgmt_ep_unregister(ep_binding,if_id,binding,object_uuid,\
                status) \
                *status = RpcMgmtEpUnregister(ep_binding,if_id,binding,\
                object_uuid)
#define rpc_mgmt_inq_com_timeout(binding,timeout,status) \
                *status = RpcMgmtInqComTimeout(binding,timeout)
#define rpc_mgmt_inq_dflt_protect_level(authn_svc,protect_level,\
                status) \
                *status = RpcMgmtInqDfltProtectLevel(authn_svc,protect_level)
#define rpc_mgmt_inq_if_ids(binding,if_id_vector,status) \
                *status = RpcMgmtInqIfIds(binding,if_id_vector)
#define rpc_mgmt_inq_server_princ_name(binding_h,authn_svc,princ_name,\
                status) *status = \
                RpcMgmtInqServerPrincName(binding_h,authn_svc,princ_name)
#define rpc_mgmt_inq_stats(binding,statistics,status) \
                *status = RpcMgmtInqStats(binding,statistics)
#define rpc_mgmt_is_server_listening(binding,status) \
                *status = RpcMgmtIsServerListening(binding)
#define rpc_mgmt_set_authorization_fn(authorization,status) \
                *status = RpcMgmtSetAuthorizationFn(authorization)
#define rpc_mgmt_set_cancel_timeout(seconds,status) \
                *status = RpcMgmtSetCancelTimeout(seconds)
#define rpc_mgmt_set_com_timeout(binding,timeout,status) \
                *status = RpcMgmtSetComTimeout(binding,timeout)
#define rpc_mgmt_set_server_stack_size(thread,status) \
                *status = RpcMgmtSetServerStackSize(thread)
```

Example E-1: The DCEPORT.H RPC API Mapping File (continued)

```
#define rpc_mgmt_stats_vector_free(statistics,status) \
        *status = RpcMgmtStatsVectorFree(statistics)
#define rpc_mgmt_stop_server_listening(binding,status) \
        *status = RpcMgmtStopServerListening(binding)
#define rpc_network_inq_protseqs(protseq_vector,status) \
        *status = RpcNetworkInqProtseqs(protseq_vector)
#define rpc_network_is_protseq_valid(protseq,status) \
        *status = RpcNetworkIsProtseqValid(protseq)
/*
** Define NSI equivalents
*/
#define rpc_ns_binding_export(name_syntax,entry_name,if_spec,\
        binding_vector,uuid_vector,status) \
        *status = RpcNsBindingExport(name_syntax,entry_name,if_spec,\
        (RPC_BINDING_VECTOR *)binding_vector,uuid_vector)
#define rpc_ns_binding_import_begin(name_syntax,entry_name,if_spec,\
        object_uuid,import_context,status) \
        *status = RpcNsBindingImportBegin(name_syntax,entry_name,\
        if_spec,object_uuid,import_context)
#define rpc_ns_binding_import_done(import_context,status) \
        *status = RpcNsBindingImportDone(import_context)
#define rpc_ns_binding_import_next(import_context,binding,status) \
        *status = RpcNsBindingImportNext(import_context,binding)
#define rpc_ns_binding_inq_entry_name(binding,name_syntax,entry_name,\
        status) \
        *status = RpcNsBindingInqEntryName(binding,name_syntax,\
        entry_name)
#define rpc_ns_binding_lookup_begin(name_syntax,entry_name,if_spec,\
        object_uuid,max_count,lookup_context,status) \
        *status = RpcNsBindingLookupBegin(name_syntax,entry_name,\
        if_spec,object_uuid,max_count,lookup_context)
#define rpc_ns_binding_lookup_done(lookup_context,status) \
        *status = RpcNsBindingLookupDone(lookup_context)
#define rpc_ns_binding_lookup_next(lookup_context,binding_vector,\
        status) \
        *status = RpcNsBindingLookupNext(lookup_context, \
        (RPC_BINDING_VECTOR **)binding_vector)
#define rpc_ns_binding_select(binding_vector,binding,status) \
        *status = RpcNsBindingSelect((RPC_BINDING_VECTOR *)\
        binding_vector,binding)
#define rpc_ns_binding_unexport(name_syntax,entry_name,if_spec,\
        uuid_vector,status) \
        *status = RpcNsBindingUnexport(name_syntax,entry_name,\
        if_spec,uuid_vector)
#define rpc_ns_entry_expand_name(name_syntax,entry_name,expanded_name,\
        status)\
        *status = RpcNsEntryExpandName(name_syntax,entry_name,\
        expanded_name)
#define rpc_ns_entry_object_inq_begin(name_syntax,entry_name,
        inquiry_context,status) \
```

Example E-1: The DCEPORT.H RPC API Mapping File (continued)

```
              *status = RpcNsEntryObjectInqBegin(name_syntax,\
              entry_name,inquiry_context)
#define rpc_ns_entry_object_inq_done(inquiry_context,status) \
              *status = RpcNsEntryObjectInqDone(inquiry_context)
#define rpc_ns_entry_object_inq_next(inquiry_context,object_uuid,\
              status) \
              *status = RpcNsEntryObjectInqNext(inquiry_context,\
              object_uuid)
#define rpc_ns_group_delete(name_syntax,group_name,status) \
              *status = RpcNsGroupDelete(name_syntax,group_name)
#define rpc_ns_group_mbr_add(name_syntax,group_name,\
              member_name_syntax,member_name,status) \
              *status = RpcNsGroupMbrAdd(name_syntax,group_name,\
              member_name_syntax,member_name)
#define rpc_ns_group_mbr_inq_begin(name_syntax,group_name,\
              member_name_syntax,inquiry_context,status) \
              *status = RpcNsGroupMbrInqBegin(name_syntax,group_name,\
              member_name_syntax,inquiry_context)
#define rpc_ns_group_mbr_inq_done(inquiry_context,status) \
              *status = RpcNsGroupMbrInqDone(inquiry_context)
#define rpc_ns_group_mbr_inq_next(inquiry_context,member_name,status) \
              *status = RpcNsGroupMbrInqNext(inquiry_context,member_name)
#define rpc_ns_group_mbr_remove(name_syntax,group_name,\
              member_name_syntax,member_name,status) \
              *status = RpcNsGroupMbrRemove(name_syntax,group_name,\
              member_name_syntax,member_name)
#define rpc_ns_mgmt_binding_unexport(name_syntax,entry_name,if_id,\
              vers_option,uuid_vector,status) \
              *status = RpcNsMgmtBindingUnexport(name_syntax,entry_name,\
              if_id,vers_option,uuid_vector)
#define rpc_ns_mgmt_entry_create(name_syntax,entry_name,status) \
              *status = RpcNsMgmtEntryCreate(name_syntax,entry_name)
#define rpc_ns_mgmt_entry_delete(name_syntax,entry_name,status) \
              *status = RpcNsMgmtEntryDelete(name_syntax,entry_name)
#define rpc_ns_mgmt_entry_inq_if_ids(name_syntax,entry_name,\
              if_id_vector,status) \
              *status = RpcNsMgmtEntryInqIfIds(name_syntax,entry_name,\
              if_id_vector)
#define rpc_ns_mgmt_handle_set_exp_age(ns_handle,expiration_age,\
              status) \
              *status = RpcNsMgmtHandleSetExpAge(ns_handle,expiration_age)
#define rpc_ns_mgmt_inq_exp_age(expiration_age,status) \
              *status = RpcNsMgmtInqExpAge(expiration_age)
#define rpc_ns_mgmt_set_exp_age(expiration_age,status) \
              *status = RpcNsMgmtSetExpAge(expiration_age)
#define rpc_ns_profile_delete(name_syntax,profile_name,status) \
              *status = RpcNsProfileDelete(name_syntax,profile_name)
#define rpc_ns_profile_elt_add(name_syntax,profile_name,if_id,\
              member_name_syntax,member_name,priority,annotation,status) \
              *status = RpcNsProfileEltAdd(name_syntax,profile_name,if_id,\
              member_name_syntax,member_name,priority,annotation)
```

Example E-1: The DCEPORT.H RPC API Mapping File (continued)

```
#define rpc_ns_profile_elt_inq_begin(name_syntax,profile_name,\
          inquiry_type,if_id,if_vers_option,member_name_syntax,\
          member_name,inquiry_context,status) \
          *status = RpcNsProfileEltInqBegin(name_syntax,profile_name,\
          inquiry_type,if_id,if_vers_option,\
          member_name_syntax,member_name,inquiry_context)
#define rpc_ns_profile_elt_inq_done(inquiry_context,status) \
          *status = RpcNsProfileEltInqDone(inquiry_context)
#define rpc_ns_profile_elt_inq_next(inquiry_context,if_id,member_name,\
          priority,annotation,status) \
          *status = RpcNsProfileEltInqNext(inquiry_context,if_id,\
          member_name,priority,annotation)
#define rpc_ns_profile_elt_remove(name_syntax,profile_name,if_id,\
          member_name_syntax,member_name,status) \
          *status = RpcNsProfileEltRemove(name_syntax,profile_name,\
          if_id,member_name_syntax,member_name)
#define rpc_object_inq_type(object_uuid,type_uuid,status) \
          *status = RpcObjectInqType(object_uuid,type_uuid)
#define rpc_object_set_inq_fn(inq_fn,status) \
          *status = RpcObjectSetInqFn(inq_fn)
#define rpc_object_set_type(object_uuid,type_uuid,status) \
          *status = RpcObjectSetType(object_uuid,type_uuid)
#define rpc_protseq_vector_free(protseq_vector,status) \
          *status = RpcProtseqVectorFree(protseq_vector)
#define rpc_server_inq_bindings(binding_vector,status) \
          *status = RpcServerInqBindings((RPC_BINDING_VECTOR **)\
          binding_vector)
#define rpc_server_inq_if(if_spec,type_uuid,mgr_epv,status) \
          *status = RpcServerInqIf(if_spec,type_uuid,mgr_epv)
#define rpc_server_listen(max_calls,status) \
          *status = RpcServerListen(2,max_calls,0)
#define rpc_server_register_auth_info(princ_name,auth_svc,\
          get_key_func,arg,status) \
          *status = RpcServerRegisterAuthInfo(princ_name,auth_svc,\
          get_key_func,arg)
#define rpc_server_register_if(if_spec,type_uuid,mgr_epv,status) \
          *status = RpcServerRegisterIf(if_spec,type_uuid,mgr_epv)
#define rpc_server_unregister_if(if_spec,type_uuid,status) \
          *status = RpcServerUnregisterIf(if_spec,type_uuid,0)
#define rpc_server_use_all_protseqs(max_call_requests,status) \
          *status = RpcServerUseAllProtseqs(max_call_requests,NULL)
#define rpc_server_use_all_protseqs_if(max_call_requests,if_spec,\
          status) \
          *status = RpcServerUseAllProtseqsIf(max_call_requests,\
          if_spec,NULL)
#define rpc_server_use_protseq(protseq,max_call_requests,status) \
          *status = RpcServerUseProtseq(protseq,max_call_requests,NULL)
#define rpc_server_use_protseq_ep(protseq,max_call_requests,endpoint,\
          status) \
          *status = RpcServerUseProtseqEp(protseq,max_call_requests,\
          endpoint,NULL)
```

Example E-1: The DCEPORT.H RPC API Mapping File (continued)

```
#define rpc_server_use_protseq_if(protseq,max_call_requests,if_spec,\
         status) \
         *status = RpcServerUseProtseqIf(protseq,max_call_requests,\
         if_spec,NULL)
#define rpc_string_binding_compose(object_uuid,protseq,netaddr,\
         endpoint,options,binding,status) \
         *status = RpcStringBindingCompose(object_uuid,protseq,\
         netaddr,endpoint,options,binding)
#define rpc_string_binding_parse(string_binding,object_uuid,protseq,\
         netaddr,endpoint,options,status) \
         *status = RpcStringBindingParse(string_binding,object_uuid,\
         protseq,netaddr,endpoint,options)
#define rpc_string_free(string,status) *status = RpcStringFree(string)
#define uuid_create(uuid,status) *status = UuidCreate(uuid)
#define uuid_to_string(uuid,string,status) \
         *status = UuidToString(uuid,string)
#define uuid_from_string(string,uuid,status) \
*status = UuidFromString(string,uuid)
#define true 1
#define false 0
/*
** Define exception handling equivalents
*/
#if defined (__RPC_WIN16__) || defined (__RPC_DOS__)
#define TRY \
     {           \
     int _mODE_fINALLY_; \
     int _exception_code; \
     ExceptionBuff exception; \
     _exception_code = RpcSetException(&exception); \
     if (!_exception_code) \
     {
#define CATCH_ALL \
       _mODE_fINALLY_ = false; \
       RpcLeaveException(); \
       } \
       else \
       {
/*
 * #define CATCH(X) \
 *    }else if ((unsigned long)RpcExceptionCode()==(unsigned long)X) {
 */
#define FINALLY \
       _mODE_fINALLY_ = true; \
       RpcLeaveException(); \
       } {
#define ENDTRY \
        } \
       if (_mODE_fINALLY_ && _exception_code) \
           RpcRaiseException(_exception_code); \
       }
```

Example E-1: The DCEPORT.H RPC API Mapping File (continued)

```
#endif /* WIN16 or DOS */
#if defined (__RPC_WIN32__)
#define TRY                 try {
/* #define CATCH(X) \
 *                          } except (GetExceptionCode() == X ? \
 *                              EXCEPTION_EXECUTE_HANDLER : \
 *                              EXCEPTION_CONTINUE_SEARCH) {
 */
#define CATCH_ALL           } except (EXCEPTION_EXECUTE_HANDLER) {
#define FINALLY             } finally {
#define ENDTRY              }
#endif /* WIN32 */
/*
** DCE Status code mappings
*/
#ifndef rpc_s_ok
#define rpc_s_ok                        RPC_S_OK
#endif
#define rpc_s_no_more_bindings          RPC_S_NO_MORE_BINDINGS
#ifndef error_status_ok
#define error_status_ok                 RPC_S_OK
#endif
#define rpc_s_invalid_arg               RPC_S_INVALID_ARG
#define rpc_s_invalid_string_binding    RPC_S_INVALID_STRING_BINDING
#define rpc_s_no_memory                 RPC_S_OUT_OF_MEMORY
#define rpc_s_wrong_kind_of_binding     RPC_S_WRONG_KIND_OF_BINDING
#define rpc_s_invalid_binding           RPC_S_INVALID_BINDING
#define rpc_s_protseq_not_supported     RPC_S_PROTSEQ_NOT_SUPPORTED
#define rpc_s_invalid_rpc_protseq       RPC_S_INVALID_RPC_PROTSEQ
#define uuid_s_invalid_string_uuid      RPC_S_INVALID_STRING_UUID
#define rpc_s_invalid_endpoint_format   RPC_S_INVALID_ENDPOINT_FORMAT
#define rpc_s_inval_net_addr            RPC_S_INVALID_NET_ADDR
#define rpc_s_invalid_naf_id            RPC_S_INVALID_NAF_IF
#define rpc_s_endpoint_not_found        RPC_S_NO_ENDPOINT_FOUND
#define rpc_s_invalid_timeout           RPC_S_INVALID_TIMEOUT
#define rpc_s_object_not_found          RPC_S_OBJECT_NOT_FOUND
#define rpc_s_already_registered        RPC_S_ALREADY_REGISTERED
#define rpc_s_type_already_registered   RPC_S_TYPE_ALREADY_REGISTERED
#define rpc_s_already_listening         RPC_S_ALREADY_LISTENING
#define rpc_s_no_protseqs_registered    RPC_S_NO_PROTSEQS_REGISTERED
#define rpc_s_cthread_create_failed     RPC_S_OUT_OF_THREADS
#define rpc_s_unknown_mgr_type          RPC_S_UNKNOWN_MGR_TYPE
#define rpc_s_unknown_if                RPC_S_UNKNOWN_IF
#define rpc_s_no_bindings               RPC_S_NO_BINDINGS
#define rpc_s_no_protseqs               RPC_S_NO_PROTSEQS
#define rpc_s_cant_create_socket        RPC_S_CANT_CREATE_ENDPOINT
#define rpc_s_comm_failure              RPC_S_SERVER_UNAVAILABLE
#define rpc_s_server_too_busy           RPC_S_SERVER_TOO_BUSY
#define rpc_s_connect_no_resources      RPC_S_OUT_OF_RESOURCES
#define rpc_s_not_supported             RPC_S_CANNOT_SUPPORT
#define rpc_s_call_failed               RPC_S_CALL_FAILED
```

Example E-1: The DCEPORT.H RPC API Mapping File (continued)

```
#define rpc_s_protocol_error             RPC_S_PROTOCOL_ERROR
#define rpc_s_cant_bind_socket           RPC_S_CANNOT_BIND
#define rpc_s_fault_remote_no_memory     RPC_S_SERVER_OUT_OF_MEMORY
#define rpc_s_unsupported_type           RPC_S_UNSUPPORTED_TYPE
#define rpc_s_fault_int_div_by_zero      RPC_S_ZERO_DIVIDE
#define rpc_s_fault_addr_error           RPC_S_ADDRESS_ERROR
#define rpc_s_fault_fp_div_by_zero       RPC_S_FP_DIV_ZERO
#define rpc_s_fault_fp_underflow         RPC_S_FP_UNDERFLOW
#define rpc_s_fault_fp_overflow          RPC_S_FP_OVERFLOW
#define rpc_s_fault_invalid_tag          RPC_S_INVALID_TAG
#define rpc_s_fault_invalid_bound        RPC_S_INVALID_BOUND
#define rpc_s_no_entry_name              RPC_S_NO_ENTRY_NAME
#define rpc_s_invalid_name_syntax        RPC_S_INVALID_NAME_SYNTAX
#define rpc_s_unsupported_name_syntax    RPC_S_UNSUPPORTED_NAME_SYNTAX
#define uuid_s_no_address                RPC_S_UUID_NO_ADDRESS
#define rpc_s_max_calls_too_small        RPC_S_MAX_CALLS_TOO_SMALL
#define rpc_s_string_too_long            RPC_S_STRING_TOO_LONG
#define rpc_s_binding_has_no_auth        RPC_S_BINDING_HAS_NO_AUTH
#define rpc_s_unknown_authn_service      RPC_S_UNKNOWN_AUTHN_SERVICE
#define ept_s_invalid_entry              EPT_S_INVALID_ENTRY
#define ept_s_cant_perform_op            EPT_S_CANT_PERFORM_OP
#define ept_s_not_registered             EPT_S_NOT_REGISTERED
#define rpc_s_no_interfaces_exported     RPC_S_NO_INTERFACES_EXPORTED
#define rpc_s_incomplete_name            RPC_S_INCOMPLETE_NAME
#define rpc_s_invalid_vers_option        RPC_S_INVALID_VERS_OPTION
#define rpc_s_no_more_members            RPC_S_NO_MORE_MEMBERS
#define rpc_s_nothing_to_unexport        RPC_S_NOTHING_TO_UNEXPORT
#define rpc_s_interface_not_found        RPC_S_INTERFACE_NOT_FOUND
#define rpc_s_entry_already_exists       RPC_S_ENTRY_ALREADY_EXISTS
#define rpc_s_entry_not_found            RPC_S_ENTRY_NOT_FOUND
#define rpc_s_name_service_unavailable   RPC_S_NAME_SERVICE_UNAVAILABLE
#define uuid_s_internal_error            RPC_S_INTERNAL_ERROR
#define rpc_s_internal_error             RPC_S_INTERNAL_ERROR
#define rpc_s_not_rpc_tower              RPC_S_CANNOT_SUPPORT
/*
** DCE Exception mappings
*/
#define rpc_x_ss_char_trans_open_fail    RPC_X_SS_CHAR_TRANS_OPEN_FAIL
#define rpc_x_ss_char_trans_short_file   RPC_X_SS_CHAR_TRANS_SHORT_FILE
#define rpc_x_ss_in_null_context         RPC_X_SS_IN_NULL_CONTEXT
#define rpc_x_ss_context_mismatch        RPC_X_SS_CONTEXT_MISMATCH
#define rpc_x_ss_context_damaged         RPC_X_SS_CONTEXT_DAMAGED
#define rpc_x_invalid_bound              RPC_X_INVALID_BOUND
#define rpc_x_invalid_tag                RPC_X_INVALID_TAG
#define rpc_x_no_memory                  RPC_X_NO_MEMORY
#define rpc_x_comm_failure               RPC_S_SERVER_UNAVAILABLE
#define rpc_x_invalid_binding            RPC_S_INVALID_BINDING
#define rpc_x_invalid_naf_id             RPC_S_INVALID_NAF_IF
#define rpc_x_invalid_rpc_protseq        RPC_S_INVALID_RPC_PROTSEQ
#define rpc_x_invalid_timeout            RPC_S_INVALID_TIMEOUT
#define rpc_x_object_not_found           RPC_S_OBJECT_NOT_FOUND
```

Example E-1: The DCEPORT.H RPC API Mapping File (continued)

```
#define rpc_x_protocol_error             RPC_S_PROTOCOL_ERROR
#define rpc_x_protseq_not_supported      RPC_S_PROTSEQ_NOT_SUPPORTED
#define rpc_x_server_too_busy            RPC_S_SERVER_TOO_BUSY
#define rpc_x_unknown_if                 RPC_S_UNKNOWN_IF
#define rpc_x_unknown_mgr_type           RPC_S_UNKNOWN_MGR_TYPE
#define rpc_x_unsupported_type           RPC_S_UNSUPPORTED_TYPE
#define rpc_x_wrong_kind_of_binding      RPC_S_WRONG_KIND_OF_BINDING
#define uuid_x_internal_error            RPC_S_INTERNAL_ERROR
#define rpc_x_connect_no_resources       RPC_S_OUT_OF_RESOURCES
#define rpc_x_invalid_endpoint_format    RPC_S_INVALID_ENDPOINT_FORMAT
#define rpc_x_string_too_long            RPC_S_STRING_TOO_LONG
#define rpc_x_incomplete_name            RPC_S_INCOMPLETE_NAME
#define rpc_x_invalid_arg                RPC_S_INVALID_ARG
#define rpc_x_invalid_name_syntax        RPC_S_INVALID_NAME_SYNTAX
#define rpc_x_entry_not_found            RPC_S_ENTRY_NOT_FOUND
#define rpc_x_unsupported_name_syntax    RPC_S_UNSUPPORTED_NAME_SYNTAX
#endif
```

Index

A

Access Control List, 66
  (see ACL)
  (see also authorization; secu-
    rity)
ACF, choosing binding methods
    with, 58
  defined, 58
  described, 21
ACF attributes
  [code], 62
  [comm_status], 60
  [fault_status], 60
  [in_line], 62
  [nocode], 62
  [out_of_line], 62
ACL, CDS, for nsid access, 66
  entries, controlling access
    with, 133
  manager procedure, 132
acl_edit program, setting DCE
    server ACLs, 134
  using for nsid, 67
administration, 63-73
  of DCE server ACL entries,
    133
administrator, for distributed
    computing services, 66
advertising the server, 109-112

allocating memory, in Microsoft
    RPC client, 27
  in Microsoft RPC server, 32
API, differences, 141-153
API sets, 136
applications, cross-environment,
    15
  (see also cross-environment
    applications)
arrays, 49-51
  conformant, 50
  example of use, 51-52
  fixed, 50
  varying, 50
**at-most-once execution seman-
    tics**, 53
Attribute Configuration File, (see
    ACF)
authentication, of clients by DCE
    servers, 131
  specifying in an ACF, 58-59
authorization, by DCE servers,
    131-132
  of Microsoft RPC clients, 132
automatic binding, deciding on,
    79
  overriding, 83

About the Authors

Ward Rosenberry is a technical-writing consultant, concentrating on technologies for the computer and communications industry. Ward has distinguished himself writing about the Open Software Foundation's Distributed Computing Environment since 1989, when he helped write Digital Equipment Corporation's original DCE submission documents. He then continued his association with DCE as Digital's documentation project leader for DCE Version 1.0. Ward is a co-author of *Understanding DCE*, published by O'Reilly & Associates in 1992. This book describes the OSF DCE, explaining how people and networks benefit from its use.

He graduated from the University of Lowell in 1979 with a B.A. in English. Ward, his wife Patricia Pestana, and their two children, William and John, live in North Chelmsford, Massachusetts.

Jim Teague works as a Principal Software Engineer for Digital Equipment Corporation. He has been involved in distributed computing since relocating to Digital's Bellevue, Washington site (often referred to as "DECwest") in 1989 and is one of the two original members of what has evolved into the Windows NT Systems Group.

Jim joined Digital in 1981 after doing programming for a number of projects at Oak Ridge National Laboratory in Oak Ridge, Tennessee. He graduated from East Tennessee State University in 1978, with a B.S. in Computer Science, and from the University of Tennessee in 1981, with a M.S. in Computer Science.

In addition to his contribution to the technical side of this book, Jim deserves some credit for keeping Ward alive by sending him an infusion of caffeine from Seattle's premier coffee roaster.

Jim and his wife Salley Anderson live in Redmond, Washington with their Irish setter, Cooper, and their cat, Wiley.

From the best-selling The Whole Internet *to our Nutshell Handbooks, there's something here for everyone. Whether you're a novice or expert UNIX user, these books will give you just what you're looking for: user-friendly, definitive information on a range of UNIX topics.*

Using UNIX

Connecting to the Internet: An O'Reilly Buyer's Guide **NEW**

By Susan Estrada
1st Edition August 1993
188 pages
ISBN 1-56592-061-9

More and more people are interested in exploring the Internet, and this book is the fastest way for you to learn how to get started. This book provides practical advice on how to determine the level of Internet service right for you, and how to find a local access provider and evaluate the services they offer.

!%@:: A Directory of Electronic Mail Addressing & Networks **NEW**

By Donnalyn Frey & Rick Adams
3rd Edition August 1993
458 pages, ISBN 1-56592-031-7

The only up-to-date directory that charts the networks that make up the Internet, provides contact names and addresses, and describes the services each network provides. It includes all of the major Internet-based networks, as well as various commercial networks such as CompuServe, Delphi, and America Online that are "gatewayed" to the Internet for transfer of electronic mail and other services. If you are someone who wants to connect to the Internet, or someone who already is connected but wants concise, up-to-date information on many of the world's networks, check out this book.

Learning the UNIX Operating System **NEW**

By Grace Todino, John Strang & Jerry Peek
3rd Edition August 1993
108 pages, ISBN 1-56592-060-0

If you are new to UNIX, this concise introduction will tell you just what you need to get started and no more. Why wade through a six-hundred-page book when you can begin working productively in a matter of minutes? This book is the most effective introduction to UNIX in print. This new edition has been updated and expanded to provide increased coverage of window systems and networking. It's a handy book for someone just starting with UNIX, as well as someone who encounters a UNIX system as a visitor via remote login over the Internet.

The Whole Internet User's Guide & Catalog

By Ed Krol
1st Edition September 1992
400 pages, ISBN 1-56592-025-2

A comprehensive—and best-selling—introduction to the Internet, the international network that includes virtually every major computer site in the world. The Internet is a resource of almost unimaginable wealth. In addition to electronic mail and news services, thousands of public archives, databases, and other special services are available: everything from space flight announcements to ski reports. This book is a comprehensive introduction to what's available and how to find it. In addition to electronic mail, file transfer, remote login, and network news, *The Whole Internet* pays special attention to some new tools for helping you find information. Whether you're a researcher, a student, or just someone who likes electronic mail, this book will help you to explore what's possible.

Smileys

By David W. Sanderson, 1st Edition March 1993
93 pages, ISBN 1-56592-041-4

Originally used to convey some kind of emotion in an e-mail message, smileys are some combination of typographic characters that depict sideways a happy or sad face. Now there are hundreds of variations, including smileys that depict presidents, animals, and cartoon characters. Not everyone likes to read mail messages littered with smileys, but almost everyone finds them humorous. The smileys in this book have been collected by David Sanderson, whom the *Wall Street Journal* called the "Noah Webster of Smileys."

UNIX Power Tools

By Jerry Peek, Mike Loukides, Tim O'Reilly, et al.
1st Edition March 1993
1162 pages
(Bantam ISBN)
0-553-35402-7

Ideal for UNIX users who hunger for technical—yet accessible—information, *UNIX Power Tools* consists of tips, tricks, concepts, and freely-available software. Covers add-on utilities and how to take advantage of clever features in the most popular UNIX utilities. CD-ROM included.

Learning the Korn Shell **NEW**

By Bill Rosenblatt
1st Edition June 1993
363 pages, ISBN 1-56592-054-6

This new Nutshell Handbook is a thorough introduction to the Korn shell, both as a user interface and as a programming language. Provides a clear explanation of the Korn shell's features, including *ksh* string operations, co-processes, signals and signal handling, and command-line interpretation. Also includes real-life programming examples and a Korn shell debugger *(kshdb)*.

Learning perl **NEW**

By Randal L. Schwartz, 1st Edition November 1993 (est.)
220 pages (est.), ISBN 1-56592-042-2

Perl is rapidly becoming the "universal scripting language". Combining capabilities of the UNIX shell, the C programming language, *sed*, *awk*, and various other utilities, it has proved its use for tasks ranging from system administration to text processing and distributed computing. *Learning perl* is a step-by-step, hands-on tutorial designed to get you writing useful perl scripts as quickly as possible. In addition to countless code examples, there are numerous programming exercises, with full answers. For a comprehensive and detailed guide to programming with Perl, read O'Reilly's companion book *Programming perl*.

Programming perl

By Larry Wall & Randal L. Schwartz
1st Edition January 1991, 428 pages, ISBN 0-937175-64-1

Authoritative guide to the hottest new UNIX utility in years, co-authored by its creator. Perl is a language for easily manipulating text, files, and processes.

Learning GNU Emacs

By Deb Cameron & Bill Rosenblatt
1st Edition October 1991
442 pages, ISBN 0-937175-84-6

An introduction to the GNU Emacs editor, one of the most widely used and powerful editors available under UNIX. Provides a solid introduction to basic editing, a look at several important "editing modes" (special Emacs features for editing specific types of documents), and a brief introduction to customization and Emacs LISP programming. The book is aimed at new Emacs users, whether or not they are programmers.

sed & awk

By Dale Dougherty, 1st Edition November 1990
414 pages, ISBN 0-937175-59-5

For people who create and modify text files, *sed* and *awk* are power tools for editing. Most of the things that you can do with these programs can be done interactively with a text editor. However, using *sed* and *awk* can save many hours of repetitive work in achieving the same result.

MH & xmh: E-mail for Users & Programmers

By Jerry Peek, 2nd Edition September 1992
728 pages, ISBN 1-56592-027-9

Customize your e-mail environment to save time and make communicating more enjoyable. *MH & xmh: E-mail for Users & Programmers* explains how to use, customize, and program with the MH electronic mail commands available on virtually any UNIX system. The handbook also covers *xmh*, an X Window System client that runs MH programs. The new second edition has been updated for X Release 5 and MH 6.7.2. We've added a chapter on *mhook*, new sections explaining under-appreciated small commands and features, and more examples showing how to use MH to handle common situations.

Learning the vi Editor

By Linda Lamb, 5th Edition October 1990
192 pages, ISBN 0-937175-67-6

A complete guide to text editing with *vi*, the editor available on nearly every UNIX system. Early chapters cover the basics; later chapters explain more advanced editing tools, such as *ex* commands and global search and replacement.

UNIX in a Nutshell:
For System V & Solaris 2.0

By Daniel Gilly and the staff of O'Reilly & Associates
2nd Edition June 1992, 444 pages, ISBN 1-56592-001-5

You may have seen UNIX quick reference guides, but you've never seen anything like *UNIX in a Nutshell*. Not a scaled-down quick-reference of common commands, *UNIX in a Nutshell* is a complete reference containing all commands and options, along with generous descriptions and examples that put the commands in context. For all but the thorniest UNIX problems this one reference should be all the documentation you need. Covers System V Releases 3 and 4 and Solaris 2.0.

An alternate version of this quick-reference is available for Berkeley UNIX.
Berkeley Edition, December 1986
(latest update October 1990)
272 pages, ISBN 0-937175-20-X

Using UUCP and Usenet

By Grace Todino & Dale Dougherty
1st Edition December 1986 (latest update October 1991)
210 pages, ISBN 0-937175-10-2

Shows users how to communicate with both UNIX and non-UNIX systems using UUCP and *cu* or *tip*, and how to read news and post articles. This handbook assumes that UUCP is already running at your site.

System Administration

Managing UUCP and Usenet

By Tim O'Reilly & Grace Todino
10th Edition January 1992
368 pages, ISBN 0-937175-93-5

For all its widespread use, UUCP is one of the most difficult UNIX utilities to master. This book is for system administrators who want to install and manage UUCP and Usenet software. "Don't even TRY to install UUCP without it!"—Usenet message 456@nitrex.UUCP

sendmail   `NEW`

By Bryan Costales, with Eric Allman & Neil Rickert
1st Edition October 1993 (est.)
600 pages (est.), ISBN 0-937175-056-2

This new Nutshell Handbook is far and away the most comprehensive book ever written on *sendmail*, a program that acts like a traffic cop in routing and delivering mail on UNIX-based networks. Although *sendmail* is the most widespread of all mail programs, it's also one of the last great uncharted territories—and most difficult utilities to learn—in UNIX system administration. The book covers both major versions of *sendmail*: the standard version available on most systems, and IDA *sendmail*, a version from Europe.

termcap & terminfo

By John Strang, Linda Mui & Tim O'Reilly
3rd Edition July 1992
270 pages, ISBN 0-937175-22-6

For UNIX system administrators and programmers. This handbook provides information on writing and debugging terminal descriptions, as well as terminal initialization, for the two UNIX terminal databases.

DNS and BIND

By Cricket Liu & Paul Albitz, 1st Edition October 1992
418 pages, ISBN 1-56592-010-4

DNS and BIND contains all you need to know about the Domain Name System (DNS) and BIND, its UNIX implementation. The Domain Name System (DNS) is the Internet's "phone book"; it's a database that tracks important information (in particular, names and addresses) for every computer on the Internet. If you're a system administrator, this book will show you how to set up and maintain the DNS software on your network.

Essential System Administration

By Æleen Frisch, 1st Edition October 1991
466 pages, ISBN 0-937175-80-3

Provides a compact, manageable introduction to the tasks faced by everyone responsible for a UNIX system. This guide is for those who use a stand-alone UNIX system, those who routinely provide administrative support for a larger shared system, or those who want an understanding of basic administrative functions. Covers all major versions of UNIX.

X Window System Administrator's Guide

By Linda Mui & Eric Pearce
1st Edition October 1992
372 pages, With CD-ROM: ISBN 1-56592-052-X
Without CD-ROM: ISBN 0-937175-83-8

This book is the first and only book devoted to the issues of system administration for X and X-based networks, written not just for UNIX system administrators but for anyone faced with the job of administering X (including those running X on stand-alone workstations). The *X Window System Administrator's Guide* is available either alone or packaged with the XCD. The CD provides X source code and binaries to complement the book's instructions for installing the software. It contains over 600 megabytes of X11 source code and binaries stored in ISO9660 and RockRidge formats. This will allow several types of UNIX workstations to mount the CD-ROM as a filesystem, browse through the source code and install pre-built software.

Practical UNIX Security

By Simson Garfinkel & Gene Spafford
1st Edition June 1991
512 pages, ISBN 0-937175-72-2

Tells system administrators how to make their UNIX system—either System V or BSD—as secure as it possibly can be without going to trusted system technology. The book describes UNIX concepts and how they enforce security, tells how to defend against and handle security breaches, and explains network security (including UUCP, NFS, Kerberos, and firewall machines) in detail.

Managing NFS and NIS

By Hal Stern
1st Edition June 1991
436 pages, ISBN 0-937175-75-7

Managing NFS and NIS is for system administrators who need to set up or manage a network filesystem installation. NFS (Network Filesystem) is probably running at any site that has two or more UNIX systems. NIS (Network Information System) is a distributed database used to manage a network of computers. The only practical book devoted entirely to these subjects, this guide is a must-have for anyone interested in UNIX networking.

TCP/IP Network Administration

By Craig Hunt
1st Edition July 1992
502 pages, ISBN 0-937175-82-X

A complete guide to setting up and running a TCP/IP network for practicing system administrators. Covers how to set up your network, how to configure important network applications including *sendmail*, and discusses troubleshooting and security. Covers BSD and System V TCP/IP implementations.

System Performance Tuning

By Mike Loukides, 1st Edition November 1990
336 pages, ISBN 0-937175-60-9

System Performance Tuning answers the fundamental question, "How can I get my computer to do more work without buying more hardware?" Some performance problems do require you to buy a bigger or faster computer, but many can be solved simply by making better use of the resources you already have.

Computer Security Basics

By Deborah Russell & G.T. Gangemi Sr.
1st Edition July 1991
464 pages, ISBN 0-937175-71-4

Provides a broad introduction to the many areas of computer security and a detailed description of current security standards. This handbook describes complicated concepts like trusted systems, encryption, and mandatory access control in simple terms, and contains a thorough, readable introduction to the "Orange Book."

UNIX Programming

Understanding Japanese Information Processing **NEW**

By Ken Lunde
1st Edition September 1993 (est.)
450 pages (est.), ISBN 1-56592-043-0

Understanding Japanese Information Processing provides detailed information on all aspects of handling Japanese text on computer systems. It tries to bring all of the relevant information together in a single book. It covers everything from the origins of modern-day Japanese to the latest information on specific emerging computer encoding standards. There are over 15 appendices which provide additional reference material, such as a code conversion table, character set tables, mapping tables, an extensive list of software sources, a glossary, and much more.

lex & yacc

By John Levine, Tony Mason & Doug Brown
2nd Edition October 1992
366 pages, ISBN 1-56592-000-7

Shows programmers how to use two UNIX utilities, *lex* and *yacc*, in program development. The second edition of *lex & yacc* contains completely revised tutorial sections for novice users and reference sections for advanced users. The new edition is twice the size of the original book, has an expanded index, and now covers Bison and Flex.

High Performance Computing **NEW**

By Kevin Dowd, 1st Edition June 1993
398 pages, ISBN 1-56592-032-5

High Performance Computing makes sense of the newest generation of workstations for application programmers and purchasing managers. It covers everything, from the basics of modern workstation architecture, to structuring benchmarks, to squeezing more performance out of critical applications. It also explains what a good compiler can do—and what you have to do yourself. The book closes with a look at the high-performance future: parallel computers and the more "garden variety" shared memory processors that are appearing on people's desktops.

ORACLE Performance Tuning **NEW**

By Peter Corrigan & Mark Gurry
1st Edition September 1993 (est.)
650 pages (est.), ISBN 1-56592-048-1

The ORACLE relational database management system is the most popular database system in use today. With more organizations downsizing and adopting client/server and distributed database approaches, system performance tuning has become vital. This book shows you the many things you can do to dramatically increase the performance of your existing ORACLE system. You may find that this book can save you the cost of a new machine; at the very least, it will save you a lot of headaches.

POSIX Programmer's Guide

By Donald Lewine, 1st Edition April 1991
640 pages, ISBN 0-937175-73-0

Most UNIX systems today are POSIX-compliant because the Federal government requires it for its purchases. However, given the manufacturer's documentation, it can be difficult to distinguish system-specific features from those features defined by POSIX. The *POSIX Programmer's Guide*, intended as an explanation of the POSIX standard and as a reference for the POSIX.1 programming library, helps you write more portable programs.

Understanding DCE

By Ward Rosenberry, David Kenney & Gerry Fisher
1st Edition October 1992
266 pages, ISBN 1-56592-005-8

A technical and conceptual overview of OSF's Distributed Computing Environment (DCE) for programmers and technical managers, marketing and sales people. Unlike many O'Reilly & Associates books, *Understanding DCE* has no hands-on programming elements. Instead, the book focuses on how DCE can be used to accomplish typical programming tasks and provides explanations to help the reader understand all the parts of DCE.

Guide to Writing DCE Applications

By John Shirley
1st Edition July 1992
282 pages, ISBN 1-56592-004-X

A hands-on programming guide to OSF's Distributed Computing Environment (DCE) for first-time DCE application programmers. This book is designed to help new DCE users make the transition from conventional, nondistributed applications programming to distributed DCE programming. Covers the IDL and ACF files, essential RPC calls, binding methods and the name service, server initialization, memory management, and selected advanced topics. Includes practical programming examples.

Power Programming with RPC

By John Bloomer
1st Edition February 1992
522 pages, ISBN 0-937175-77-3

RPC, or remote procedure calling, is the ability to distribute the execution of functions on remote computers. Written from a programmer's perspective, this book shows what you can do with RPC's, like Sun RPC, the de facto standard on UNIX systems. It covers related programming topics for Sun and other UNIX systems and teaches through examples.

Managing Projects with make

By Andrew Oram & Steve Talbott
2nd Edition October 1991
152 pages, ISBN 0-937175-90-0

make is one of UNIX's greatest contributions to software development, and this book is the clearest description of *make* ever written. This revised second edition includes guidelines on meeting the needs of large projects.

Software Portability with imake   **NEW**

By Paul DuBois
1st Edition July 1993
390 pages, 1-56592-055-4

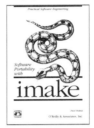

imake is a utility that works with *make* to enable code to be complied and installed on different UNIX machines. This new Nutshell Handbook—the only book available on *imake*—is ideal for X and UNIX programmers who want their software to be portable. It includes a general explanation of *imake*, how to write and debug an *Imakefile*, and how to write configuration files. Several sample sets of configuration files are described and are available free over the Net.

UNIX for FORTRAN Programmers

By Mike Loukides
1st Edition August 1990
264 pages, ISBN 0-937175-51-X

This book provides the serious scientific programmer with an introduction to the UNIX operating system and its tools. The intent of the book is to minimize the UNIX entry barrier and to familiarize readers with the most important tools so they can be productive as quickly as possible.

UNIX for FORTRAN Programmers shows readers how to do things they're interested in: not just how to use a tool such as *make* or *rcs*, but how to use it in program development and how it fits into the toolset as a whole. "An excellent book describing the features of the UNIX FORTRAN compiler *f77* and related software. This book is extremely well written." — American Mathematical Monthly, February 1991

Practical C Programming

By Steve Oualline
2nd Edition January 1993
396 pages, ISBN 1-56592-035-X

C programming is more than just getting the syntax right. Style and debugging also play a tremendous part in creating programs that run well. *Practical C Programming* teaches you not only the mechanics of programming, but also how to create programs that are easy to read, maintain, and debug. There are lots of introductory C books, but this is the Nutshell Handbook! In the second edition, programs now conform to ANSI C.

Checking C Programs with lint

By Ian F. Darwin
1st Edition October 1988
84 pages, ISBN 0-937175-30-7

The *lint* program is one of the best tools for finding portability problems and certain types of coding errors in C programs. This handbook introduces you to *lint*, guides you through running it on your programs, and helps you interpret *lint's* output.

Using C on the UNIX System

By Dave Curry
1st Edition January 1989
250 pages, ISBN 0-937175-23-4

Using C on the UNIX System provides a thorough introduction to the UNIX system call libraries. It is aimed at programmers who already know C but who want to take full advantage of the UNIX programming environment. If you want to learn how to work with the operating system and to write programs that can interact with directories, terminals, and networks at the lowest level you will find this book essential. It is impossible to write UNIX utilities of any sophistication without understanding the material in this book. "A gem of a book. The author's aim is to provide a guide to system programming, and he succeeds admirably. His balance is steady between System V and BSD-based systems, so readers come away knowing both." — SUN Expert, November 1989

Guide to OSF/1

By the staff of O'Reilly & Associates
1st Edition June 1991
304 pages, ISBN 0-937175-78-1

This technically competent introduction to OSF/1 is based on OSF technical seminars. In addition to its description of OSF/1, it includes the differences between OSF/1 and System V Release 4 and a look ahead at DCE.

Understanding and Using COFF

By Gintaras R. Gircys
1st Edition November 1988
196 pages, ISBN 0-937175-31-5

COFF—Common Object File Format—is the formal definition for the structure of machine code files in the UNIX System V environment. All machine-code files are COFF files. This handbook explains COFF data structure and its manipulation.

Career

Love Your Job!   **NEW**

By Dr. Paul Powers, with Deborah Russell
1st Edition August 1993
210 pages, ISBN 1-56592-036-8

Do you love your job? Too few people do. In fact, surveys show that 80 to 95 percent of Americans are dissatisfied with their jobs. Considering that most of us will work nearly 100,000 hours during our lifetimes (half the waking hours of our entire adult lives!), it's sad that our work doesn't bring us the rewards—both financial and emotional—that we deserve. *Love Your Job!* is an inspirational guide to loving your work. It consists of a series of one-page reflections, anecdotes, and exercises aimed at helping readers think more deeply about what they want out of their jobs. Each can be read individually (anyplace, anytime, whenever you need to lift your spirits), or the book can be read and treated as a whole. *Love Your Job!* informs you, inspires you, and challenges you, not only to look outside at the world of work, but also to look inside yourself at what work means to you.

How to Get Information about O'Reilly & Associates

The online O'Reilly Information Resource is a Gopher server that provides you with information on our books, how to download code examples, and how to order from us. There is also a UNIX bibliography you can use to get information on current books by subject area.

Connecting to the O'Reilly Information Resource

Gopher is an interactive tool that organizes the resources found on the Internet as a sequence of menus. If you don't know how Gopher works, see the chapter "Tunneling through the Internet: Gopher" in *The Whole Internet User's Guide and Catalog* by Ed Krol.

An easy way to use Gopher is to download a Gopher client, either the tty Gopher that uses curses or the Xgopher.

Once you have a local Gopher client, you can launch Gopher with:

```
gopher gopher.ora.com
```

To use the Xgopher client, enter:

```
xgopher -xrm "xgopher.rootServer:
gopher.ora.com"
```

If you have no client, log in on our machine via telnet and run Gopher from there, with:

```
telnet gopher.ora.com
login: gopher (no password)
```

Another option is to use a World Wide Web browser, and enter the http address:

```
gopher://gopher.ora.com
```

Once the connection is made, you should see a root menu similar to this:

```
Internet Gopher Information Client v1.12
    Root gopher server: gopher.ora.com

->1. News Flash! -- New Products and
     Projects of ORA/.
   2.About O'Reilly & Associates.
   3.Book Descriptions and Information/
   4.Complete Listing of Book Titles.
   5.FTP Archive and E-Mail Information/
   6.Ordering Information/
   7.UNIX Bibliography/

Press ? for Help, q to Quit, u to go up a
menu                        Page: 1/1
```

From the root menu you can begin exploring the information that we have available. If you don't know much about O'Reilly & Associates, choose About O'Reilly & Associates from the menu. You'll see an article by Tim O'Reilly that gives an overview of who we are—and a little background on the books we publish.

Getting Information About Our Books

The Gopher server makes available online the same information that we provide in our print catalog, often in more detail.

Choose Complete Listing of Book Titles from the root menu to view a list of all our titles. This is a useful summary to have when you want to place an order.

To find out more about a particular book, choose Book Descriptions and Information; you will see the screen below:

```
Internet Gopher Information Client v1.12
    Book Descriptions and Information

->1.New Books and Editions/
   2.Computer Security/
   3.Distributed Computing Environment
     (DCE)/
   4.Non-Technical Books/
   5.System Administration/
   6.UNIX & C Programming/
   7.Using UNIX/
   8.X Resource/
   9.X Window System/
  10.CD-Rom Book Companions/
  11.Errata and Updates/
  12.Keyword Search on all Book
     Descriptions <?>
  13.Keyword Search on all Tables of
     Content <?>
```

All of our new books are listed in a single category. The rest of our books are grouped by subject. Select a subject to see a list of book titles in that category. When you select a specific book, you'll find a full description and table of contents.

For example, if you wanted to look at what books we had on administration, you would choose selection 5, System Administration, resulting in the following screen:

```
             System Administration

   1.DNS and BIND/
   2.Essential System Administration/
   3.Managing NFS and NIS/
   4.Managing UUCP and Usenet/
   5.sendmail/
   6.System Performance Tuning/
   7.TCP/IP Network Administration/
```

If you then choose Essential System Administration, you will be given the choice of looking at either the book description or the table of contents.

```
    Essential System Administration

->1.Book Description and Information.
  2.Book Table of Contents.
```

Selecting either of these options will display the contents of a file. Gopher then provides instructions for you to navigate elsewhere or quit the program.

Searching For the Book You Want

Gopher also allows you to locate book descriptions or tables of contents by using a word search. (We have compiled a full-text index WAIS.)

If you choose Book Descriptions and Information from the root menu, the last two selections on that menu allow you to do keyword searches.

Choose Keyword Search on all Book Descriptions and you will be prompted with:

Index word(s) to search for:

Once you enter a keyword, the server returns a list of the book descriptions that match the keyword. For example, if you enter the keyword DCE, you will see:

```
Keyword Search on all Book Descriptions:
                   DCE

-> 1.Understanding DCE.
   2.Guide to Writing DCE Applications.
   3.Distributed Applications Across DCE
     and Windows NT.
   4.DCE Administration Guide.
   5.Power Programming with RPC.
   6.Guide to OSF/1.
```

Choose one of these selections to view the book description.

Using the keyword search option can be a faster and less tedious way to locate a book than moving through a lot of menus.

You can also use a WAIS client to access the full-text index or book descriptions. The name of the database is

O'Reilly_Book_Descriptions.src

and you can find it in the WAIS directory of servers.

Note: We are always adding functions and listings to the O'Reilly Information Resource. By the time you read this article, the actual screens may very well have changed.

E-mail Accounts

E-mail ordering promises to be quick and easy, even faster than using our 800 number. Because we don't want you to send credit card information over a non-secure network, we ask that you set up an account with us in advance. To do so, either call us at 1-800-998-9938 or use the application provided in Ordering Information on the Gopher root menu. You will then be provided with a confidential account number.

Your account number allows us to retrieve your billing information when you place an order by e-mail, so you only need to send us your account number and what you want to order.

For your security, we use the credit card information and shipping address that we have on file. We also verify that the name of the person sending us the e-mail order matches the name on the account. If any of this information needs to change, we ask that you contact order@ora.com or call our Customer Service department.

Ordering by E-mail

Once you have an account with us, you can send us your orders by e-mail. Remember that you can use our online catalog to find out more about the books you want. Here's what we need when you send us an order:

1. Address your e-mail to: order@ora.com
2. Include in your message:
   - The title of each book you want to order (including ISBN number, if you know it)
   - The quantity of each book
   - Method of delivery: UPS Standard, Fed Ex Priority...
   - Your name and account number
   - Anything special you'd like to tell us about the order

When we receive your e-mail message, our Customer Service representative will verify your order before we ship it, and give you a total cost. If you would like to change your order after confirmation, or if there are ever any problems, please use the phone and give us a call—e-mail has its limitations.

This program is an experiment for us. We appreciate getting your feedback so we can continue improving our service.

How to Order by E-mail

E-mail ordering promises to be quick and easy. Because we don't want you sending credit card information over a non-secure network, we ask that you set up an account with us before ordering by e-mail.

To find out more about setting up an e-mail account, you can either call us at (800) 998-9938 or select `Ordering Information` from the Gopher root menu.

O'Reilly & Associates Inc.
103A Morris Street, Sebastopol, CA 95472

(800) 998-9938 • (707) 829-0515 • FAX (707) 829-0104 • order@ora.com

How to get information about O'Reilly books online

• If you have a local gopher client, then you can launch gopher and connect to our server:
`gopher gopher.ora.com`
• If you want to use the Xgopher client, then enter:
`xgopher -xrm "xgopher.rootServer: gopher.ora.com"`
• If you want to use telnet, then enter:
`telnet gopher.ora.com   login: gopher    [no password]`
• If you use a World Wide Web browser, you can access the gopher server
by typing the following http address:
`gopher://gopher.ora.com`

W E ' D   L I K E   T O   H E A R   F R O M   Y O U

Company Name _____

Name _____

Address _____

City/State _____

Zip/Country _____

Telephone _____

FAX _____

Internet or *Uunet* e-mail address _____

Which O'Reilly book did this card come from? _____

Is your job: ❑ SysAdmin? ❑ Programmer?
❑ Other? What?_____

Do you use other computer systems besides UNIX? If so, which one(s)?
_____

Please send me the following:

❑ A free catalog of titles

❑ A list of bookstores in my area that carry O'Reilly books

❑ A list of distributors outside of the U.S. and Canada

❑ Information about bundling O'Reilly books with my product

O'Reilly & Associates Inc.

(800) 998-9938 • (707) 829-0515 • *FAX* (707) 829-0104 • order@ora.com

How to order books by e-mail:

1. Address your e-mail to: order@ora.com
2. Include in your message:
   - The title of each book you want to order
     (*an ISBN number is helpful but not necessary*)
   - The quantity of each book
   - Your account number and name
   - Anything special you'd like us to know about your order

_____

O'Reilly Online Account Number

Use our online catalog to find out more about our books (see reverse).